AMERICAN
DREAM
DEFERRED

AMERICAN DREAM DEFERRED

Black Federal Workers
in Washington, DC, 1941–1981

FREDERICK W. GOODING JR.

University of Pittsburgh Press

"Harlem (Dream Deferred)" by Langston Hughes is reprinted by permissions of Harold Ober Associates Incorporated. Copyright © 2018.

Published by the University of Pittsburgh Press, Pittsburgh, Pa., 15260
Copyright © 2018, University of Pittsburgh Press
All rights reserved
Manufactured in the United States of America
Printed on acid-free paper
10 9 8 7 6 5 4 3 2

Cataloging-in-Publication data is available from the Library of Congress

ISBN 13: 978-0-8229-4539-0

Cover art: (*clockwise from top left*): Chicago Post Office, circa 1970. United States Postal Service; Washington, DC, Post Office, circa 1958. United States Postal Service; Ella Watson, black-collar worker, 1942. Library of Congress; Letter Carriers in Mobile, Alabama, 1956. United States Postal Service.

Cover design: Melissa Dias-Mandoly

To all touched by the lives of black workers, lest their labors be in vain

CONTENTS

ACKNOWLEDGMENTS

Thank you to my family. Thank you to my academic mentors from Georgetown University. Thank you especially to all black federal workers who have gone before us, and those who are yet to come.

AMERICAN
DREAM
DEFERRED

Figure 1. *The Washington Family*, Oil painting by Edward Savage, 1796.

PAINTING THE PICTURE OF BLACK FEDERAL WORKERS

Slightly to the left of center in the painting is a refined gentleman sitting in a chair with his legs crossed. The chair sits on a checkerboard-design floor. Farther to the gentleman's left is a globe; behind him through an open window can be seen well-tended crops that span a sprawling plantation. On the other side of the table sit two women, one younger and the other older, interacting with a map. Meanwhile, a young boy stands at rapt attention at the stately gentleman's immediate side, clutching a compass in the same hand that rests on the globe. This eighteenth-century scene convincingly portrays the posh gentleman as a man of means, civility, and respect in accordance with the grand manner style of paintings popularized at the time wherein subjects were depicted in their idealized, not actual state. Heightening the picture's focus on the main subjects is that instead of being inside of a regular room, they appear to be onstage, ornately displayed and centrally placed in front of large, draping orange curtains that border the painting. On closer inspection, however, one can observe that five subjects are present, not just the four readily seen around the table.

What is significant about the bordering orange curtains is that they appear to camouflage the presence of a Negro slave, whose body is outlined on the far right side of the painting, but who lacks definitive facial features in contrast to the central subjects. While the actual identity of the enslaved individual is unconfirmed, what is definite is that this 1796 Edward Savage painting, *The Washington Family*, effectively memorialized the first president of the United States of America, George Washington.[1]

In exploring the world of black federal workers in Washington, DC, it is appropriate, albeit ironic, to begin by invoking the name of one of the nation's first and most famous government employees, General George Washington. The main thrust and core argument of the following text on black federal public sector workers in Washington is essentially captured by the scene depicted in Savage's 1796 portrait. Washington's presence speaks to the very heart of the American Dream—the concept that hard workers who apply themselves will be rewarded for their labors.[2] The American Dream, while not absolute for all Americans, involves variable interpretations of "success," most of which correspond to themes of financial security, meaningful personal relationships, respect from peers, and esteemed social positions. While progress toward this American Dream can arguably be measured socially, artistically, or politically, it is likely that in America's capitalistic economy, financial growth remains one of the most influential metrics for measuring progress toward this dream.

George Washington certainly represented the upward drive of the American Dream ethos, ascending to the presidency after having started from relatively modest means earlier in life. There is no question that Washington labored to prove himself by demonstrating valor and leadership on the battlefield in addition to prudence and economy in his personal business affairs. No one gifted Washington the presidency—he earned it based on the profound goodwill he enjoyed from his peers. As the highest-ranking federal officer of a fledgling republic, Washington was especially sensitive to his public image; he wanted his presence to reflect the highest ideals of all Americans and is thus widely credited for establishing dignity and respect in the office of the presidency.

In considering the American Dream framework and the excellent model established by one of its pioneering public servants, it is also essential to evaluate the presence of the lone Negro slave in *The Washington Family* portrait. This individual also probably has aspirations to fulfill the American Dream—or at least his conception of it—which may differ from Washington's, but remains consistent in substance. After all, pursuit of the American Dream has been no less intense for black Americans than for any other Americans. Anyone even vaguely familiar with the history of blacks in the United States of America is keenly aware of the complex web of emotions, thoughts, and actions encompassing both triumph and tribulation over several centuries, ever since the *White Lion* ship arrived in Jamestown, Virginia, with the first recorded shipment of enslaved Africans in 1619.

In evaluating how the American Dream was historically perceived by African Americans, it is important to recall that dating back to what I call the "era of enslavement," black Americans have traditionally always been economically disadvantaged relative to whites.[3] Black labor has not enjoyed the same degree of financial success that has marked the continuous gains of whites in the private sector over the same time period. In addition to successful, long-standing, blue chip, white-owned companies like Caswell-Massey, DuPont, and Colgate, the ability of a crafty entrepreneur to pursue an open-ended income by sparing no mercy—or expense—along the way has been personified by some infamous robber barons and captains of industry of the early twentieth century (e.g., John D. Rockefeller, Cornelius Vanderbilt, J. P. Morgan), all of whom were white males. The private sector, in employing standard rules of Darwinian theory (e.g., "survival of the fittest") has traditionally disregarded blacks as key contributors to free market economic advancement insofar as many working blacks do not control the means of their own production. This largely remained true until the federal government, much like Washington in his first presidency, took the lead in showing how the descendants of slaves could in fact contribute meaningfully to the growth of a dominant global superpower.

The United States' role as a dominant global superpower was essentially concretized with its involvement in the Second World War. The country's conversion from an agricultural force to an industrial powerhouse was completed in the postwar boom when economic growth translated into increased individual growth for many Americans. Many industries shifted gears to wartime production and new economic opportunities for employment were created in response to pressures for labor to maintain high rates of production. Not only did white women enter the workforce in unprecedented numbers, but blacks of both genders found new entry points to the American economy as well. One of the main points of entry was the federal public sector.

DREAM DEFERRED

This book, *American Dream Deferred*, is a complex study that explores two competing and at times contradictory core concepts: the American Dream and a critique of the American Dream embodied in the poem "Harlem (Dream Deferred)" by Langston Hughes. In the poem Hughes demonstrates his genius by encapsulating in just eleven lines the ongoing struggle for economic security, dignity, and respect experienced by many blacks in pursuit of the American Dream:

What happens to a dream deferred?
Does it dry up
like a raisin in the sun?
Or fester like a sore—
And then run?
Does it stink like rotten meat?
Or crust and sugar over—
like a syrupy sweet?
Maybe it just sags
like a heavy load.
Or does it explode?

Many historians accurately chronicle the public sector as a rich source of employment for black Americans in contrast to the more hostile and discriminatory environment in the private sector environment. In addition to the increased economic security these public sector jobs provided, many blacks became emboldened to increase their levels of political participation while on the job via public sector union membership. What is often intimated but never adequately explored is the degree and level of resistance faced by black federal employees while embracing their new roles as professionals in society. In other words, the American Dream was not easy to realize for black workers, even when they were directly employed as federal civil servants for America itself. Despite the heavily publicized battles for freedom and pride in the mainstream media during the civil rights movement, many black public sector employees privately waged battles for dignity and respect within the confines of their newfound employment. Using the few legal and social mechanisms at their disposal to exert pressure for grassroots change, these employees were resourceful in creating new solutions to an old problem that simply would not go away easily or quietly.

American Dream Deferred explores the tensions of two core concepts (the American Dream and Dream Deferred) with the nation's capital serving as the background setting. Washington, DC, is not only the capital city that represents the seat of power and policy of the American people and its government, it also represents events similar to those that occurred in many large metropolitan areas once deindustrialization helped spark mass suburbanization in the postwar era. More blacks became employed in the public sector to keep the large urban centers operational once openings were created by fleeing former white inhabitants. Much like the black servant who was fortunate to be included in the painting of the Washington family, but was still only partially depicted in Savage's portrait, federal sector blacks were intimately in-

FigURE 2. Langston Hughes, one-time Washington, DC, resident, poet, and author of "Harlem (Dream Deferred)" in 1951.

volved in the construction and maintenance of federal affairs, but were mostly partial beneficiaries of their own efforts. And here is what makes Savage's
portrait so wonderfully representative of the book's central thesis: while both
the slave and Washington shared the same space in *The Washington Family*
portrait, and while both likely "worked hard" in the fulfillment of their duties,
each had different expectations and outcomes for their investment of labor.
In other words, no matter how hard the slave worked for General Washington, his American Dream would have to defer to that of his owner. No matter
how hard black federal workers worked in DC, the question remained whether
their collective American Dream would have to defer to that of their employer.

GOOD GOVERNMENT JOB

In general, black Americans considered the federal government quite favorably as a worthwhile employer, and therefore felt encouraged to pursue these
jobs as a preferred option. For instance, Gladys Derricotte was well-known
in her family circle for repeatedly doling out this simple, direct advice to her
children and other relatives over the years: "Go on and get yourself a good
government job!"[4]

Derricotte was adamant because this same advice had worked for her.
Originally hailing from Texas, Derricotte moved to the nation's capital in
1947 to search for government work, having heard from relatives that the Government Accountability Office (GAO) was hiring. Thirty-five years later, Derricotte retired from the public sector along with her husband Randolph, who
worked just as long as a civil servant in the postal service. In the interim, the
Derricottes were able to realize (at least part of) their American Dream by
purchasing a home, enjoying a solid middle-class lifestyle, and sending their
children to college. Two of their daughters, Denise Derricotte and Michelle
Peyton, followed their parents' lead and became federal government employees and homeowners as well. When Gladys Derricotte's granddaughter, Tisha
Derricotte, also became a GAO employee like her grandmother, she became
the third generation of black workers in just one family to seek the American
Dream through federal employment in Washington, DC.

While not the norm, the Derricottes' experience was not unusual. The idea
of a "good government job" was very prevalent in the African American community during 1941–81. In fact, federal employment benefited countless black
families whose breadwinners earned stable salaries outside of the restrictive
agricultural, manufacturing, and service sectors in which African Americans
had traditionally toiled before the Second World War (e.g., seven out of every
ten employed black women were restricted to domestic work in 1940).[5] Government work also served as an entrée to higher-ranking jobs for black em-

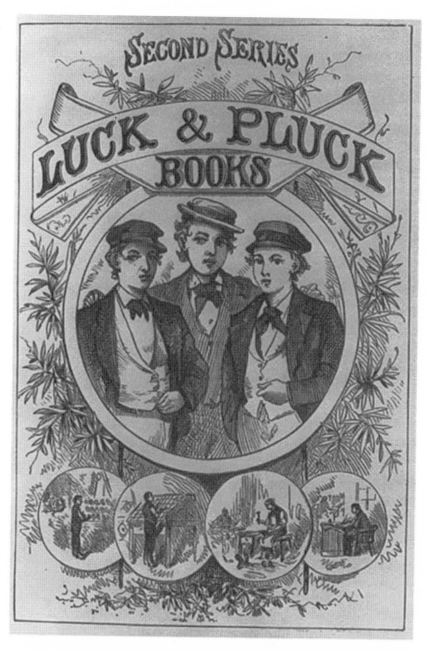

FIGURE 3. An illustration from Horatio Alger's "Luck & Pluck" series, circa 1874. Library of Congress.

ployees who lacked high school diplomas or college degrees.[6] Whereas black workers routinely suffered exclusion from comparable higher-paying, professionally ranked jobs in the private sector, the federal government provided broader access to clerical, semiprofessional, and in some cases, professional positions. Such unprecedented access to economic opportunity prompted Gloster Current, a former top official of the National Association for the Advancement of Colored People (NAACP), to facetiously call the federal government "the largest civil rights organization" in the country.[7]

While the federal government's structural approach to fairness certainly challenged historical socioeconomic norms for blacks, federal employment ultimately did not substantively change black economic stratification. This sobering story of underpaid and underpromoted black federal workers illustrates that the public sector was no complete safe haven from the constant occurrence of racial discrimination, which merely adapted and evolved over the decades. The culmination of this research is my effort to challenge the overly optimistic thinking that black northern migration to cities such as Washington, DC, during and after the Second World War, while understandably fraught with some shortcomings, was overall a boon to the African American condition. Despite several decades of workplace rights activism and changing racial attitudes, black federal workers remained deeply marginalized on the job.

This book explains the seemingly intractable subjugated status of black federal workers. For at first blush, the primary movement of blacks up north, and secondarily into federal jobs certainly fostered *change over time* with respect to a growing black middle class. In fact, so many black workers successfully descended upon Washington, that E. Franklin Frazier observed that due to the "large numbers of Negroes employed in the federal government, Negroes in the nation's capital had incomes far above those in other parts of the country." Furthermore, these higher incomes enabled blacks to "engage in forms of consumption and entertainment that established [federal employment's] pre-eminence among American Negroes."[8] Full economic citizenship was finally within grasp for many a black worker who otherwise did not fit the mold of a young, upstart white male courting American Dream success as described in a typical Horatio Alger novel (e.g., *Luck & Pluck*).

What was *consistent over time* was the ever-adapting nature of racial discrimination that essentially neutralized any collective gains that had amassed. My research is part of a vivid, historical understanding that shows even though black federal workers in DC were "better off" than those blacks who remained trapped in depressed southern economies, they were nonetheless consistently restricted from upwardly mobile economic and social growth opportunities.

The data bear out my argument that lower wages and slower raises for black workers stubbornly persisted in spite of official federal interventions from above and black-initiated grassroots efforts from below. My book examines the irony of how a "good government job" did not secure freedom as much as it secured the fantasy of freedom. The fact remained: *if blacks were thus restricted in the public sector, they were similarly restricted in the private sector, if not more so.* As a barometer of collective progress, black public sector workers are an overlooked group for insight into blacks' socioeconomic status today.

BLACK-COLLAR WORKERS

The best histories have focused on the mere advent of black government employment and how it has increased significantly and substantially around the Second World War. In other words, the quantitative analysis has been well-documented. Less known is what these jobs meant over time to African Americans themselves; the qualitative literature is thin on evaluating the modest quality of such employment and what black workers did to improve their conditions. Most accounts that mention black workers focus on the white actors or institutions that shaped the surrounding conditions of employment. For instance, Joseph Slater's work, while thoroughly documenting public workers' trials and tribulations in organizing against state actors and pushing the public sector from peripheral to primary importance in the labor movement, inexplicably omits black workers from his otherwise excellent analysis of unionizing. Similarly, Nancy MacLean's work effectively introduces job discrimination as the key battleground for the civil rights movement, but only touches on black workers as part of her larger focus on white women and Mexican workers as protected groups. Few studies deal with black federal workers as the center of their own postwar narrative; the specific history of these workers themselves remains largely unexamined. Yet existing narratives of public employees, black workers, and postwar black progress cannot be understood without taking black federal workers and their history into account.

History, of course, is the study of change over time, but it is often overlooked that change is a concept fraught with relativity—a concept that is uniquely dependent on its opposite, constancy. To properly evaluate any change relative to the past, one must also measure what has remained constant or consistent over time. Since the inception of their relationship with the United States of America, African Americans have had a difficult relationship with labor. The African American experience is unique in having been characterized by legally restricted opportunities in the job market, romantic racialist notions of blacks being best suited only to serve or entertain whites, or flat out racist notions of presumed incompetence and lack of intelligence necessary for gainful employment.

In the aftermath of the era of enslavement, a short-lived "radical" Reconstruction period gave way to a rigged economy in the South whereby blacks navigated labor spaces that were similar in social and economic tone to slavery, except that the working dynamics operated by different names. Sharecropping, convict lease programs, and apprenticeship programs for vagrant black youths were all transparent in their design to subjugate black labor and its black laborers. Black Codes and the subsequent institutionalization of Jim Crow segregation after the turn of the century all contributed to a dire economic outlook that would make even Horatio Alger blush.

For example, Eric S. Yellin cogently described how "the American state has been complicit in racism and black poverty" with the Wilson administration's decision to segregate blacks in federal employment in the wake of Reconstruction. At a cabinet meeting on April 11, 1913, President Woodrow Wilson made no objection to Postmaster Alfred Burleson's recommendation to segregate the federal workforce, which meant that no safe haven existed for black laborers. While many federal agencies declined to do so, several prominent agencies such as the Treasury Department and Bureau of Engraving and Printing followed the segregationist lead of Burleson who wanted all rail line and local postal service window positions made "lily white."[9] Burleson wasted little time in advancing his segregationist agenda; President Wilson was scarcely in office for one month, having been inaugurated on March 4, 1913.[10] So many progressive reformers signed on to the idea of workplace segregation because it represented efficiency for the government. Disparaging narratives in circulation at the time about blacks being associated with dirty politics made the whitening of government a simple and rational choice, rather than a racist one. Yellin ominously observed that "if radical reconstruction offered a chance for the United States to fulfill its founding promises, Wilsonian discrimination revealed the extent to which the state continued to be implicated in the nation's failures."[11]

American Dream Deferred picks up this narrative of the federal government's involvement in both the hope and failure of African American actualization. The narrative of limited black economic opportunity was further cemented with the widespread hardships brought about by the Great Depression. In the Jim Crow era, limited resources for whites most certainly meant limited to no resources for blacks. For instance, federal initiatives such as the Social Security Act of 1935, which explicitly excluded agricultural and domestic workers from its protections, served to further ostracize blacks from the ever-elusive American Dream. But in wartime, the prioritization of domestic discrimination was trumped by the need for global goodwill. Many historians, including Margaret C. Rung, note that nontraditional employment opportunities did not just open up generally during the Second World War, but that specifically "the federal government led the way in providing new employment opportunities for women and African Americans."[12]

Enthusiasm was initially high about the economic and social significance of the war to blacks. Andrew Kersten notes, "More recently, historians have tempered the notion of the 1940s as 'watershed' or 'revolution' in the Black experience, but still emphasize its significance in presaging the modern Civil Rights Movement."[13] During this "watershed" blacks built an infrastructure of political action through the black press, the growth of the NAACP, and the founding of other significant civil rights groups, such as the Congress of Racial Equality (CORE). African Americans in the military gained access to education, training for new jobs, and the tantalizing experience of greater freedom in countries like England and France. In turn, many African Americans on the home front moved away from agrarian incomes, learned new job skills, and improved their quality of life by fleeing Jim Crow segregation in the South. Government policy also underwent a significant shift during the war and by the end of the war, fighting for civil rights became a central part of the liberal agenda.

It is thus accurate to state that the meticulously organized data of Desmond King and others paints a poignant picture of change over time. Further analysis is nevertheless required regarding what specific types of changes transpired over time. Political and symbolic changes aside, direct and substantive economic changes have been slower to come for blacks in the federal workplace. This is why I do not share Rung's optimism when she states that for "African Americans and second and third generation Americans, working for the federal government provided an opportunity to prove one's employment ability and one's worth as an American."[14] If anything, economic stagnation has been the predominant narrative for blacks since their initial contact with the federal sector; this economic marginalization has been consistent and institutionalized over time. Ultimately, the collective black federal workers' experience demonstrates that the worth of a black American civil servant is disproportionately discounted.

While economic prosperity has never been guaranteed to American citizens, the hope and promise of financial well-being have been freely shared. It is fascinating to observe how, over time, despite significant political and social change, continuous challenging economic conditions have remained for black Americans as a whole, notwithstanding exceptional individual cases, which do not challenge the overarching rule. This idea of consistent economic marginalization is encapsulated in the term "black-collar workers," which I offer as a distinct interpretation of this dynamic as reflected in federal employment in the nation's capital.

Many colors have been used to categorize workers in labor circles since the Great Depression. Upton Sinclair coined the term "white-collar worker" as early as the 1930s to refer to professional grade workers who presumably wear a shirt with a white collar (and tie) to work. A blue-collar worker is one who typically labors on an hourly wage in factory or industrial settings (in uniform) in contrast to a white-collar worker who usually commands a higher salary for an administrative or managerial position. The white- and blue-collar workers contrast with the more recent designation of pink-collar workers in the 1990s, which represents women in the service industries.

In this book, as opposed to referencing manual laborers in exclusively dirty and dangerous industries, *black-collar workers* will refer to the dynamic of black federal workers (despite their manual, professional, or service status) who remained economically marginalized just because of their black identity, or the black skin that touches their collar. Whereas other "collar" designations refer to workers by function, this term organizes workers by identity, as the consequences of having a black identity in the federal workplace are distinct and separate from general issues common to workers with particular functions in the economy. This work further develops what Thomas Sugrue termed "racialized inequality" of black workers, which was not merely the by-product of inevitable, uncontrollable market forces at work. Rather black-collar workers represent the concerted efforts of many individuals from numerous federal agencies that influenced national policies. Just as Joseph Slater demonstrated that government employees became just as important to the American political economy as private sector workers after the Second World War, I argue that black government workers are key to appreciating the overall stunted socioeconomic status of black laborers in both the public and private spheres.

CONSTITUTIONAL RESPONSIBILITY

The disparate, spread-out nature of the federal government has made it difficult to research as a single cohesive unit. Yet the study of black federal workers during the period between 1941 and 1981 readily illustrates that the workers' black identity is what made the phenomena of lower wages and slower raises consistent across different federal agencies, various professional specialties, and diverse educational backgrounds. This makes Philip Rubio and Paul Tennassee's exclusive works on black postal workers significant: the quasi-governmental agency was sufficiently large enough to warrant independent study, in contrast to other agencies with markedly different behavioral characteristics. As fewer works explore the degree to which isolated struggles and triumphs of unionizing inside the postal service were replicated by black workers in myriad other federal agencies, my contribution comes largely through the broader profile of nonpostal, nonmilitary, nondefense workers.

While many different federal agencies operate independently of one another, protecting their budgetary fiefdoms with fervor, one national Constitution serves as a common denominator among them all to promote the general welfare. For federal workers most especially, I frame this collective encumbrance as a "constitutional responsibility." My general topic is not new, but my specific focus builds on the idea that if there was ever an area of the nation's economy where people stood the best chance of realizing the American Dream, it would be in the public sector. Transparent entrance examinations, public scrutiny, and accountability all contribute toward having a system that appears and operates in a fair manner to uphold public trust.[15]

If there is one sector of the American economy that can make the argument for idealist principles of fair play in a meritocratic marketplace, where participants fairly keep what they earn, it might well be the federal government. After all, the federal government is fundamentally about the "business" of America, its operations and policies, many of which are influenced to varying degrees by seminal documents such as the Declaration of Independence (e.g., "We hold these truths to be self-evident . . .") and the Constitution of the United States (e.g., "To secure these rights . . ."), which outline the tenets of a functional democratic republic. In one of the most remarkable displays of human rhetoric, in his 1963 "I Have a Dream" speech, Dr. Martin Luther King Jr. even seized on this concept to make his influential point: "When the architects of our republic wrote the magnificent words of the Constitution and the Declaration of Independence, they were signing a promissory note to which every American was to fall heir."

I acknowledge that no written express obligation presupposes that the government must promise to help people make money and become independently wealthy. Yet I am persuaded by Dr. King's assertion that this promissory note was indeed "a promise that all men . . . would be guaranteed the inalienable rights of life, liberty and the pursuit of happiness."[16] Thus, under principles of equal access and "fair play," pursuing potential wealth (i.e., happiness?) unhindered by the frustrating friction of racial discrimination I argue is implicit. No specific language in the Constitution forbids racial discrimination, but equity and fairness are key undergirding principles that make up much of what composes the noble American idea and the great American experiment.

One fascinating place to further explore this concept of presumed accountability, or constitutional responsibility, is the public sector. The private sector is always "free to be discriminating" and choose whomever it wishes to employ for whatever reason, but the public sector is designed to serve all citizens alike. Despite different agencies focusing on various populations and regions throughout the country, the bottom line is revealed in data on black-collar workers who on average have consistently suffered economically compared to their white counterparts. The historian Letitia Woods Brown, one of the first black women to earn a PhD in history from Harvard University, observed that "slavery and the slave trade in the nation's capital were a constant source of embarrassment to men who espoused democratic equalitarian principles."[17] Time was to tell whether systemic racial discrimination would prove to be just as embarrassing, for the American Dream was equally as tenuous for those working directly for the American government as for those working in the private sector—if not more so.

In accordance with this constitutional responsibility, the federal public sector began to quickly outpace the private sector in its effort to eliminate racial discrimination soon after the Second World War. In a marked departure from Wilsonian policies, President Harry S. Truman remarked, "We cannot be satisfied until all our people have equal opportunities for jobs . . . and until all our people have equal protection under the law. . . . There is a serious gap between our ideals and some of our practices. This gap must be closed."[18] Accordingly, the federal government created several opportunities for federal agencies and their employees to address the gap that Truman referenced. From 1941 to 1981, every president except Gerald Ford issued an executive order to directly address racial discrimination in the workplace (see chapter 4, table 4.1). At least three federal commissions studied the matter intently, gathering data and making recommendations for change; in addition, individual agencies investigated their own internal affairs. Nearly every administration also introduced new or refined grievance measures, frequently referencing the sensitive and symbolic nature of federal service and its high visibility.[19] A major legal effort to eradicate workplace discrimination came with Title VII of the 1964 Civil Rights Act, which created the Equal Employment Opportunity Commission (EEOC). However, it was not until 1972 that the EEOC was authorized to levy sanctions in both the federal and private sectors.

The influence of the EEOC was nevertheless more limited than its architects cared to admit. New antidiscrimination policies and procedures required implementation by employees and administrators who were not inclined to change their old habits so quickly, if at all. While no longer barred from specific jobs that were explicitly reserved for whites, many blacks still encountered more subtle forms of racism as manifested in lower wages and slower promotions.[20] As black federal workers realized the extent of their plight, they began to organize and resist. Indeed, their employment opportunities were not brought about due to "a shift in white attitudes. Rather, they were a result of decades of activism and policy making—boycotts, pickets, agitation, riots, lobbying, litigation, and legislation."[21] Active black federal workers organized job actions through local branches of organizations like the National Urban League (NUL), the NAACP, various labor unions, local grassroots activists like Julius Hobson, and individual challenges to agency officials. Many black federal workers took great pride in their work and in the government that hired them to serve. It was more remarkable that so many black federal workers remained loyal to their jobs, even if they risked their livelihoods or spent years of their lives fighting for such equal opportunities.

Many actors in federal employment openly embraced the concept that the federal government had an obligation to fight for equal opportunity. President Dwight D. Eisenhower once stated: "On no level of our national existence can inequality be justified. Within the federal government itself, however, tolerance of inequality would be odious. What we cherish as an ideal for our nation as a whole must today be honestly exemplified by the federal establishment."[22] Thus, by developing the construct of constitutional responsibility, this book explores the contours of what Samuel Krislov meant when he wisely observed that the "symbolic role of public position should not be overlooked. In seeking to implement the goal of greater equality in society generally government has a special responsibility to come to others with clean hands."[23] In other words, just as "the father of Harlem radicalism" Hubert Harrison suggested, one of the best methods to test the strength of American democracy is through historical analysis of African Americans. As Harrison declared that African Americans are the "touchstone of the modern democratic idea," the collective triumphs and tribulations of American blacks have brought to bear in living color both evil and cruel actions wrought upon them by fellow Americans. More specifically, the contours and limits of American democracy can be seen through the working experiences of black employees of the federal government.[24]

A REPRESENTATIVE CITY

The locale of this study is the heart of American federal employment—Washington, DC. I have deliberately chosen DC as the setting for a case study because of the high concentration of federal jobs within the city limits. The capital city represents a trend that occurred in many urban areas after the mass migration of blacks to northern cities both during and after the Second World War. In exploring the collective experience of black federal workers in DC, spanning the presidencies from Roosevelt to Reagan, this book explores the intersection of public sector labor and black labor, and thus contrasts with existing studies that deal with the two separately. The book examines the working lives of black federal employees and their efforts to improve their status from the Second World War to the early 1980s. Because "the color line between black and white has remained America's most salient social division," the experiences of Washington and other cities with significant populations of black public sector workers have much in common.[25]

Several push and pull factors contributed to the groundswell of black labor in DC. One major push came from the increasing mechanization of Southern agriculture. More machinery meant less labor was required to work the lands, which translated into fewer jobs available for blacks.[26] A significant pull factor was the promise of an improved lifestyle outside of the South. Under the Jim Crow order, a white superior did not feel pressure to pay a black worker his or her fair market value, making these workers perpetually vulnerable to exploitation. Additional factors pulling black laborers away from the South included the fervent pace of increased economic activity taking place in major northern urban centers as industrial mobilization hit full stride during the war. This exodus was widely supported in publications such as the *Chicago Defender* and others with the message that anywhere but the South held the promise of a better life.

The representative function of Washington, DC, as the nation's capital meant that the extent to which blacks were successful in federal jobs had outsized significance for blacks nationwide, since "discrimination in Washington was never merely another example of southern Jim Crow: it was evidence of the white supremacy at the heart of the nation."[27]

While DC had no manufacturing industries that attracted blacks during the Great Migrations from 1915 to the 1950s, similar to cities like Chicago, Pittsburgh, and New York, black newcomers did find jobs in DC's burgeoning public sector. While smaller in absolute size, DC had a higher proportion of blacks than metropolises such as New York, Detroit, Pittsburgh, or Philadelphia during the postwar era.[28] By 1950, blacks composed a third of the population in Washington and would reach a majority over 70 percent just two decades later.[29]

As federal agencies based in Washington grew in size and number, so did the national presence of black federal government workers. Numbering less than a thousand at the turn of the century, the numbers of black government employees swelled to over a quarter of a million nationwide during the Second World War.[30]

Moreover, during the war, the nation's capital became the undisputed center of a blossoming federal workforce. In 1946, only the state of California could boast more federal employees (247,600) than Washington, DC (235,100), although the state was nearly twelve times larger in population.[31] At the turn of the century, less than 1 percent of federal employees were black. But this proportion rose to 11.9 percent in 1944, including 41,566 in Washington.[32]

With such a rapid increase in the black population came a steep learning curve; blacks and whites separated by many social conventions outside of work now had to labor together on the job. As with any new arrangement, there were initial conflicts. In theory, black citizens working for the federal government were entitled to full dignity and respect. In practice, Jim Crow social customs dictated a social hierarchy that placed black dignity and respect under constant threat. In an effort to better understand this conflict between theory and practice as it related to black citizens, President Truman established a Committee on Civil Rights. The committee warned in its 1947 report that for "Negro Americans, Washington is not just the nation's capital. It is the point at which . . . the South becomes 'Jim Crow.' If he stops in Washington, a Negro may dine like any other man in the Union [train] Station, but as soon as he steps out into the capital, he leaves such democratic practices behind."[33]

But the irony that the epicenter of a leading democratic global superpower was contaminated with racial discrimination was not lost on black activists. In contrast to static accounts of new antidiscrimination policies, this research explores the true limits of American identity through the strategies employed by black federal workers to leverage the powerful federal government's verbiage against itself. Many federal employees took advantage of a growing civil rights consciousness and attempted to force the government's hand toward implementing equity in view of the nearly constant racial discrimination they faced on the job. Moreover, the development of the Cold War forced U.S. officials to oppose racism and Jim Crow customs domestically rather than risk key international alliances by contradicting their rhetoric about global democracy.[34]

Activists wisely understood that the federal government had a complex role in both serving as a leader in setting standards for the public sector and in following public opinion. The transparency and openness of federal government records also meant that the public sector was more vulnerable to shifting public consensus about jobs and discrimination. Racial discrimination was especially acute and overt in the federal ranks before the Second World War as a reflection of larger American society at the time. Yet when discrimination became less acceptable to the general public (e.g., heightened awareness through the civil rights movement), federal agencies were forced to address such inequities in the workplace. Address they did. Eliminate they did not.

CHAPTER SUMMARIES

To understand and depict the nuanced struggle of black federal workers in Washington, DC, in chapter 1, I establish the importance of DC as a growing city during the Second World War that attracted the attention of many blacks looking for work. The U.S. government achieved unprecedented levels of production during the Second World War, which would not have been possible without the contribution of an increased number of black workers. However, the federal government maintained mostly segregated workspaces for the new black workers it tepidly "welcomed," but in fact earnestly and desperately *needed* on the job. This chapter highlights how even an unusually progressive agency, the Office of Price Administration (OPA), struggled with overcoming entrenched customs of segregation. During this time, there is little official record of black resistance to such treatment, probably because workers had few official outlets on the job to address such grievances.

In chapter 2, I look at the federal government's first steps, just after the Second World War ended, to eliminate discrimination on the job. In 1946, President Truman established a federal panel to investigate racial discrimination, which published recommendations on how to combat it. The report marked a federal shift from passive observer to concern and study in the face of ongoing discrimination; this shift was assisted by the prodding of small but vocal public sector unions, Cold War pressures, and an evolving liberal agenda. This chapter details how the President's Committee on Civil Rights (PCCR) provided legislators with concrete data that would later prove influential in changing federal policy. Despite a strong mandate from the president, action was far from uniform as many heads of federal agencies denied that any racial problems even existed, while others failed to realize how their standard hiring practices harmed the career prospects of black federal workers.

In chapter 3, I analyze white resistance to increased pressure to bring about racial equality in the federal workplace. From 1948 to 1959, after the dissolution of the Fair Employment Practice Committee in 1946, the federal government continued to move away from structural discrimination in the federal workplace and, for the first time, mandated low-level dispute resolution procedures to recognize the grievances of black federal employees. Many blacks in Washington, DC, continued to draw benefits from federal employment in contrast to existing private sector jobs, but still had to contend with the deeply ingrained practice of racial harassment on the job. While racial discrimination increasingly became less permissible publicly, federal agencies, their supervisors, and many white employees still practiced it out of habit or spite. Accordingly, individual black federal workers protested and advocated for change through local chapters of the NAACP and NUL. New workplace protocols—such as the use of independent arbiters—emboldened many black workers who pushed their federal agencies to take a harder stance against discrimination. Others went outside the workplace and used the NAACP and NUL to amass data and file lawsuits.

Chapter 4 focuses on the political gains enjoyed by black federal workers from 1960 to 1969. The Civil Rights Act of 1964 included provisions that represented the strongest stand the federal government had ever taken to do away with workplace discrimination. Emboldened by the black freedom movement, many black federal workers sought to take advantage of both the new EEOC and the protections offered by Title VII of the 1964 act. This occurred simultaneously when the government, for the first time ever, recognized limited collective bargaining rights for all federal workers. This intersection of black workers' rights with the increased legitimacy of public sector unionism was initially a boon to black federal workers. Chapter 4 also details the dogged efforts of Julius Hobson, a former federal employee turned community activist, to maintain pressure on the federal government for workplace equality. Hobson relentlessly used data collection, pamphleteering, petitions, case law, Title VII of the 1964 Civil Rights Act, and any other tool at his disposal well into the 1970s, which suggests that the historian Nancy MacLean overstated the case when she asserted that Title VII of the 1964 Civil Rights Act was a "a powerful tool with which to open entry into the economic mainstream."[35] This chapter shows the immediate, suffocating backlog of cases that effectively neutralized much of the good that Title VII and the EEOC was theoretically to bring for aggrieved black workers—even though black federal workers were not included in Title VII's protections until close to a decade after its original passage. Hence, the data demonstrate that racial disparities persisted more covertly, as Rogers M. Smith's analysis maintains: even at the apex of racial liberalism (e.g., civil rights movement), federal policies paradoxically reinforced racial inequalities in the manner of their execution.[36]

Finally, in chapter 5, I explain why and how many black federal workers formed a nonunion, professional advocacy organization of their own—Blacks In Government (BIG)—in 1975, a good decade after the civil rights movement had birthed the most groundbreaking federal antidiscrimination mechanism to date, the EEOC. While blacks were always active in asserting their agency for change in the federal workplace, Blacks In Government was a direct and organized response to the shortcomings of past federal mechanisms that failed to effectively solve nagging problems of lower wages and slower promotion rates for black federal workers.

For instance, black postal workers first organized themselves as an industrial union called the National Alliance of Postal Employees (NAPE) in 1913, and later expanded their focus to include all federal employees. However, the union lost considerable political influence when it was not recognized as a bargaining agent during the reorganization of the postal service in the early 1970s, despite the fact that a significant part of workers striking for change were black, inner city postal workers. Hence, BIG's broad search for practical solutions to the common economic malaise afflicting many black federal workers across agency lines led to a 1979 conference held in Washington, DC, designed to teach black federal employees how to best prepare for career advancement. No longer content to wait for the government to make equality a reality, members and supporters of BIG decided to help themselves through a more structured organizational format.

With respect to how efforts to organize workers after the civil rights movement dwindled considerably, Joseph McCartin provides an excellent history of one smaller, specific group of federal workers.[37] By the early 1980s, public sector unionism had weakened considerably because of a strike by the Professional Air Traffic Controllers Organization (PATCO) that failed to generate broad labor support. As McCartin illustrates, before that fateful strike, public sector unionism had helped air traffic controllers, nearly all of whom were white, to improve their working conditions. In contrast, my study describes the obstacles black federal workers faced from a wider array of different agencies in seeking to advance their careers, especially in organizing a larger constituency unified along more abstract definitions of shared racial identity.

While air traffic controllers experienced plenty of turbulence in getting their union to a respectable position of power, there was little doubt among members about their larger group identity, forged through the shared experiences of rigorous and stressful training and work. Since the African American experience is far from monolithic, my research shows that organizing black federal workers primarily based on their racial identity was even more challenging than organizing workers who shared the same job function, which likely contributed to the continued maintenance of black-collar worker status over the decades. Given the broader, muddier interpretations of race, black workers had to create internal consensus as well as gain consensus with the external forces they faced. The chapters in this book illustrate black agency in wrestling with these questions surrounding socioeconomic identity, rather than only showing black federal workers as passive reactors to policy decisions made by high-profile, white political actors.

By the late 1970s, while more blacks had acquired supervisory positions with larger incomes across varied federal agencies, few obtained the new Senior Executive Service (SES) positions created for the most elite federal workers. As a result, at the beginning of the Reagan era, it was still as uncommon as it had been forty years earlier for any black federal worker to supervise large numbers of white employees. My study ends in 1981; the election of President Ronald Reagan and the decline of unionizing and federal employment growth were two trends that had significant consequences for black workers who were precariously positioned near the bottom of most economic wage scales. My research investigates the documented contextual changes for black federal employment between the eras of Wilsonian progressivism and Reagan conservatism.

With transparent hiring practices, steady and secure benefits, and a theoretical mandate for fair play, federal employment certainly looked promising. First, however, black-collar workers chronically suffered from lower wages and slower raises. Second, government-led, anti-racist employment policies were consistently manipulated and marginalized over the years. Third, black workers ultimately suffered the indignity of working for a system that simply did not work for them. When viewing the big picture of black federal employment from these three angles of historical analysis, it becomes readily apparent how the status of black federal public sector workers in Washington is encapsulated in the grand scene depicted in Savage's 1796 portrait, *The Washington Family*. Black workers were included in the picture, but largely brushed to the side of the larger economic picture.

My research shows how black government workers continued to believe in the promise of the American Dream and struggled in different ways to achieve it during a period noted for increasing racial liberalism. The public sector offered an improvement over a more openly hostile and discriminatory private sector, and in addition to greater economic security, many blacks increased their levels of political participation through membership in public sector unions. In contrasting the virtues of the public sector versus the private sector, it is vital to recall that one's income is theoretically unlimited in the private sector. Meanwhile, many black federal workers struggled for years just to obtain improved compensation in a large and coordinated wage system that had hard caps or fine limitations on one's earning potential.

By definition, it was (and still is) impossible for any black federal employee to earn more than a million dollars annually through wages alone; many chief executive officers working on Wall Street would seriously frown on such a restriction.[38] The implications of this socioeconomic dynamic cannot be overlooked. Blacks faced limitations in the job market where wages were limited in the public sector, and likely faced even greater restrictions where wages were less limited in the more remunerative private sector. In the struggle waged by black-collar workers for higher wages and faster raises, the economic stakes were still relatively low compared to the traditional earning power exhibited by whites in the private sector since time immemorial.

The Derricottes and other black families would agree that working for the federal public sector was definitely a "good government job," all things considered. However, my book contravenes the wholesale historiography that characterizes federal employment for blacks as "good government jobs." They may have been good jobs, but the question remains whether they were *great jobs*. Although the historian Thomas Sugrue declares that "no institution played a greater role than government in breaking the grip of poverty and creating a black middle class," the grip may have been broken but not obliterated.[39] Historical tensions regarding keeping blacks "in their place" are nowhere made more manifest than here, for if anything, the opportunity cost of being a black-collar worker (i.e., lower wages and slower raises) is incalculable. The idea that blacks should be satisfied—if not gracious and grateful—for a mere good job is an inadequate analysis. Such logic is reminiscent of how Southerners complained about "impudent Negroes" who would not stay in their place. African Americans should be free to pursue excellence in all its forms, including workplace economic equality. What is largely missing from the "good job" debate is dialogue and critique about how good jobs objectively could have been made greater. To criticize these good jobs as not good enough is to move from this sunken place, and perhaps toward a more encouraging reality that might better capture the idea of the American Dream, and not an *American Dream Deferred*.

CHAPTER 1

"BOY! LOOK AT ALL THESE GOVERNMENT GIRLS!"

BLACK OPPORTUNITY IN THE NATION'S CAPITAL, 1941–1945

School of Social Work student Dorothy M. Boggess came to Washington, DC, from Atlanta, Georgia, in the spring of 1941 to obtain a job as a federal typist. Although Boggess could have continued her graduate studies at Atlanta University, a local newspaper advertising the federal salary of $1,440 a year caught her eye since this salary was unprecedented for a black female worker in the South. The average Georgian stenographer, without the benefit of an advanced education, made only $1,000 annually at the time.[1] Boggess therefore took a qualifying typing exam at her local post office to determine whether migrating North would be a beneficial option. Shortly after receiving a favorable test score, Boggess received a telegram asking her to report to DC on April 4, 1941. She postponed her social work studies and left for the nation's capital to join the ranks as a "government girl" or "G-girl" at the War Department (now known as the Department of Defense). In contrast to the untold number of black women who stayed behind, Boggess immediately began to earn a larger, steadier, more secure income up North. Yet the irony was that Boggess's wages, while better in every respect than Southern rates, were still less than what the average Northern white worker earned performing the same type of job in DC.

Boggess's migration to Washington, DC, fit within a broader pattern; as many as 300 G-girls arrived daily throughout the early 1940s and during

1940–41, over 24,000 government girls came to DC alone.[2] Scarcely a month after the Pearl Harbor attack, *Good Housekeeping* magazine observed, "There's a new army on the Potomac—the bright-eyed, fresh-faced young Americans who have poured into Washington from remote farms, sleepy little towns, and the confusion of cities, to work for the government in a time of national emergency. Every morning they flow, like bright rivers, into the maws of the great buildings."[3]

G-girls in particular, fully exploited the window of opportunity created by war's social upheaval. Not only did G-girls flock to the nation's capital in hopes of attracting gainful employment opportunities, but they also attracted much positive attention in the process. In addition to having a military plane christened in their name, the G-girl experience was fodder for at least one Hollywood movie (*Government Girl*, 1943) and they were prominently featured in mainstream publications such as *Good Housekeeping*.[4] Further capitalizing on G-girl popularity, the *Washington Times-Herald* published a recurring feature, Jane's Journal, which chronicled the daily experiences of the fictional Jane Meredith, "a small-town girl who came to Washington to join the swelling ranks of Government workers,"[5] thereby underscoring the ubiquitous G-girl experience, although it was exclusively framed through a white lens. Curiously, none of Jane's Journal installments contained any overt hints of what Washington, DC, historian Constance McLaughlin Green termed "the secret city," or the growing number of black citizens that rapidly grew to a third of the city's population by the end of the 1940s.[6] In none of the accompanying photographs for Jane's Journal, which included depictions of Jane boarding the trolley or waiting listlessly in a cafeteria line, is she seen with or next to anyone of color. Although a growing number of incoming black women served the federal government just as faithfully, the euphemism "G-girl" was primarily reserved for white women.[7]

"G-girl" soon became the catchall designation to describe young, upwardly mobile women who flocked to Washington in search of stable government work. A native of Louisville, Kentucky, Boggess successfully matriculated at Kentucky State University, earning a degree in sociology. She assuredly had a sense of her political being and place, having attended a historically black college and university (HBCU) and having joined the first Greek letter sorority organized primarily for African American women, Alpha Kappa Alpha, during her senior year in 1939. As a college graduate, Boggess's first full-time employment (while simultaneously taking classes) was largely secretarial work for the president of another HBCU, Atlanta University, which likely made the War Department's offer more enticing for a young college graduate with long-term career aspirations of becoming an effective social worker.[8]

Boggess's career could only go so far if she remained in the South where most women her age at that time were working full-time either in agricultural or domestic trades.[9] Domestic work was not necessarily "beneath" Boggess now that she was a recent college graduate, it was simply more costly in terms of time and security. For starters, domestic work in the South replicated social dynamics reminiscent of the era of enslavement inasmuch workers were often on twenty-four-hour call: privacy and personal time were concepts reserved for white workers. Moreover, far too many black domestic workers were asked or forced to perform "additional duties" that had little to do with cleaning and that posed a risk to the worker's personal safety and welfare.[10] Given the dearth of options for black women outside of domestic and agricultural work, working as a G-girl provided migrating black workers the possibility for increased social standing and financial autonomy.[11]

Hence, as a rare black female college graduate, the young and enterprising Boggess likely saw Washington, DC, as more than just a capital city that bridged the North and South, but as a testing ground to see whether her personal quest for life, liberty, and the pursuit of happiness in the working world (i.e., her American Dream) could continue unencumbered. During an age when racial segregation was legally enforced, Boggess learned all too quickly that black workers like herself remained largely segregated from the mainstream in ways that their white coworkers were not—especially in the federal workplace.

It is no secret that the federal government had practiced segregation for nearly three decades before Boggess arrived in Washington. Physically dividing federal workers into separate workspaces by race dates back to when President Woodrow Wilson issued his April 11, 1913, decree, if not earlier informally. Wilson's observance of a segregated workforce prompted a direct response from black postal workers who organized an industrial union to extend across craft lines that same year, entitled the National Alliance of Postal Employees (NAPE). However, black federal workers like Boggess were still on their own; not until the mid-1960s did NAPE open its membership to all federal employees.

When Boggess first started her federal job, she was assigned to a segregated typing pool in the old Munitions Building in the 1900 block of Constitution Avenue, NW—there were only five black women in her unit. As the first black clerical employees in the War Department, their presence certainly did not go unnoticed. For, in addition to navigating the generic G-girl struggles that Jane Meredith faced in an unfamiliar urban environment, black workers like Boggess contended with the additional, distressing reality of racial discrimination in frequently hostile working environments. In the 1940s, people knew the nation's capital as a place where, "the seat of Federal Government is located in an area predominately 'south' in attitude, etiquette, customs and conventions."[12] Hence, Washington likely seemed more familiar to black Southern migrants as a "sleepy, southern town" than a foreign, industry-heavy metropolis such as Chicago or New York.

Notwithstanding Washington's Southern pace and feel, many other blacks besides Boggess began to view federal employment in the nation's capital as a promising avenue for economic and social advancement. As black War Manpower Commission employee Lucia M. Pitts noted in 1942: "Negroes, like other American citizens, helped build America, love America, want to defend America, but they must have their rightful share not only of woe and tribulation and sacrifice, but of economic opportunity and faith in America."[13] Pitts's eloquent juxtaposition of African Americans' desire to help America's cause as a way to directly help their own cause corresponds to historian Timothy C. Dowling's observations on a similar thought pattern during the Civil War nearly a century earlier. Dowling notes that many blacks saw the armed conflict as an "opportunity to prove that blacks were solid, skilled, proud, contributing members of American society and thus deserved the full benefits of U.S. citizenship," just as many blacks "proved" their loyalty by volunteering for Union or Confederate forces.[14] Lucia M. Pitts made this quid pro quo connection of full commitment to the country in exchange for full benefits of citizenship of that same country when she further observed, "America cannot win a war if thirteen million of her citizens are left out of it."[15] In other words, Pitts clearly identified a theoretical, if not moral, responsibility between her federal employer and the ideals for which they both labored.

Contrary to Pitts's concern, the federal government did not leave all thirteen million of its African American citizens out of the war effort; it actively hired blacks at a rate never seen before in the whole history of the country. The nation's capital quickly became a specific landing point for the estimated million black workers who migrated west or north during the Second World War, where the average black income rose faster in 1940–50 than in any other decade during the twentieth century.[16] Table 1.1 illustrates the explosive growth trajectory of the number of black federal employees. This chart is somewhat deceptive if one focuses only on the percentage of total black employees in the third column, as the rate of growth between 1938 and 1943 indicates an increase of only two percentage points. Yet, since the total number of federal employees in the entire nation also grew overall, the rate of relative black employee growth appears statistically insignificant relative to the whole. What is most significant is the second column, which enumerates the actual number of black employees. Here, the table reads more impressively that within the

Table 1.1. Nationwide growth of black federal employees, 1900–1944

Year	Total Employees	Total Negro Employees	Percent Negro of Total Employees
1900	232,000	868	.4
1910	384,088	22,540	5.9
1912	395,460	19,729	5.0
1918	917,760	45,000	4.9
1928	540,867	51,882	9.6
1933	572,091	53,000	9.8
1938	861,914	82,000	9.8
1944	2,295,614	273,971	11.9

Source: John Hope II and Edward E. Shelton, "The Negro in the Federal Government," *Journal of Negro Education* 32, No. 4 (Autumn 1963), 372. The first Great Migration may explain the percentage jump from 1918 to 1928 during the First World War. "As a result of World War I, an estimated seven hundred thousand to one million blacks left the South." Joe William Trotter Jr., "The Great Migration," *OAH Magazine of History* 17, no. 1 (October 2002), 31.

same five-year period of 1938 to 1943, the number of black federal employees more than tripled, which more than qualifies the Second World War as a watershed moment in the history of black economic development. Overall, the growth of black federal employees is remarkable, considering that the federal government, which had employed fewer than 1,000 blacks at the turn of the century, employed more than a quarter of a million black workers nationwide by 1944 (table 1.1).

In Washington, DC, alone, the National Urban League (NUL), a black civic organization focused on equity in the workplace and economic advancement of the black community, reported that "there were less than 10,000 Negro workers in the Federal government in 1938; in 1944, there were 41,566."[17] While the number of black federal workers in Washington, DC, was relatively insignificant at the onset of U.S. involvement in the Second World War, their number grew exponentially from that point for the next three decades, forever altering the "face" of American government. Only the brisk hiring pace that peaked at 4,000 new workers monthly made these high black employment levels and hiring rates even possible, although normal hiring patterns were dictated by the Civil Service Commission, which used a centralized, competitive examination system for lower grade positions.[18] While there is scant evidence to confirm that agencies routinely relaxed their hiring standards during wartime, the creation of emergency agencies increased demand for new rapid hires.[19]

But most of these positions, as filled by (white) women and blacks, were eliminated after the war due to obsolescence or were filled by returning servicemen who according to the Selective Service Act of 1940 had "super-seniority," and were able to reclaim their prewar jobs within ninety days of military discharge.[20] The pool of civilian workers was significantly narrowed with the expansion of the Veterans' Preference Act in 1948 to include mothers of veterans in addition to widows, wives, and veterans themselves. Many workers hired during the war were told that their jobs were temporary as no policy provisions were in place to protect these jobs.

Tensions arose not necessarily from the performance of black workers on the job, as many were competent and able to learn quickly. In fact, many unions did not feel threatened by this new incursion of employees as they saw the effort as a temporary, but necessary evil, and often maneuvered to prevent temporary workers from becoming permanent hires. Instead, tensions developed among black and white workers because of the strong impulse of many white workers to reject blacks once they started arriving in large numbers and, in some cases, once they held supervisory positions over white workers. More telling are the "hate strikes" documented during wartime staged by white American workers who refused to work alongside or under those select few black workers who were upgraded to jobs formerly held by whites.[21]

Black workers had to contend with more than the antics and tactics of racists on an individual level; many agencies such as the Treasury Department and Bureau of Engraving and Printing held fast to long-standing segregationist policies at the institutional level—even in light of supply and demand dynamics that dictated the hiring of black workers as sound economic policy. The contentious circumstances surrounding the federal government's embrace of black federal workers are thus significant because they provide insight into black employees' sustained treatment as "black-collar workers."

WAGING WAR

As black workers took advantage of war labor shortages to secure employment in the federal government, they quickly learned that the government operated differently from most other employers. Unlike the less-regulated and more openly discriminatory private sector, the federal government, to comply with regulations it imposed on private companies, was more obligated to treat its employees fairly. For example, high-profile agencies such as the Department of Labor were mandated by law to look after the welfare of wage earners of the United States of America and specifically to "advance their opportunities for profitable employment."[22] Given this context, I frame the theoretical, legal, and possibly moral obligation instinctively identified by Lucia M. Pitts and others as the federal government's "constitutional responsibility."

The transition of the federal government from segregation to equal opportunity was gradual and conflicted. Up until this point, proponents of racial integration attempted to leverage their arguments on an economic analysis for a more efficient workplace. That is, the urgent need for manpower during wartime meant that the government simply could not afford to discriminate among its labor pool, which would consequently limit its overall productivity. For example, in 1942, the Congress of Industrial Organizations (CIO) founder and labor leader Sidney Hillman called "employers' attention to the wastefulness of importing labor from distant areas or raiding the employment rolls of competitive firms when unused Negro labor remained available."[23] Once federal agencies actually hired black employees in larger numbers, Jim Crow segregationist customs stubbornly trumped federal ideals, and black employees were consistently limited to "black-collar jobs," or job opportunities with lower wages and slower raises relative to their white coworkers.

For instance, while Boggess's federal salary helped her earn more than virtually any stenographer, typist, or secretary throughout the entire state of Georgia, she still commanded a wage rate that was toward the bottom of the federal pay scale—$1,440 was comparable to a low-ranking Clerical, Administrative, and Fiscal Service (CAF-2) position.[24] While nonetheless part of the federal service, it was common to see black employees performing janitorial duties at the Federal Security Agency or cutting lawns for the Department of Interior; in other words, many blacks held manual and menial job functions similar to the jobs limited to blacks in the private sector. Relatively speaking, Boggess was placed in a better position than many because she was able to perform low-level clerical work, instead of being placed in a job requiring more physically demanding labor.

The DC chapter of the NUL noted early in 1940 that "the majority of [black federal] workers here as elsewhere, are in the lower occupational brackets, and therefore generally poorly paid."[25] The Washington Urban League (WUL) was the District of Columbia's local chapter of the national organization, the NUL. Founded in 1910, the NUL shared many of the same goals as other national civic organizations such as the National Association for the Advancement of Colored People (NAACP). Yet the NUL was not as racially integrated as the NAACP and focused more on workplace equity, as symbolized by its logo of a lone equal sign inside a circle and by its mission to "enable African Americans to secure economic self-reliance, parity, power and civil rights." The NUL was hardly engaging in conjecture; official data on occupational groupings for

Table 1.2. Major occupational groups of federal government workers in DC (excluding national defense and postal service), 1940

Occupation	White male	White female	Negro male	Negro female
Total	39,918	34,535	5,428	2,376
Professional and semiprofessional	8,222	1,775	95	71
Managers and officials	3,128	420	26	9
Clerical and kindred workers*	18,675	28,964	1,989	471
Craftsmen, foremen, and kindred workers	2,176	81	116	12
Operatives and kindred workers	1,600	1,613	724	440
Protective service workers	3,109	36	145	4
Service workers, except protective workers	757	1,496	569	1,281
Laborers, including farm workers	2,100	96	1,734	81

Note: *The term "kindred workers" refers to "similarly related job positions."

Source: U.S. Bureau of the Census, 1940 National Census, 609–12.

black federal workers in DC in 1940 reveals a "disproportionate concentration of Negro workers in the lower grades," with essentially no black workers in the upper-level professional or managerial ranks (table 1.2).[26]

As table 1.2 illustrates, whereas the majority of white workers ranked as clerical or higher, most black workers were in lower-grade positions performing maintenance, custodial, janitorial, or landscaping work inside federal buildings or on federal lands. The jobs of most black federal workers were thus similar to those they held in the private sector when the war effort first began. For example, a survey of 14 federal departments in April 1942 found that out of a total of 171,103 personnel, 9.1 percent were black, of whom "a mere 2.3 per cent were in positions other than junior or custodial ones."[27] Aside from an increase in pay above wages for standard domestic or agricultural work, it was unclear how else blacks initially benefited from federal employment; the jobs they happened to land did little to challenge the predominant social narrative that saw urban blacks as employable primarily in service positions.

PICTURING GOOD JOBS

Still, given the dearth of alternatives for transplanted and displaced black workers (e.g., domestic or service industries), such public sector opportunities were indeed attractive. Most black workers considered federal jobs to be "good jobs" inasmuch as they offered decent wages and a measure of long-term stability—a rare and alien concept regarding black laborers in the Jim Crow private sector. In addition to higher pay, the prevailing perception that the hiring process in the federal sector was more transparent and fair than in the private sector also made those jobs "good." For instance, Boggess's blind-ranking typing exam suggested that her ability rather than her skin color would determine the trajectory of her future federal career.[28]

Additionally, as early as 1940, the black newspaper, *Washington Tribune*, noted that threshold rules of transparency aided many blacks in taking the exams and qualifying for civil service jobs. Yet, once blacks started working for an agency, equal opportunities to succeed and advance within the agency were inconsistent at best. As a result, the *Tribune* noted that black applicants "have been subject to every trick of discrimination which the prejudiced [federal] appointing officers have been able to devise."[29] Despite the presence of agency protocols that discouraged racial discrimination, it nonetheless persisted.

Evaluating black-collar jobs is a complex task because these newfound positions were simultaneously fruitful and frustrating for black federal employees. While a black professional class existed in nearly every urban area, South or North—however small—federal positions in Washington proved very inviting to a large number of migrating blacks looking for work. Federal employment was the fruitful solution that provided stable, secure, and competitive pay in an environment more shielded from conventional types of discrimination. Many of these same workers had the frustrating revelation that racism was still operative, even within vetted federal agencies. Black-collar workers rarely enjoyed salaries or careers that matched those of their white coworkers, even for the same jobs. By 1947, 89.4 percent of black federal workers in DC had salaries less than the median average for whites.[30] While the federal government can and should be lauded for some of its innovative efforts to address racial discrimination in the workplace, ultimately it did little to fundamentally, systemically change or dismantle the overarching narrative of black economic marginalization consistent with the black-collar worker analysis. The fact that this "last line of defense" also succumbed to racism was indeed sobering for many black employees who migrated to the North.

An employee of the Farm Security Administration (FMSA), Ella Watson, is another clear example of these frustrating black-collar experiences that were defined partly or completely by race. Watson was the subject of the iconic 1942 Gordon Parks photograph *American Gothic*, which depicts her holding upright both a broom and mop in front of a large American flag inside the FMSA offices where she worked.[31] Parks was the fifteenth child of black Kansas sharecroppers who survived the Depression. Parks was therefore well familiar with the humbling concept of poverty as blacks were routinely worse off than whites due to institutional barriers that prevented and isolated blacks from obtaining nearly as much relief as white families from President Franklin D. Roosevelt's New Deal policies, which were designed to alleviate poverty both during and after the Depression. One notable example is that the Social Security Act of 1935 specifically excluded domestic and agricultural workers, who not coincidentally constituted two of the largest occupational categories in the black community at the time.

It was not until Parks arrived in the nation's capital, however, that he began to experience direct, daily racism—perhaps having interpreted his upbringing and condition as "normal" for rural living. Parks, as a professional photographer, a rare job for an African American, himself broke the color barrier when he first started working for the FMSA in 1942. He was bitterly displeased with Washington's "shocking level of bigotry in a city that contained the symbols of American democracy." Parks was horrified by the fact that "white restaurants made me enter through the back door. White theaters wouldn't even let me in the door."[32] He turned his frustration into ambition and subsequently accepted a challenge from his supervisor Roy Stryker to attempt to capture the racism he felt within the two-dimensional space of a photograph. Adding to the challenge was that he had to capture someone else's anguish and frustration and frame the picture correctly.

Recognizing the true import of the federal government's "constitutional responsibility," he soon realized that "photographing bigotry was very difficult," so he focused on "the evil of its effect . . . discernible in the black faces of the oppressed and their blighted neighborhood lying within the shadows of the Capitol." In other words, American democracy could not only be tested, but documented in the faces and lives of American workers—black federal workers, that is. Parks thus challenged the conventional definition of the "average American" by showing a black-collar employee in Ella Watson who worked just as hard for her American Dream, but perhaps had less to show for it.

In Parks's famous *American Gothic*, the missing buttons on Watson's dress, along with her blank stare and solitude, contrast perfectly with the 1930 Grant Wood painting of a farmer in the wake of the Great Depression. Parks's *American Gothic* photograph was a poignant reimaging of Wood's work of the same name depicting a stoic farmer holding a pitchfork, standing beside a woman (variously interpreted as his daughter or his wife) who looks equally stolid in front of their white Iowan farmhouse. In addition to her worn dress, Watson's face was worn as well; while it is true to state that she worked in the FMSA offices, it is equally important to clarify the type of work she performed—she was a government charwoman, or janitor, who faithfully cleaned the FMSA

Figure 4. Ella Watson, black-collar worker, 1942. Library of Congress.

offices nightly for twenty-five years. She started work at 5:30 p.m.—a time when most G-girls were leaving to go home or out on the town and indulge in their social and economic freedoms.

Not as socially or economically free as Jane Meredith or other typical G-girls who came to Washington, Watson had unfortunately arrived in the nation's capital with "racial baggage"; she lacked early parental support after her mother died and her father's life was taken by a lynch mob. She struggled through high school, got married and became pregnant, but received the news that her husband had accidentally been shot, which happened only two days before the birth of their daughter. Now widowed, Watson likely saw the North as a way to escape the violence and death that plagued her in the South. Watson's daughter had two children out of wedlock by the time she was eighteen, but died herself only two weeks after giving birth to the second child.[33] Thus, Watson was still affected by death and now encumbered with the responsibility of raising her deceased daughter's two children, one of whom was a paraplegic, in her tiny one-bedroom apartment. This parentless, widowed, childless grandmother was nonetheless committed to supporting the only lives connected to her. Probably because she did not have a college degree like Boggess, Watson had to accept a lower annual salary of $1,080.

At the FMSA offices, she had to settle for an even lower public opinion of her value and worth. In her work, Watson had to clean the office of a white female manager who began in federal employment at the same time as Watson with the same level of experience. Watson received a lower salary than her white "colleague" despite receiving a higher initial performance rating.[34] Here is where the federal government's policy of transparency failed Watson: what mattered most was that she was a black-collar employee. On paper, rating higher in performance than her white colleague, Watson should have been the logical first choice for promotion in a system operating best by placing the highest-qualified individuals in place. In reality, however, Watson had to endure immense injury to both pride and psyche in having to clean the office of a lower-rated colleague. The federal government's policy of transparency left no mystery as to who was the higher-rated candidate. The only mystery that remained was how denying Watson's promotion made logical, ethical, or capitalistic sense. Said Parks of his controversial *American Gothic* depiction, "I didn't care about what anybody else felt. That's what I felt about America and Ella Watson's position inside America."[35] Indeed what was clear was that Watson's lowly position encapsulated the frustration of black-collar workers who suffered the indignity of knowing that the only logical explanation for their social and economic plight was the illogical nature of racism.

It was a pity that neither Ella Watson nor Dorothy Boggess, who unlike Jane Meredith, had a publisher willing to chronicle her life in journal form as being among the first African American employees *ever* employed at the War Department. However, Boggess did note that her mere presence "caused quite a stir. The messengers and maintenance workers would peek in the door to see if the unit actually existed."[36] Before Dorothy Boggess joined the federal government, her enrollment in social work studies already signaled her desire to escape the domestic labor track that had ensnared so many black women:

nearly 60 percent of all black female laborers nationwide worked as private household workers at that time.[37] Whereas for Ella Watson, the unfortunate irony was that after finding employment with the federal government outside of the South, she still found herself working odd hours cleaning up after others for another quarter of a century, despite migrating North to presumably improved conditions. And yet it was likely Watson's "good" government job that led her to stay in DC for as long as she ultimately did.

STAYING IN DC

With hundreds of new workers arriving daily in DC, black and white government workers alike had another problem besides finding equitable, gainful employment. They had to secure adequate housing, and, given the growing demand and dwindling supply, this task proved more and more difficult.[38] With respect to skyrocketing demand, the nation's capital was so teeming with the constant flow of incoming workers that one white G-girl remarked that for her daily morning commute, "going to work on street cars and buses is like being packed in slave ships."[39] If Jane Meredith reported that she endured stress in searching for a suitable housing option, then housing options were especially limited for blacks in a city that was still quite openly segregated.[40]

Certain DC neighborhoods were "off-limits" to blacks due to practices of redlining, whereby real estate agents flatly refused to show blacks properties outside of areas marked in red on their office real estate maps, and due to racial covenants, where property owners agreed or promised not to allow blacks to take possession of the property. As late as 1948, the Washington Real Estate Board pronounced: "No property in a white section should ever be sold, rented, advertised, or offered to colored people. In case of doubt, advice from the Public Affairs Committee should be obtained."[41] The sum total of these many and varied barriers to entry prompted historian Francine Cary to note that moving "to the District proved far easier than finding a place to live and earning a decent wage. Segregation in housing allowed blacks only a limited range of housing options."[42]

In 1941, the same year that Boggess arrived in Washington, the limited range of housing options essentially meant that she could only live in "the black part of town." Although the nation's capital was technically open to all Americans, the black part of DC consisted of three principal areas: (1) the white-dominated Northwest quadrant with a pocket of black middle- and upper-class residents stretching from U Street to LeDroit Park, (2) the more racially and class-mixed Southeast quadrant, and (3) the black-dominated slums of the Southwest quadrant. In the early 1940s, black residents scarce-

FIGURE 5. Economic prosperity was not a given in the nation's capital, several federal workers were limited to housing options in DC's slums.

ly penetrated any points west of 16th Street or Rock Creek Park in the upper Northwest, the lone exception being a small inkblot of black life dubbed the "Gold Coast," inhabited by a mostly professional black class north on 16th Street, not far from DC's northwest border with Silver Spring, Maryland.[43]

While unable to secure government housing, Boggess was able to avoid the dreaded "black neighborhoods" of Tiber Creek and Swampoodle; two Southwest neighborhoods that constantly suffered from frequent flooding and foul aromas. There, a garbage disposal at New Jersey and K Streets in addition to a garbage crematory at the foot of South Capitol on the corner of T Street burned coal constantly to incinerate garbage and dead animals daily. Dead bodies were also numerous in Southwest Washington; it was home to the DC Morgue for many years. Although built to resemble a chapel to soften its visual presence, complete with a spire and stained glass, the morgue's location at 7th and Water Streets was directly due to the frequent drowning of victims in the Potomac nearby. Southwest DC also became home to the city's poorest newcomers who found shelter in DC at the expensive proposition of no electricity or running water. Southwest alley dwellers "were employed in farming, governmental jobs from clerks to janitors, and the burgeoning dock work

FIGURE 6. Sunbathers on the sidewalk in the back of Idaho Hall at Arlington Farms, 1943.

along the waterfront." These living conditions starkly contrasted with the idyllic postwar suburban utopias sprouting up in nearby Montgomery County, Maryland, or Arlington County, Virginia.

Once Dorothy Boggess left her northbound train at Washington Union Station, she had to navigate a city highly segregated along residential and commercial lines. For example, her first residence in DC was the all-black Phyllis Wheatley YWCA off Rhode Island Avenue, named after the first female black published poet. But her stay there was brief; she was fortunate to transfer to a single room inside a private home soon afterward. Perhaps Boggess's relatively smooth transition influenced her positive praise of Washington, DC, as "the place where colored southerners could escape the field or kitchen and work indoors for the government."[44] Thus, for many black and white federal workers, government housing became a welcome option because it was affordably priced, well-maintained, close to work, and often roommate-free.[45] However, only white G-girls like Jane were eligible to live in Arlington Farms, a large, sprawling government housing complex in the Washington suburb of Alexandria, Virginia.

This type of preferential treatment for whites was not isolated, for Evalyn Walsh McLean (last private owner of the Hope Diamond) sold her Northwest Tenleytown Road, summer estate, Friendship, property to the federal government for $1,000,000 on December 31, 1941. McLean stipulated converting and developing the residence into temporary—but segregated—housing for white government workers.[46] With more than 6,000 rooms accommodating more than 8,000 workers, Arlington Farms cost $24.50 a month in rent. Meanwhile, Negro G-girls had to live in segregated public housing, which isolated and stigmatized the workers because of their race.[47] In response to the exclusively white Arlington Farms, the federal government agreed to build three small dormitories for Negro girls adjacent to the black neighborhood of LeDroit Park and Howard University in Northwest DC: Slowe, Midway, and Wake Halls.[48] Wake Hall, the first residence dormitory for Negro G-girls located at Oklahoma Avenue and Twenty-Fourth Street, Northeast, housed close to 800 girls. While Midway was opened to 75 new residents without much fanfare, Alcott Hall for white G-girls was opened with a congressional reception attended by officials from the Federal Public Housing Authority.

Lucy D. Slowe Hall was designed by the black architect Hilyard Robinson and was built by the Defense Homes Corporation in 1943, while the other two dormitories reserved for segregated housing, Midway and Wake Halls, were constructed by Samuel Plato, a rare black American contractor who built over forty government buildings in his lifetime. Lucy D. Slowe Hall, owed its namesake to one extraordinary educator, the first U.S. black female to win a national championship (American Tennis Association, 1917) and a founder of the oldest black female sorority in the country, Alpha Kappa Alpha—which coincidentally was founded at the HBCU Howard University in 1908. Located at Third and U Street, Northwest, inside the attractive and highly desirable LeDroit Park neighborhood, Slowe Hall was built at a cost of $760,000 and opened on December 15, 1942. Slowe Hall contained 277 single rooms that rented for $7 weekly and 22 double rooms that rented at $6 per person weekly. By January 12, 1943, the building was only 50 percent occupied due to the administrative neglect of not prioritizing the needs of Negro G-girls, which created an outcry among area leaders despite the severe shortage of housing for workers in DC. The new Negro hall was managed by W. Spurgeon Burke on behalf of the Defense Homes Corporation and targeted black women living in

FIGURE 7. Lucy D. Slowe Hall, first government residence built exclusively for Negro women, 1943.

DC for less than one year in anticipation of 35,000 more black women arriving between January and July of 1943.

Segregation in work and housing at the federal agency and private housing levels was difficult enough, but blacks also suffered from social segregation as well. Blacks remained excluded from the whites-only social clubs and were restricted in taking advantage of the cosmopolitan attractions of downtown Washington, since so many restaurants, department stores, and movie theaters refused to serve black people.[49] For example, the *Negro Motorist Travel Guide*, published listings of segregated facilities to prepare wary black visitors to Washington, with more than sixty addresses mostly around U Street and Florida Avenue. Jim Crow was alive and well in the nation's capital; the city, although smaller in size, had just as many segregated listings in the *Travel Guide* than some states in the South. The guidebook's creator, Victor H. Green, created the book as a means to spare traveling blacks undue humiliation and also served the nation as a federal employee (Harlem postal worker) before leaving for more friendly territory in the travel agency business.

As a direct by-product of segregationist practices in DC, the three small

Negro dormitories (or rather, the cafeterias and lounges inside them) became huge cultural resources where black workers and military servicemen alike could meet, eat, and socialize. George Green, a former enlisted man, recalled, "I met my wife [at the black dormitory Lucy D. Slowe Hall] forty-five years ago. I was a military man. Tenth Calvary. We used to ride horses down Pennsylvania Avenue. A friend of [my wife] introduced me. We used to court right there in the [Slowe] lounge."[50] Negro dorms served as a citadel or safe haven from the socially destructive discriminatory forces in the private economy. Rather than risk physical or verbal abuse or embarrassment, many black federal employees used the Negro dorms as a social base to include members of the black community (not just federal workers) in various social occasions, celebrations, and even dances outside of the white world from which they were restricted. The cruel irony was that during the war effort, black and white federal workers were colleagues working for the same country during the day, but forced to avoid each other like enemies from different territories the minute they got off work.

DISCRIMINATION AT THE AGENCY LEVEL: INSIDE THE OFFICE OF PRICE ADMINISTRATION

While segregation operated as a general barrier, adversely affecting black-collar workers in employment, housing, and social circles, four specific barriers directly shaped the black-collar experience on the job in the federal government bureaucracy during the Second World War—physical, economic, bureaucratic, and barriers ironically deemed "nonexistent." The experiences of black workers in one significant executive agency—the Office of Price Administration (OPA)—illustrate this fruitful and frustrating reality. The OPA played a key role in regulating the economy by implementing price controls and administering the rationing system. The agency, as described by its director of personnel, Everett Reimer, was the creation of a small group of young, mostly Jewish attorneys who were in fierce competition with other agencies over jurisdictional matters influencing the OPA's reach and ability to fulfill its mission. Just a few months after the Japanese attack on Pearl Harbor, the OPA had over 60,000 employees nationwide with a field organization consisting of "7,000 local boards, 300 rent offices, 70 district offices and 9 regional offices." According to Reimer, there "literally was not time for the [racial] prejudice of individuals to become consolidated," particularly when, as Jews, so many officials experienced and were sensitive to morally questionable social ostracism as well.[51]

Although black workers composed just 2.1 percent of the OPA's workforce, the agency nonetheless emerged as one of the more progressive federal agencies based on its treatment of black-collar workers at the time.[52] Part of this positive legacy is thanks to the leadership of the OPA administrator from 1943 until the end of the war, Chester Bowles, who built a solid reputation as a leftist-leaning, independent political thinker. Bowles, according to Reimer, "gave more attention to the problem of race discrimination than any of OPA's other administrators" and was "the first of OPA's Administrators to discuss the question of discrimination personally with the heads of the field offices."[53]

One of Bowles's early acts was to amend local OPA board member selection policies to allow for more minority representation. Bowles also required district offices to include minorities to better represent and serve their districts. These changes directly resulted in the hiring (by a federal agency) of blacks to do professional work for the very first time in some Southern states. Further, besides just issuing memorandums from the national office, Bowles held regular meetings to encourage his program deputies to treat black employees fairly both on the job and in the field. While directly responsible for only a small portion of OPA hiring decisions, Bowles's mandates helped create an encouraging environment of racial acceptance on the job.

PHYSICAL BARRIERS

Bowles's management style was quite unorthodox compared to that in the vast majority of federal agencies that observed racial segregation as part of everyday protocol. Historian Karen Anderson suggests that in many cases, physical segregation was seen as a necessary tactic by white managers seeking to minimize and quell unrest among the majority of their white workers. White female employees were apprehensive about sharing the same physical workspaces with blacks, while white men were more anxious about their rank, pay and promotion rates being demonstratively higher relative to black male workers. Physically separating white and black federal employees was a cost-efficient way to allay these fears of both male and female white workers.[54]

Federal agencies routinely segregated black and white federal workers by positioning filing cabinets and other furniture so as to isolate and cordon off black workers from whites in the same section of the same agency.[55] In fact, on an inspection tour of the newly built Pentagon, President Franklin D. Roosevelt noted four restrooms placed "along each of the five axes that connect the outer ring to the inmost on each floor of the building." When he inquired about the reason for such prodigality of lavatory space, when only two at each axis were necessary, "the President was informed that nondiscrimination required as many rooms marked 'Colored Men' and 'Colored Women' as 'White Men' and 'White Women.'" Thus, in the name of *nondiscrimination*, twice the number of allowable bathrooms were built to ensure equal, but segregated access to the facilities in the federal workplace. Federal administrators also placed screens and partitions between black and white workers to ease white staff members' irrational apprehensions of being too close to black workers possibly becoming defiled in the process.[56]

However, even the OPA, with its unusually liberal chief administrator, also enforced physical segregation, thereby creating tension between black and white employees at the agency. Housed inside the Old Census Building, the OPA separated cafeteria lines and dining rooms by race during wartime. After many whites occupied the "Negro line" and cafeteria in order to cut down wait time, blacks did the same to the white facilities in response. But one OPA official remarked, defensively: "[W]hat is important is that while there were at that time many prejudiced persons in OPA they did not set the pattern for the majority as they usually do."[57]

Shortly after the war, the OPA's Personnel Office attempted to improve racial relations by creating an internal policy dictating that official parties "could not be planned by any organizational unit which all members of the unit could not attend." Washington, as a highly segregated city, left the agency with few options, with some segregationist facilities "bending" their rules "to the extent of permitting mixed groups in private dining rooms." But the OPA had its own struggle with discrimination. Reimer reported problems with unsuccessful racial and social mixing in the recreation room and numerous incidents "in which white girls became fearful of Negro men"—disturbing and unchallenged narratives that sounded eerily reminiscent of the misguided rationales shared in or around many Southern lynching grounds now found themselves echoing and reverberating down federal hallways up North.[58] Not to mention, many white OPA administrators objected to the composition of all-black pricing boards, even if lawfully constructed in certain urban areas where blacks were concentrated, under the auspices that such all-black boards would appear "discriminatory." Meanwhile, the composition of all-white pricing boards proliferated in both the North and South and blacks were routinely denied opportunities to purchase scarce goods during the era of price control.

In response to these tensions, the Printing and Distribution Branch of the OPA in 1943 took the unprecedented step of commissioning a fact-finding committee to investigate charges of racial disparities. The fact-finding committee was established in response to stinging charges of discrimination brought by the United Federal Workers of America (UFWA), a left-leaning, interracial union that had about 10,000 black members nationwide by 1944.[59] The committee conducted extensive interviews and learned, unsurprisingly, that black expectations for equal treatment conflicted with the white predilection for segregationist customs. For example, the fact-finding committee heard the testimony of a black employee, Mrs. Robb, who originally had a desk job working on the nationwide census with the Census Bureau, housed in the Department of Commerce since 1913. Because of Robb's fair complexion, she was mistaken for white. After white colleagues discovered her racial identity, they immediately placed Robb in the stockroom, physically and psychologically distanced from her former white colleagues.[60] Her experience was far from unique. The committee determined there "was and is physical as well as organizational segregation of Negro employees of the Branch. In some sections with both Negro and white employees, the seating arrangement is such that the Negroes are grouped together."[61]

The UFWA had a close relationship with the officials of the OPA as well as its black employees. Everett Reimer noted that the UFWA was "a consistent, vigorous and intelligent protagonist and watchdog of the cause of nondiscrimination."[62] Individual supervisors and administrative officers of the OPA were also members of the UFWA. This nexus encouraged the OPA Personnel Office in particular to "develop a sense of mission with regard to the rights of minority group members."[63] Soon after the OPA made its nondiscrimination policy public early in the war effort, the union took the bold step of bringing discrimination charges against a white deputy administrator for failing to promote qualified blacks in his unit—an uncommon move at the time given underdeveloped antidiscrimination protocols. After the hearing board presented a draft report of its findings, the deputy administrator resigned, which "bolstered the union's confidence in the good faith of the management, [and] strengthened its bargaining power with operating executives."[64]

At the same time, many federal agencies reinforced existing segregation by contracting with job placement services such as the United States Employment Service (USES), which maintained separate reception desks and working sections for blacks and whites within its own agency offices. Such stark physical separation made it difficult for prospective black employees to start their careers without feeling racially inadequate. In addition to physical segregation on the job, blacks faced literal physical scrutiny during the application process for such federal jobs.

With the common "Rule of Three" practice, federal employers looking for candidates would distill applicants down to three finalists and pick the most qualified applicant for the job, notwithstanding the fact that the applicant's photo was attached as a requirement. Only the top three names were forwarded to hiring officials, with hiring preferences provided to veterans who "floated" to the top of lists thanks to the Veterans' Preference Acts of 1919 and 1944, in recognition of their service, sacrifice, and skills. This "Rule of Three" practice was predictably abused in a discriminatory manner against black applicants when the protocol required inclusion of the applicants' photographs—a practice discontinued based on the intervention and advocacy of NAPE and the NAACP. Since three pictured candidates received consideration simultaneously, it was difficult to establish that top black candidates were specifically not selected due to discrimination. Black postal workers in NAPE and the NAACP nevertheless successfully campaigned to abolish the photograph practice in 1941, citing a disproportionate influence on black candidates who were passed over at a rate more than twenty times that of their similarly situated white counterparts. Aside from the expensive practice of obtaining a photograph, which already disproportionately affected black candidates, what was truly costly for black employees was that more often than not they were screened out of jobs because employers knew their race beforehand.[65]

ECONOMIC BARRIERS

It was clear from the time blacks entered the federal workforce en masse that black federal workers consistently earned lower salaries than fellow white employees performing the same type of work. The difficulty in analyzing economic data in isolation is that low salary levels alone do not reveal de facto discriminatory patterns. On the one hand, a few black employees of the OPA made as much as $6,500, or nearly three times the median for whites at the agency, which undoubtedly was an encouraging sign of racial progress.

Moreover, this salary disparity explains how an agency like the OPA could—accurately—boast a growing number of blacks, but few in upper-level, higher-paying positions. A 1944 press release announced that "Negro employment in the National Office of the Office of Price Administration has risen to 12 percent of the total force, from 1½ percent in January, 1943." The same press release celebrated that the OPA had received a plaque from the UFWA for having the best race-relations policy among government agencies. The same press release also hinted at the rarity of upper-level black employees when it listed the occupations of those blacks in the OPA's Enforcement Department as consisting of "a senior attorney, an investigator, statistical clerks, typists."[66] While an attorney is undeniably in an upper-level position, grouping in black typists suggests a liberal classification to mask the dearth of total upper-level blacks employed.

A staggering 65 percent of blacks working at the OPA never progressed higher than Grade 1, where the annual salary was just $1,260.[67] Those black employees who commanded higher salaries, perhaps unsurprisingly, had received a higher education (e.g., as a lawyer, economic statistician, or accountant), which was true for only a minuscule proportion of all blacks employed

Table 1.3. School attendance by age for the Washington Metropolitan District, 1940

Age	Total	White No.	White Percent	Negro No.	Negro Percent
Attending school	157,629	117,800	74.7	33,694	21.3
15 years	11,940	8,909	74.6	2,958	24.7
16–17 years	19,538	15,373	78.6	3,954	20.2
18–19 years	10,820	8,883	82.0	1,755	16.2

Source: U.S. Bureau of the Census, 1940 National Census, 971.

nationwide at the time. In 1940, only 1.3 percent of blacks obtained a bachelor's degree or higher; before the doors of federal employment opened, a lack of education was a concrete institutional barrier to social mobility as higher education was a virtual prerequisite for entry and advancement in many of the professional trades.[68]

Obtaining a higher education was not simple for black employees who wanted to improve their standing in the workplace, insofar as black students tended to drop out of high school in greater numbers than did whites. In DC, for example, school attendance percentages for the year 1940 were roughly the same for both races until students reached the age of fifteen. By then, more black students began leaving school to look for work, likely experiencing compelling economic pressures at home, which accounts for inferior high school graduation rates in contrast to their white counterparts (see table 1.3). The percentage of black students drops precipitously as the age of the student increases. The lack of schooling opportunities and quality education put many black employees at a severe disadvantage when competing for anything other than entry-level jobs in the federal government.

The ubiquity of black employees in the OPA in lower-level positions reveals the relationship between education and employment levels; 87.5 percent of all black employees in March of 1945 occupied the two lowest pay categories (see table 1.4). Unsurprisingly, this group sustained the largest amount of attrition after the war (i.e., over 40 percent), a further indication of their vulnerability and perceived expendability.

However, educational disparities only illuminate part of the reasons that black employees working side-by-side with white employees in the same agency still received different treatment despite performing the same work and having similar backgrounds. For instance, Arlene Neal was a black, married mimeograph operator at the OPA with a beginning classification of CAF-1, a

Table 1.4. Types of jobs that use professional and clerical skills held by Negroes in OPA regional and district offices with number and salary range for each type

Types of jobs	No. of Negroes employed		Salary range
	March 1945	November 1945	
I. Attorneys associated with Price, Rationing, and Enforcement	9	6	$3,200–4,600
II. Price, Rationing, and Rent Director, Executives, Examiners, Inspectors, Aides, and Interviewers	41	43	$1,620–4,600
III. Information Officers	14	5	$2,000–3,800
IV. Administrative Officers	17	8	$3,200–3,800
V. Investigators	43	41	$1,800–3,800
VI. Economists, Accountants	5	2	$2,000–3,800
VII. Stenographers, Typists, Clerks	891	501	$1,260–3,600
VIII. Machine Operators	14	20	$1,260–1,620
Totals	1,034	626	

Note: The larger salary range and broader range of job functions may explain the number of black workers listed in Category II. The number of workers in Category V, Investigators, may be explained by a concerted strategy by the OPA chief Chester Bowles who was "anxious" to have staff carry out: "Full use of Negroes, or members of other minorities, not only as regular staff members but in positions where it is important to have persons who know intimately the needs of the various minority groups within the particular region."

Source: Office of Price Administration, "Analysis of Reports on Negro Employment in All Field Offices," November 30, 1945, Box 7, RPCCR; Office of Price Administration, "Memorandum: Special Assistant to the Administrator on Racial Relations," November 25, 1944, Box 7, RPCCR.

pay rate of $1,260, and a superior performance record. In 1943, Neal learned from her supervisor that she had "reached her peak" in the section after a year's time. Neal's supervisor directed her to take a typist training course to prepare her for a lateral move. Rather than give her a promotion and pay upgrade in her field of specialization, the OPA fired Neal. But the white worker who was hired to take Neal's old job received an immediate raise to $1,620, which constituted a more than 30 percent increase over Neal's old pay despite performing Neal's same duties.[69] Statistical data demonstrate that only 10 percent of white employees across all educational levels worked at Grade 1 versus 65 percent of all black employees. This discrepancy suggests that white colleagues and supervisors valued and evaluated each other's work differently from that of black-collar workers. In other words, more than educational disparities, a blatant preference for white workers by other white workers was a challenge few black workers could consistently prevent or address without incurring severe economic consequences.

Another example of economic segregation was the 1943 case of OPA employee John A. Alexander, a black assistant file clerk, classified as CAF-3, and paid $1,620 annually.[70] Despite earning strong marks for past job performance, Alexander applied for a promotion three separate times, but his supervisors denied him on each occasion. Adding to his frustration, on each application Alexander learned that his supervisors offered the promotion to white males—even though they had not applied for the given position. When his superiors found no one willing to accept the promotion, rather than offer it to Alexander who applied thrice previously, the agency abolished the position altogether and created two new jobs that ranked lower than the original position for which he had applied. A new white employee filled one of the new positions, and Alexander filled the other. Alexander's promotion ordeal demonstrated the agency's reluctance to give blacks in the workplace more power and responsibility at work since the promotion would have placed Alexander in charge of some whites. The OPA "resolved" the problem, but only by forcing Alexander to share his responsibilities with a new white employee who had much less seniority.

Interviewed for the job of senior clerk of the Printing and Distribution Branch of the OPA, Alexander said that when he missed the first and second vacancies, he thought little of the matter. When he missed the third job vacancy, however, he began to realize, "It was my color which was keeping me down, I felt pretty much in the dumps."[71] Alexander's comments remind us that economic barriers not only represented the direct financial costs of not being able to advance one's career, but also a psychological cost that was even more difficult to precisely calculate.

BUREAUCRATIC BARRIERS

In addition to physical and economic barriers in the federal workplace, black employees had to navigate bureaucratic barriers that were subtler and more difficult to surmount. Over time, racist notions of black incompetence persisted even as black bodies became more common in federal workspaces. The increase of black employees working with whites at various federal agencies over an extended period of time might suggest increased familiarity and a relaxing of racial tensions as tasks were completed. However, under the flexible principle of black-collar workers, the narrative or description of black inferiority merely shifted to fit new circumstances. Thus, while new policies and legal apparatuses for fighting discrimination emerged during the postwar period, whites reinscribed race discrimination in new structures, erecting new barriers that constrained blacks from gaining entrance to the highest-paid, most prestigious positions in the federal government. It was not a question of competency, for it was a matter of compatibility with the employee's black identity. While overtly offensive and obvious racist reasons were not necessarily articulated directly to the black-collar employee, the end result was that the black employee's economic prospects were marginalized and invalidated, all in the name of a blameless, faceless bureaucracy. This notion is false since the bureaucracy is composed of numerous individuals who never took responsibility for their actions, which had collective damaging results.

Furthermore, it was harder for isolated, higher-ranking black employees to defend themselves against such subtle barriers, particularly when so few of them ascended to the bureaucracy's upper ranks and had little familiarity with the nuanced nature of internal politics. More than being blocked from view by obstructive file cabinets or receiving a smaller paycheck, bureaucratic segregation spoke to black-collar workers' marginalized experience as employees because most whites ultimately saw them as inherently incompatible and incompetent. Hence, a major reason for the lower pay or physical separation was the shared, collective sentiment that blacks were simply less competent, less capable of management, or less cohesive within the workplace.

Federal employment was unique in that it provided one of the first large-scale American working environments in which blacks and whites actually *worked together* within the same space, as most black laborers were strictly segregated by function, pay, and importance in the South. While the supply and demand dynamics of the Second World War made the prospect of additional black laborers as contributors more attractive, black workers were still less desired as colleagues by whites. For example, in an exhaustive study about segregation in the nation's capital, one white manager of a federal agency offered this simple defense for rejecting black employees: "I was afraid of losing a number of the very good [white] girls I had."[72] Black employees were perhaps needed, but not wanted.

While such fearful attitudes reflected Jim Crow conventions, they nonetheless betrayed core ideals of equity, or constitutional responsibility, that the federal government supposedly pledged to uphold. For instance, the OPA fact-finding committee discovered that "Negroes were not promoted to vacancies in sections other than Stock and Duplicating. In terms of the total numbers of white and Negro clerical personnel in the Branch there were proportionately four times as many promotions of whites as of Negroes from the period August 1 to October 16, 1942."[73] This trend against black promotion displayed in the OPA was unfortunately not unique at the time. The OPA was nevertheless unique in enjoying a reputation for being more progressive than most federal agencies when it came to racial relations. If one of the more progressive federal agencies was promoting white employees at a rate roughly four times that of black employees, this likely says less about the OPA and more about the federal employment landscape as a whole. Such employment, while fruitful in contrast to hard domestic or agricultural labor, was nonetheless frustrated by Jim Crow conventions that dictated disparate treatment for black and white employees working for the same agency, for the same government, in the same country.

Bureaucratic segregation led directly to the "ghettoization" of black labor, which kept most blacks at the lower salary levels, prevented them from advancing in their careers, and often isolated them from upwardly mobile white employees. For instance, table 1.5 demonstrates that before the end of the war in 1945, 93 percent of all black employees at the OPA national office in DC were being paid at least $2,000 or less. Meanwhile, in the same agency in the same city, 77 percent of all white employees making at least $2,000 or more. Such data amassed by the OPA at the onset of the postwar era war is highly valuable inasmuch as it was quite rare—the OPA was a trendsetter in its maintenance of a transparent set of statistical records as many agencies did not amass and collect such racial data unless expressly asked to do so. In fact, federal agencies would not be required to report racial data until passage of the Civil Rights Act decades later in the mid-sixties and the creation of the Equal Employment Opportunity Commission.

What makes the OPA data even more disconcerting is the fact that there were nearly seven times the number of white employees as black, which controverts general principles of supply and demand that might suggest fewer federal black employees held higher paying positions since there were a smaller number of upper echelon positions available. If anything, shocking salary disparities between black and white workers persisted in federal public sector circles akin to those disparities prevalent in the private sector that so many blacks sought to escape by migrating north. In the progressive OPA alone, while the overwhelming majority of the nearly 500 black workers received less than $2,000, nearly half that total of white employees (i.e., 237) commanded salaries of more than three times that amount—$6,500. While the heavy concentration of black employees at the lower pay grades likely corresponds to

Table 1.5. Summary table, types of salaries held by Negroes, OPA national office

All employees	All levels	$6,500 and up	$5,600	$4,600	$3,800	$3,200
	3723	237	356	526	377	326
Negro employees	493	0	4	3	4	8
Percent Negro of total	13	0	1	1	1	2

All employees	$2,600	$2,000	$1,800	$1,620	$1,440	$1,320
	269	408	693	367	111	43
Negro employees	12	39	145	174	72	32
Percent Negro of total	4	10	21	5	65	74

Source: Office of Price Administration, "Analysis of Reports on Negro Employment in All Field Offices," November 30, 1945, Box 7, RPCCR.

the lack of increased education (see table 1.3), at the same time, not all white employees at the higher pay grades had the benefit of higher education. Many whites were promoted without the aid of education as the deciding factor. Thus, the absence of black employees in the upper-level federal positions contrasted sharply with the heavy preponderance of white workers who occupied them (see table 1.5).

Not only were many blacks simply not privy to direct political access that translated into personal direct gain in the federal system, but a feedback loop was created wherein white managers and administrators only justified black workers' inferior pay and inferior placements since such low-grade positions were already dominated by black presence. Another practical bureaucratic barrier was the lack of exposure black workers sustained in upper-management circles even if they harbored plans of upward mobility; most low-grade positions were heavier on manual and menial labor and required little or no interaction with white coworkers. This psychological framing helped maintain the unequal status quo. In a segregated workplace, the constant exclusion of blacks from informal conversations and training opportunities and limited leadership experiences in the white-collar world of federal employment stunted the career growth of any black employee before it began.

For those federal agencies employing a large proportion of white-collar employees, there was little, if any, black representation. For example, table 1.6 illustrates how the Securities and Exchange Commission had over 1,000 em-

Table 1.6. Federal departments with over 1,000 employees, 1941

Department	Total	Black	Percent
SEC	1,001	5	.5
RR Retirement Board	1,168	8	.68
Home Owners' Loan	1,210	5	.41
Farm Credit Administration	1,307	27	2.07
FHA	1,431	14	.98
Recon Fin Corp	1,463	47	3.21
Federal Emergency Relief Administration, Public Works	1,665	494	29.67
ICC	1,789	11	.61
VA	2,142	88	4.11
WPA	2,142	88	4.11
Labor	2,290	150	6.55
Justice	2,454	77	3.14
Soc Sec Bd.	2,519	23	.91
Post Office	4,378	735	16.08
General Accounting Office	4,959	151	3.04
Commerce	5,065	222	4.38
War	5,235	197	3.76
GPO	5,399	1,043	19.32
Navy	10,740	146	1.36
Agriculture	11,850	352	2.97

Source: "Tribune Columnist Shows that Executive Branch of Federal Government Employs 9,717 Negroes against 115,552 Whites," *Washington Tribune,* July 5, 1941.

ployees located in Washington, DC, in 1941, but only five were black (.005 percent). That same year, the General Accounting Office had 4,959 employees working in DC, with only 151 black (3.04 percent). Where black workers occupied a significant proportion of the workforce (i.e., 10 percent or more), it was largely in agencies that required a large number of manual and menial laborers (e.g., Public Works, the Post Office, and the Government Printing Office) and where, unlike working inside a shared office space, they were unlikely to consistently share a physical space with whites.

Not all blacks were disempowered or devoid of contact with upper echelon jobs that had administrative clout—on paper, that is. In contrast to Dorothy Boggess who came to Washington, DC, at the beginning of the Second

World War in search of federal employment, Dr. Robert C. Weaver represents a high-ranking, black official who left both his federal job and the nation's capital toward the end of the war due to bureaucratic barriers that he found too great to surmount. While the gender, timing, and employment status of Boggess and Weaver differ, their stories reveal the working conditions black-collar employees faced at varying places in the employment hierarchy.

Unlike Boggess, Dr. Weaver did not have to start his federal career from the bottom of the political hierarchy with an entry-level job after taking a blind typing exam. A DC native and Dunbar High School graduate, Weaver became a rare, high-ranking black federal employee who represented the empowering possibilities of government employment. Having earned a PhD in economics at Harvard University, Weaver was fast-tracked into leadership, having been named a director in the War Manpower Commission. Weaver saw his directorship of Minority Group Services with the War Manpower Commission as a viable means of implementing change for other black Americans. All his education, experience, and training still failed to fully prepare and protect him from the sting of black-collar treatment. After some time on the job, Weaver felt that too much theorizing stood in the way of effective policies to increase job and housing opportunities beneficial to black Americans—his chief complaint being the lack of autonomy and authority to perform his job.

Although Dr. Weaver felt he was "enmeshed in a maze or irrelevant and unimportant functions," while working for the government, he nonetheless saw federal employment as a key source of jobs for the black community. He wanted to ensure that such jobs would continue to be available, and increase in peacetime as well as during wartime.[74] In early 1944, despite his having worked for the federal government in a high-ranking, high-powered position for eight years, Weaver resigned in frustration over what he termed to his own "administrative impotence." After leaving his government office, he wrote *Negro Ghetto*, a book that outlined his thoughts on why black poverty was unique and so difficult to overcome.[75] Weaver's resignation signaled that, despite his numerous attempts to change federal employment policy, change was slow in coming—especially in the higher ranks where bureaucratic protocols were directly shaped.

Dr. Weaver's commentary is telling, as few blacks had more direct access to federal power than he. As an unofficial member of President Roosevelt's "Black Cabinet," a term coined by the noted black female federal employee and educator Mary McLeod Bethune, Dr. Weaver's federal career trajectory of having successfully "made it to the table," only to be effectively marginalized in actual authority and responsibility presaged the black-collar status of most black federal workers. Despite his early misgivings, Weaver eventually

FIGURE 8. Robert C. Weaver, a pioneering black federal worker who was also unafraid to critique his employer. Library of Congress.

became the first African American to be *officially* appointed as a full-fledged cabinet member when he served as the U.S. secretary for Housing and Urban Development for President Lyndon B. Johnson from 1966 to 1968. At this early stage before the war ended, Dr. Weaver's pessimism concerning fundamental, systemic economic change for blacks was still too great. Later in his career, he came "full circle" to work again for the federal government on an issue about which he was passionate—inadequate and impoverished housing for urban blacks. Nevertheless it cannot be overlooked that early in his career when arguably he had more to risk, he had the courage of his convictions to resign from a federal government apparatus that he felt was not working.

Relatively speaking, however, more blacks were gainfully employed by the federal government than ever before. Further complicating evaluation were small flashes of encouraging success experienced by many other black federal workers. For example, Bethune not only was appointed head of the Division of Negro Affairs for the National Youth Administration (NYA), a New Deal program created in 1935, but also was instrumental in obtaining equal pay for black youths working in the program.[76] However, it should be noted that the equal pay initiative was largely limited to all-black working units, and limited to 10 percent of all total funds (reflective of the black population at the time) although blacks constituted more than 20 percent of all poor people during the Depression Era. Jobs created by the NYA were also mostly temporary, and only provided occupational training opportunities for youth between the ages of sixteen and twenty-five.[77] In other words, although the equal pay Bethune secured was laudable and groundbreaking, such efforts were mostly for segregated, transient high school and college students and excluded full-time working adults in the federal sector. It should also be noted that once the NYA was disbanded in 1943 after Congress refused to fund it further, Bethune never worked for the federal government again.

"NONEXISTENT" BARRIERS

Likely due to implicit pressures associated with constitutional responsibility, many federal agency heads tried to avoid appearing unfair to their black employees—at least publicly. Although the existence of racial discrimination was observed privately, federal agency leadership rarely acknowledged it openly—at least in the province of their own particular agency or fiefdom. For example, on December 3, 1945, OPA chief Chester Bowles wrote a letter to United States Civil Service commissioner Arthur S. Flemming detailing various racial problems in Flemming's agency.

Since the war had ended, many black OPA employees were "reduced-in-force" as the agency sustained overall cuts. However, unlike most agencies, many OPA officers routinely made the effort to find jobs with other agencies for their employees. While scant data exist to definitively corroborate the the trend, it is likely given the milieu of socioeconomic and political factors surrounding black employment that a disproportionate number of black employees—especially those in menial positions—were "reduced-in-force" disproportionately in contrast to white employees. An OPA report issued after war details how from the period of November, 1945 to March 1946, the number of Negro attorneys associated with price rationing and enforcement was reduced only from 9 to 6, whereas Negro stenographers, typists, and clerks went down from 891 to 501.[78]

Frustrated by reports from the OPA's Personnel Division that several "reduced-in-force" black employees were having difficulty getting transfers to the United States Civil Service, Bowles drafted an internal memorandum listing several specific examples of racial discrimination that he became aware of as an upper-level white administrator. Chief among Bowles's allegations were: (1) that the State Department specified white, Gentile messengers for jobs to the exclusion of anybody else, (2) that the Weather Bureau in the Department of Commerce inquired for transfer applicants of "light complexion," (3) that the Naval Research Laboratory indicated they lacked facilities for "Negro employees," and (4) that the Civil Aeronautics Administration (CAA) stopped considering a prospective applicant after learning the applicant had attended the HBCU Howard University.[79]

Bowles's inflammatory memo was accidentally leaked to the press, prompting an outcry from the federal agencies he accused of practicing discrimination. Bowles then drafted a more generic, politically benign letter that he authorized for release to the public. He apologized and rescinded his comments by sending separate, personal apologies to the head of every agency mentioned in his letter.[80] CAA chief T. P. Wright's response to Bowles's apology reveals the understandable desire to avoid appearing discriminatory, despite concrete data suggesting otherwise. Wright clarified for Bowles that the alleged discriminatory CAA action in refusing to consider an HBCU, or black, graduate, "was not made by the Personnel Office of the Civil Aeronautics Administration, but by the Personnel Office of another Federal agency. It is indeed unfortunate that the CAA was erroneously mentioned in your letter."[81] Tellingly, Wright's letter did not convey the name of the other federal agency involved, or confront the discriminatory conduct carried out by another federal agency, or condemn the incident's occurrence under federal auspices. More important, the letter sought exculpation in order to protect the CAA's interagency reputation and prevent it from being unfairly impugned any further.

To be fair, Bowles's original motivations may not have been entirely altruistic. While his original memorandum dealt with the subject of racial discrimination, the effort may have been fueled more by professional indignation. While such motivations are difficult to discern from the primary sources, it is clear that Bowles modified his initial more pointed and critical tone and attempted to appease other white male administrators with personal apologies

as his first communication also risked insulting white male bravado specifically and not just general federal notions of fair play. The lack of agency many
blacks had in communicating their grievances is illustrated by the fact that the
four alarming allegations by Bowles only saw the light of day through the lens
of white males vying for administrative power and control. Revelations of racial discrimination appeared to be the mere by-product of a political struggle
as Bowles's agency originally was rebuffed in attempts to reassign workers that
it already decided to terminate. While the CAA agency head bristled over the
very suggestion that racism was infecting his domain, no substantive public
discussion emerged over the implications and possible influence of the four allegations, if they were found to be true. Also unknown is what Bowles would
say if challenged to explain why so many OPA black workers were targeted for
reduction in force in the first place.

However, in a private move suggesting that Bowles believed in the veracity
of his initial criticism, despite his subsequent public backpedaling, a month
later he instructed his black administrative assistant, Frances Williams, to
take an informal poll to gauge additional reaction to his original memorandum. The "Negro public" expressed that Bowles's memo "lifted my spirits"
and "spoke when no else would." In contrast, for the "section of the white
public I know," Ms. Williams reported that some white respondents generally thought, "It is just what I expected from Bowles." White officials in the
OPA found the memo "unfortunate," "crazy," and an example of "bad timing."
There was no indication in the poll of what would constitute better timing to
address allegations of racial discrimination, if they were true.

All of the aforementioned barriers meant that many black federal employees remained largely unprotected from blatant acts of discrimination by their
white coworkers. White workers were loath to incriminate one another, especially in a culture and social climate where it was still acceptable to openly
disparage and devalue blacks, both individually and collectively. The normal
nature of black devaluation is evident in the case of War Department employee Jessica Valentine. In 1945, Valentine complained to the local NAACP
branch after unsuccessfully pursuing resolution of her discrimination complaint through her own agency's chain of command. Valentine, a junior statistical clerk and the only black worker in her group, testified that she "never was
warmly received by the group, but I always exchanged greetings with them,
and I endeavored to work harmoniously with them, with a detached and
business-like attitude."

Despite her "businesslike" attitude, her fellow workers and her immediate supervisor freely used the epithet "nigger" and boisterously sang the song
"catch a nigger by the toe," in her presence, laughing repeatedly as they did

so. Valentine duly documented her grievance, but no disciplinary action occurred. To add insult to injury, the uniformed head of her section told her that she was "too sensitive." To add further injury to insult, Valentine reported that the head of personnel, a Captain Weir, "immediately began to relate some anecdotes to me about Negroes that he once knew who have been called 'nigger' and how they ignored it."

Valentine's account illustrates upper administration's callous, tone-deaf approach to resolving racial friction in the federal workplace. Valentine's concerns about her career trajectory in a toxic work environment, which had been documented and acknowledged as filled with animus, coupled with the psychological stress of not knowing when the next "racial attack" might occur and from where were summarily ignored. If anything, she received an ultimatum since disciplining racist offenders was not within agency protocol. Valentine reported, in distress, "Captain Weir then said that if I felt that I was being discriminated against, and could not get along, the thing for me to do was to resign, because 'he could not fire anyone.'"[82] The War Department doubly victimized Valentine: initially with the offending behavior and then by refusing to recognize her grievance as if it had no rational basis and did not exist.

As more federal agencies hired more black employees in the wartime city, the struggle between the "theory" and "practice" of racial equality only grew more complex because blacks had access to a newfound federal job market with a wide range of economic—and by association—political implications for their roles in the larger American society. While the general idea of racial discrimination was not "new" to many of the black federal employees working at the time, many of them were working for the federal government for the first time. Thus, racial discrimination would rear its head in similar, but nonetheless different ways from those to which blacks were previously accustomed. Many black employees had to adapt and adopt tactics to resist a variety of physical, economic, bureaucratic, and "nonexistent" barriers that they did not have to consider when working out in the field or in someone's home. This is not to suggest that black workers had no agency, but rather, it addresses the difficulty of navigating a new and ever-changing landscape because over time racist notions of black incompetence had persisted, and the narrative of black inferiority merely shifted to fit new circumstances under the principle of black-collar workers.

DC AND BOGGESS BOTH CHANGE

Dorothy's original all-black unit of five eventually grew to fifteen. Fifteen then decreased to zero when the group was eventually abolished and employees were absorbed into other units with the onset of increased integration toward the end of the war. After the war, Dorothy Boggess left the War Department and enrolled in Howard University's Graduate School of Social Work to continue the studies she had initially abandoned after joining the war effort. Upon completing her studies in 1951, Boggess successfully pursued a career in the health services industry, landing jobs with the DC Health Department, DC Village, DC General Hospital, and the Department of Vocational Rehabilitation. Boggess continued a career in the public rather than the private sector—this time for the local municipal government of Washington. Like many of the black female employees who stayed in Negro dormitories like Slowe Hall, Boggess married a man who also happened to be a black federal worker; they met in the lobby of Slowe Hall even though unbeknownst to both he was already quite close to her while working at the Navy and Munitions Building.

The contrast between Boggess's story and that of Jane Meredith in Jane's Journal reflects a larger dynamic at play during a vital period in modern American history. Unlike Jane, Boggess and many other black workers like her who escaped the South, were coming north to the nation's capital for more than just a job. They were searching for more than a viable career path. They too, sought life, liberty, and the pursuit of happiness. Or so they thought. Officials in the federal government were keenly aware of this hope for real freedom. The War Department, for example, used the image of black Pearl Harbor hero Dorie Miller on recruiting posters directed at African Americans immediately after the fateful attack. Miller, a Navy cook who, without any prior training, instinctively manned a machine gun during the chaos of the surprise attack and may have shot down a Japanese plane. He received the Navy Cross for his bravery.

However, the War Department neglected to mention that, if they were to enlist, blacks were more likely to remain restricted to kitchen duty or other service jobs than to see live action handling artillery or heavy machinery, as celebrated in Miller's case.[83] The recruitment posters can more accurately be classified as glamorous propaganda; at the same time that the federal government was developing marketing materials in efforts to ease racial tensions, promote unity, and encourage support for the war against blacks, there was no discussion or thought of fundamentally changing an employment system that saw blacks as fit for menial cooking and cleaning jobs only. The Dorie Miller campaign perfectly illustrates the black-collar worker's dilemma—blacks in the federal government were needed, but not wanted. Compared to black workers in the private sector, black federal workers suffered more from this "illusion of inclusion," where the federal government used images of black workers to embellish its political mandate of an idealistic, egalitarian society that in practice offered the full benefits of American citizenship (economic freedom in particular), to a mostly white population.

Nonetheless, the iconography of Miller's hope was widespread—even after his death in the hold of a naval ship less than two years after his rise to fame. After making personal sacrifices, traveling a great distance, and agreeing to work for the federal government, more black workers were eager to start a new life of public service on their own terms. This quid pro quo analysis hearkens back to the Civil War, when many blacks reasoned that despite the North's imperfections, "proving" their loyalty and citizenship through military service and sacrifice would improve their chances of "earning" the full rights and responsibilities of American citizenship.

Historical evidence demonstrates, however, that the ultimate sacrifice was not enough to prevent the country from embracing Black Codes, sharecropping, or Supreme Court–sanctioned Jim Crow laws after the Civil War. Perhaps as a profound statement about the inferior socioeconomic leverage collectively enjoyed by blacks during the Second World War, the powerful black press ignored this precedent and rationalized that aligning with the federal government would be better than fending for themselves in the virulently racist and violent South. The federal government benefited from its popular image of transparency and was seen as less economically restrictive than the private sector due to less friction upon entry with standardized examinations and high labor demands. During wartime, initial eagerness for employment would slowly evolve into the expectation of enjoying full equality on the job as the number of black-collar workers continued to grow. This sentiment of expecting a return for one's investment as part of the American idea was captured by NAACP president Walter White who confidently declared in 1940: "It's our country, too."[84]

Gainfully employed black federal workers differed significantly from their counterparts in the private sector. While some black federal workers performed specific tasks that resembled blue-collar or service positions in private industry (e.g., operating press machines for the Government Printing Office or mowing lawns for the Department of Interior), the larger federal employment structure provided a more transparent and tangible system for career development and advancement. In short, while a committed steel worker likely had few employment options outside of the steel mill, a federal worker had several agencies that could offer lateral or upward movements based on performance and opportunity.

Auto and steel workers were adjuncts to the machinery that kept large corporations running, but black government workers gained an additional measure of esteem for they both literally and figuratively represented the face of the American government. This additional esteem, while difficult to measure in monetary terms, nonetheless had value in a Jim Crow world that rarely affirmed the competency and capability of black workers.

The Second World War provided a new window of economic opportunity for many blacks migrating to DC in search of work. However, Jim Crow practices continued during war, and the federal government maintained mostly segregated workspaces for the new black workers it welcomed on the job. Arguably, the government's most significant step toward racial equality since Reconstruction occurred on June 25, 1941, when President Franklin D. Roosevelt signed Executive Order (E.O.) 8802, which called for dismantling racial barriers in the defense contracting industry. President Roosevelt promulgated E.O. 8802 in response to black labor activist A. Phillip Randolph's plan to stage a march and rally on the Washington Mall to protest the exclusion of black workers from defense jobs.[85] Randolph's efforts to advocate for black labor in the private sector also gave black workers in the public sector an important new legal weapon to improve their status. After Randolph agreed to call off the march, E.O. 8802 also fostered the formation of the president's Fair Employment Practice Committee (FEPC) to administer the unprecedented executive order.

In reality, E.O. 8802 hardly affected the day-to-day working conditions of many workers like Boggess, but it did create the first official federal mechanism to track and monitor discrimination on the job. Placed under the War Manpower Commission in 1942, the FEPC sorely lacked powers of enforcement or investigation and dissolved four years later in 1946. Still, its existence—and weakness—underscored the need for additional resources to effectively combat the very disparities contemplated with the FEPC's creation, as 75 percent of all cases across forty-nine industries involved African Americans in the FEPC's first year.[86] While it theoretically had the ability to cancel contracts, the exigencies of war dictated that most government officials were unwilling to do so even when there was a violation. So, based upon money, the FEPC was merely an idea that never materialized into an initiative. Herbert Hill testified that not a single contract had been canceled as of 1968, "although many major government contractors have been found guilty of engaging in a variety of discriminatory employment practices."[87]

The historical record reflects government acknowledgment of racial discrimination as a labor problem as early as 1941, but effective solutions for discriminatory treatment initially lacked centralization and consistent application. Even the left-leaning OPA, which amassed a better antidiscrimination track record than most agencies, still did not stray far from the majority of agencies that aggregated most black workers in the unskilled, lowest ranks with the lowest wages. OPA administrators like Everett Reimer acknowledged the confluence of events that contributed to black federal employment rather than the singular inspiration of altruistic racial justice: "The war, the labor market, the nature of the program, the way the agency got started, and the way it grew, the fact that it was a new agency; all these contributed to the results achieved."[88] If the factors Reimer listed were necessary to provide a few black workers with working conditions only slightly better than the average black federal worker, which were arguably better than those of the average black domestic or agricultural employee, then such conditions spoke volumes about the low quality and quantity of working opportunities for black workers in the private sector.

During the Second World War, black federal workers came to the nation's capital and were rewarded with stable work that provided more promise of a future career than did most private sector jobs. As northern cities became more crowded due to the loss of Southern jobs because of increased agricultural mechanization, which prompted further migration, black workers generally met with more restrictive protocols and barriers to entering the free market economy than those experienced by most white immigrants at the turn of the century.

Public sector work thus became all the more attractive given its accessibility and stability relative to the external market forces that were starting to wreak havoc on the private sector. The private sector model shifted from welfare to warfare during the war, complete with cost-plus contracts, which guaranteed profits for enterprising proprietors, and now had to shift again once wartime ended. Thus, early in the postwar era, increased industrial automation plus reorganization of the global economy resulting in the export of millions of jobs to less developed parts of the world (i.e., China, Mexico, etc.) made entry-level private sector work more difficult to find and maintain. Public sector work, while not fully immune to the travails of the private sector, was structured and designed to better prevent concepts such as nepotism and seniority from otherwise wholly excluding capable contributors from joining the workforce.

This constitutional responsibility to be open, accessible, and presumptively fair is likely what informed a 1943 survey of federal agencies concerned with "Negro Morale," which claimed that the nation's very survival hinged on the "effectiveness with which it rights the [racial] wrongs which prevail on the home front."[89] Not only did public sector work become more plentiful, accessible, and stable, it arguably grew more politically significant to the nation's identity as a whole by the beginning of the postwar era. The federal workplace became the public, highly visible, petri dish by which all could observe how "the great democratic experiment" was progressing. Consistent with earlier periods in American history, there is often no better way to test democracy than to study its effects on the African American. A winner of the 1974 Nobel Prize in Economic Sciences, Gunnar Myrdal observed as much in his 1944 seminal work, *American Dilemma*, where he stated that the immoral treatment of the Negro was "a kind of moral dry rot which eats away at the emotional and rational bases of democratic beliefs."[90] Myrdal's report echoed the words of socialist activist Hubert Harrison a generation earlier when he described "the Negro [as] the touchstone of the modern democratic idea."[91]

Thus, one way to analyze the strength of the American democratic ideal is through the lens of black Americans who formally joined forces with the federal ranks. Unfortunately, these "black-collar workers" not only received lower wages with slower promotion rates, but also lacked sufficient economic and social leverage to reject the principle that a black-collar job with less pay was still better than no job at all. In 1944, Maurice A. Gersing of the Columbia Heights Improvement Association told the Senate District Committee that most blacks in DC "are newcomers who came here because they were told they could get good jobs, high wages and they should clean up while the cleaning is good and then go home."[92] Gersing's succinct analysis accurately describes the scenario surrounding many incoming blacks who literally changed the complexion of the federal workforce during a period of wartime need. Gersing and the federal government were still unclear about what changes lay ahead as many emigrating blacks decided against "going home" and stayed in the area seeking to call Washington, DC, their new sanctuary, just as Dorothy Boggess did.

CHAPTER 2

"STUDY LONG, STUDY WRONG"

ACHIEVEMENTS AND LIMITS OF COMMISSIONS STUDYING DISCRIMINATION IN THE FEDERAL WORKFORCE, 1945–1947

PRE-POSTWAR AMERICA

"They Read about It in Paris" reads the caption of a photograph that appears on page nine of the August 25, 1945 edition of the *Pittsburgh Courier*—one of the country's widest circulating black-owned newspapers after the Depression era, topping 200,000 at its peak. In the darkened photograph, light reflects most prominently off the face of the white-owned *Ce Soir* newspaper that announced the Japanese acceptance of the Potsdam ultimatum of July 26, 1945. The undated photo offers no clue as to when exactly these servicemen obtained the August 11, 1945, edition of this French newspaper whose headline read "Le Japon Capitule!" (Japan Surrenders!), but the photo indicates that this small audience is well-pleased. Five black male and female members of the 6888th Central Postal Directory Battalion stationed at Rouen, France—a town just two hours northwest of Paris—appear crowded around the outstretched newspaper, and five smiles are barely visible to both the strained and trained eye as they "prepare to celebrate."[1]

The *Ce Soir* article details that the British Broadcasting Company announced fourteen hours earlier that the Japanese government was preparing to accept the conditions of the Potsdam Declaration, in which President Harry Truman famously demanded that opponents surrender or suffer "prompt and utter destruction."[2] However, Truman did not formally announce the surrender until the evening of August 14, 1945, with the official ceremony following two weeks later. But shortly after Truman's initial announcement, people began to gather spontaneously and celebrate V-J Day, or Victory over Japan Day, which symbolized the formal end of the Second World War given the fact that Nazi Germany had unconditionally surrendered in Europe some three months earlier. This spontaneous American celebration was encapsulated for many years in the controversial, prize-winning photograph by *LIFE* photographer Alfred Eisenstaedt of a sailor and a nurse "kissing" in New York City's Times Square. While the identity of the pair and the consensual nature of the kiss remain in dispute, it is clear that the sailor and the nurse did not know each other had no existing relationship before V-J day. For years, this emblematic photograph embodied the mood of many Americans throughout the land at that moment—the feeling that with very little fear of the unknown, America would sally forth toward progress and prosperity, passionately embracing welcome allies along the way.

More accurately, the Eisenstaedt photo captured the mood of many *white* Americans. According to the historian John Fousek, the *Pittsburgh Courier* photo of the black servicemen in France is likely one of the few images that captures blacks celebrating the end of the Second World War.[3] Even though the black battalion members in France may have caught wind of the end of the war before most of America, ironically, their picture was published after the major celebrations had taken place. The image is a U.S. Army Signal Corps photo from the Bureau of Public Relations, which calls into question its true origin and the sincerity of its intent. Not enough information is provided to discern whether the moment captured in the photograph was spontaneous or whether it was staged to show that V-J Day affected more than just whites.

In the very same August 25, 1945, edition of the black newspaper, the *Pittsburgh Courier*, columnist Toki Schalk observed that on V-J Day, "we rode through the lanes of shouting, gesticulating folks . . . and then in sharp contrast to the white people, there were the little knots of colored people, just standing, watching. Not shouting, nor crying, nor waving their hands." Schalk's account is a sobering reminder that the celebration was not uniform for all Americans at that time. Schalk ominously continued with a foreshadowing of the black-collar worker's continued plight despite the war's conclusion when she wrote, "It wasn't that all of us don't have something to be thankful for . . . but for Negroes, another war has already started . . . the war for economic freedom."[4]

Economic freedom transitioned from an American Dream into an American reality for millions of new families as the postwar era became a very dynamic time in American history marked by profound financial growth. Now that the war was over, birthrates started to surge again after a protracted lull and "the cry of the baby was heard across the land," as historian Landon Jones put it.[5] By the end of 1946, some 3.4 million babies were born, representing an eye-popping 20 percent increase from the year before and the "baby boomer" generation represented a distinct departure from the widespread conservative approach that hindered family development in the aftermath of the Great Depression. Now that the American economy had received a substantial boost from the war, it started to transition from being a producer-based economy to a consumer-based economy, necessitating widespread change within entire industries as the Industrial Revolution showed signs of slowing down.

Moreover, there was one industry that—even in peacetime—bucked the declining trends and continued to enjoy sustained growth: the federal government. While now at peace with many previous wartime enemies, the United States was not at peace with the communist Union of Soviet Socialist Republics. While many disputes were settled leading up to V-J day, a major question remained unanswered—who would emerge as the dominant superpower, complete with a political economy that was universally accepted by other nations? In the ensuing struggle to build up America as a beacon of democracy, the United States not only invested in foreign countries abroad through arrangements such as the North American Treaty Organization (NATO), it also made significant investments domestically through the build up of its military prowess and firepower. As the government grew in its role to spread democracy, so did its need for a larger military. As the population grew, so did the government.

If every cloud has a silver lining, then out of the billowing, gray clouds at Pearl Harbor on December 7, 1941, emerged a renewed sense of patriotism not felt before in the twentieth century. As the United States became involved in the Second World War, so did its commitment to exhausting all military and government resources to ensure success; out of profound loss came profound opportunity. Government girls like Dorothy Boggess recognized this opportunity and sought to personally profit as did many black Americans who migrated from the South. However, now that the war was over, this profound opportunity quickly changed and the urgent demand for black labor dissipated, although in cities like Washington, the black-collar worker remained. Now a new battle for a new American democracy began.

BACK TO WORK

Once the war ended, one new battle facing thousands of black federal workers was to successfully land long-term employment with the federal government.[6] In September 1945, Agnes E. Meyer, wife of Eugene Meyer, the editor and publisher of the *Washington Post*, warned the Washington Council of Church Women that the "adjustment of the migrant war workers and the absorption of the returned veteran by the local community" called for a highly coordinated effort between federal and local agencies. Meyer's motivation was to "prevent acute and widespread hardship . . . especially of Negroes."[7] Her comments were prescient in light of the 1944 Veterans' Preference Act that explicitly allowed for super-seniority, which translated into massive displacement of temporary black workers as returning white veterans (as well as their mothers, wives, and widows) reclaimed their prewar jobs.

Before many agencies rescinded their temporary war service positions, the federal government assisted as great a number of workers as possible with lateral transfers to perform similar work with those agencies that survived the war. In most cases, employees had to reapply for jobs with no guarantee of being rehired. However, black federal employees disproportionately failed to obtain transfers or permanent employment elsewhere.[8] In fact, black federal workers were "affected two and one-half times as severely as white workers" by unemployment since so many had held service positions that only lasted for the duration of the war.[9] Once the war ended, the value of black federal workers decreased dramatically in the eyes of many white administrators as the supply-and-demand pressures shifted. The very same administrators who had desperately counted on black workers during dire times saw their need for black workers quickly faded in peacetime.

For many agencies, a return to peacetime also meant, at least initially, a return to prewar Jim Crow traditions that stifled black workers' opportunities and clouded their once bright future. Research by local DC unions and civic organizations showed that in the aftermath of the war, agencies such as the Department of Labor and Department of Commerce explicitly stated that they had "clerical positions for white workers but not for Negroes."[10] Even the United States Employment Service (USES), although expressly responsible for fair job placements for all eligible applicants, maintained "separate interview units for black and white workers, kept separate files of job applicants, and on request, referred applicants to employers on the basis of race."[11] Thus, the transition from war to a peacetime economy severely threatened economic advances made by blacks employed in the federal government.

The irony was that the positive Second World War working experience of blacks and whites collaborating for the same government only solidified the fact that blacks had one set of expectations for the future, while whites had another. White veterans returned to Washington, DC, expecting to claim new jobs, but conversely, black workers (women in particular) wondered whether they would have to reclaim their old subservient jobs. However, too many blacks were hired and entrenched within the federal ranks to be easily moved out or reduced in force entirely.[12] It is likely that the government did not fully anticipate the new long-term labor problems that would arise from its decision to hire blacks temporarily just to solve its immediate labor shortage problem.

For many white workers, the "liberty" to participate in a free market economy without direct competition from an equally qualified class of laborers was likely taken for granted during the prewar Jim Crow era. This historically restrictive economic dynamic was now under assault after the war—at least in public sector circles. Black workers repeatedly faced resistance from new white "colleagues" who wanted nothing more than to return to more familiar times when blacks were not coworkers, but were easily co-opted into completing tasks as subordinates.

Norah D. Stearns, a white editor with the U.S. Geological Survey, demonstrated the difficult conceptual transition that lay ahead for federal workspaces seeking to integrate both white and black workers once the war concluded. Shortly after V-J Day in December 1945, she stated: "I have no doubt that most former domestics will go back to housework, but conditions must be changed. Intelligently-run housekeeping bureaus should be established to put domestic work on the same basis as industrial and governmental jobs."[13] Commenting on postwar job contraction, Stearns essentially argued that black female workers should leave the federal workplace and return to domestic labor, or "go back to housework." Additionally, by directing her comments to "former domestics," Stearns is not referencing all G-girls of all types (à la Jane Meredith), but rather employs a euphemism for black female workers. The narrative of domestic black female workers was particularly dominant during this time when nearly two-thirds "of all nonwhite women in the experienced labor force in all occupations were in [domestic service] fields in 1940."[14]

Again, Stearns was not so much espousing racist drivel as she was being "rational" in her reflection of the indelible image of blacks operating primarily in a service capacity as reinforced and reflected in mainstream popular culture. A twenty-year study conducted by the Graduate School of Business Administration at UCLA noted that in 1946, the overwhelming majority of blacks depicted in mainstream commercial advertisements "were depicted in the ads as having laborer or service jobs: maid, waiter, slave, field hand, personal servant, the Aunt Jemima, or the Uncle Tom. The higher status occupations (including police and firemen) shown in the ads constituted three percent of the American Negroes."[15] Cognitively, it was especially disorienting for white workers to compete with blacks for better jobs or, simply to work alongside them in formerly all-white working environments as evidenced by white-led "hate strikes" during the war effort.[16] Thus, after the war, in returning to "normal," many whites did not see African American workers in white-collar professions or managerial settings as part of the normal order.

In recognition of the paucity of visible black professionals, it is not wholly coincidental that soon after the war ended, in November 1945, John H. Johnson began publishing *Ebony* magazine. In so doing, Johnson wanted to illustrate "[w]ords and pictures, *Black* words and pictures, and a *holistic presentation* of the Black image"[17] that expanded beyond the subjugated and servile images of blacks that were heavily circulated in popular culture. Up to this point in history, the average white employee's work life was unquestionably white-dominated and was made financially secure courtesy of systemic narratives that reinforced institutionalized racism—even in the purportedly more progressive North.

Less than a year into the postwar era, for instance, Neil Dalton, a senior official in the Federal Housing Administration (FHA), reasoned that the dramatic slowing of hiring new blacks in federal employment was more than mere coincidence: "From the results to date in regard to the employment of Negroes, it would seem that the search for qualified members of minority groups had proceeded neither positively nor vigorously."[18] Upon the war's conclusion, many black workers found they were the last hired and the first fired as the federal government downsized from its peak wartime levels; black workers found it especially difficult to keep their jobs, find lateral transfers, or land new jobs altogether. Fortunately for these black-collar workers, these inequities did not go completely unnoticed.

EARLY ATTEMPTS TO ADDRESS INEQUITY

With such a dramatic demographic shift in such a short period, the federal government sought to understand quickly what potential problems might arise and what solutions were feasible for all parties involved. Recognizing that the number of black workers had grown so significantly that they were likely to become a fixture of the federal workforce in DC, the government initiated investigations into the state of race relations, paying particular attention to how racial inequities affected its own workforce.

After the war, initial attempts to address racial disparities in the federal government yielded inconsistent results. Little evidence exists of consistent, race-based grievance protocols during the war, insofar as potentially latent racial tensions were likely masked by a nationalistic focus on patriotism. Furthermore, high concentrations of blacks in low-level positions coupled with a dearth of high-ranking black employees who had seniority disadvantaged employees with work-related concerns because few blacks had the ability to institute or influence any type of grievance mechanisms in the workplace. Historian Jesse Thomas Moore Jr. notes that of the "nearly 300,000 Negro government employees in 1945, approximately 70 percent were in unclassified positions." Agencies such as the Public Health Service, the Export-Import Bank, the Patent Office, the Federal Security Agency, and others, publicly acknowledged that they did not employ Negroes except as cafeteria workers or porters. The National Urban League (NUL) and other organizations chided the president for allowing federal agencies to engage in such racial discrimination without effective grievance mechanisms.[19]

The investigatory mechanisms that did exist often lacked binding power to be truly effective. Exacerbating matters was the general lack of agreement on what constituted a "discriminatory act." Virtually every federal agency had its own head who had a different philosophy as to what constituted racial discrimination. Hence, while it is possible that many instances of racial discrimination occurred, only in a few selected scenarios did the federal government publicly acknowledge the existence of racial discrimination.

For instance, in November 1945, Oliver Short, director of personnel for the Department of Commerce wrote, "Very few cases of alleged discrimination have come to my attention during the past few years." In a memorandum to other heads of bureaus and offices in the department, Short counseled that "to maintain this good record during the current [postwar] readjustment period we must carefully avoid actions that might be construed as violations of this policy." His statement emphasizes the superficial appearance of a good record, and suggests *avoidance* as a strategy for addressing any potential discrimination.

In addition, Short's self-assessment of a "good record" exhibits a curious logic—just because he was unaware of a racial complaint as "very few cases of alleged discrimination have come to my attention," he assumed that none legitimately existed.[20] The consequence of a decentralized antidiscrimination protocol at the agency level meant that agency heads and supervisors had wide latitude to define and defend against discrimination. Short's assessment of the Department of Commerce was hardly unique; in 1946 when the Civil Service Commission (CSC) conducted an investigation of all federal agencies in Washington, it found race discrimination occurred in only 58 of the 1,871 cases it investigated, a rate of just 3 percent.[21]

TRUMAN TAKES ACTION

Unlike many agency heads, President Harry S. Truman did show an interest in substantively improving race relations through direct action.[22] Perhaps Truman saw better race relations as part of the "fair deal" he promised Amer-

FIGURE 9. President Harry Truman was willing to study "the problem" immediately after the Second World War. Library of Congress.

icans. Or perhaps the mounting evidence and pressure for action during the four months since V-J Day had become too difficult to ignore. Unlike Oliver Short's assessment of the Department of Commerce, a month later on December 17, 1945, the Fair Employment Practice Committee (FEPC) chairman Malcolm Ross reported several instances in which federal agents violated federal policies against discrimination. This report was likely highly embarrassing to Truman in light of its apparent conflict with the international campaign of the United States to be a global example of democracy in the beginning stages of the Cold War. In recognizing the dual problem of disproportionate job cutbacks and discrimination against black federal employees as a serious issue worthy of a significant response, Truman responded the following day by: (1) signing Executive Order 9664 extending the life of the FEPC by six months until June 1946, and (2) issuing an antidiscrimination directive exclusively to all federal agency heads.[23]

Truman's antidiscrimination directive was unprecedented insofar as it was specifically targeted toward federal employers and did not address discrimination generally in the private sector. The president remarked, "It has come to my attention that a considerable number of loyal and qualified employees have been refused transfer and reemployment by employing [federal] agencies solely because of race and creed."[24] In the government's nascent stages of addressing internal instances of discrimination, Truman still had to walk a fine political line; he chose not to ignore an important issue but nonetheless did not confront it directly, probably to avoid alienating his trusted administrators who, as part of the executive branch of government, were charged with implementing Truman's policies.

Thus, Truman's tone was far from forceful when he stated, "I am writing to request that you make careful analysis of your personnel policies, procedures and practices in order that you can assure me that they are in accord with national law and policy."[25] Rather than unilaterally imposing a new federal policy, Truman suggested merely studying the issue further (i.e., "I am writing to request that you make careful analysis"). While Truman's December 1945 directive to stop racial discrimination was simple enough to comprehend and follow, subsequent federal correspondence illustrates the practical frustration cited by numerous agency heads in executing the president's commands. For example, roughly a month after Truman issued his directive, four black women in Washington, applied for federal employment. In January 1946, the U.S. Department of Agriculture rejected all four black candidates, but mistakenly mailed back to one applicant all four rejected applications together with an internal memorandum attached: "Attached are the applications I talked to you about. Except for color—they look like good girls."[26] The letter failed to offer any other explanation, but the reference to race as the reason for rejection suggested a casual tolerance of discrimination that would require more than one, lone presidential directive to eradicate.

Existing antidiscrimination regulations did not help these women because they were not yet federal employees. But the United Public Workers of America (UPWA) learned of the incident and argued, fruitlessly, that the rejections were racially discriminatory. Were it not for an administrative error that revealed the ugly truth, the Department of Agriculture might have successfully persuaded the rejected applicants (and others) that race was an irrelevant factor in the decision not to hire, when in fact it appeared to be the central issue. What remains unknown is how often other federal agencies denied they were discriminating against black workers in the public sector while contradicting themselves with the circulation of discriminatory messaging in private.

STUDYING THE PROBLEM FURTHER

Now that more information was bubbling forth about "inconsistencies" of treatment among all federal employees along racial lines, Truman's next response was to investigate why. Truman also had the foresight to know that tangible data more easily facilitated substantive changes in racial policy. He therefore authorized the President's Committee on Civil Rights (PCCR, or President's Committee), roughly a year after his antidiscrimination directive in Executive Order 9808 on December 5, 1946. Many historians such as Paul Gordon Lauren assert that the damning and influential report, *An American Dilemma* (1944), by the Swedish economist Gunnar Myrdal, inspired Truman to create the PCCR by framing discrimination against blacks, or racism, as an international, moral, and economic problem. Myrdal did not mince words when he, a foreign observer, stated that he saw in America a fundamental clash between "the consciousness of sins and the devotion to high ideals."[27]

Myrdal's analysis struck a chord reminiscent of Alexis de Tocqueville's influential treatise, *Democracy in America*, an 1835 account that placed America's emerging ideals into an international perspective, was lauded for its objectivity and thoroughness, and is considered a groundbreaking work in the political science and sociology fields. Truman was also influenced by black leaders who lobbied concerning the abuses suffered by black servicemen after they returned home from the war. In any case, Truman created the PCCR through the powers of an executive order, likely to avoid having to lobby for Southern congressional approval—a tactic soon to be repeated by other presidents who followed. While the committee was created in recognition of a problem, the committee's central task was not to assume a problem existed and to neutrally gather data about civil rights in general before producing a final report focused on workplace relations.

The PCCR consisted of sixteen members of various professions ranging from corporate (e.g., Charles Edward Wilson, president of General Electric) to academic (e.g., John S. Dickey, president of Dartmouth College) to legal (e.g., Franklin D. Roosevelt Jr., an attorney in private practice).[28] As with any committee, levels of participation varied from the irritated and mildly disinterested to the exacting and serious. In May 1947, Dickey displayed his irritation and disinterest when he wrote, "I am still by no means clear how much longer I am going to be able to stay with this assignment. Just since getting back several extremely important and demanding responsibilities have come up and I am now at a point where something has got to give and, as Miss Cleveland adds, I should much prefer that it was not myself." Meanwhile, labor leader Boris Shiskin took his responsibility quite seriously and wrote to the PCCR's executive director two weeks after Dickey did, noting his dismay that group protocols were not observed, "Inasmuch as the taking of the oath of office by

FIGURE 10. The President's Committee on Civil Rights intuitively acknowledged constitutional responsibility with the overarching symbology of Washington, DC, as the seat of federal activity. Library of Congress.

the Committee was suggested by me, I would like to take this opportunity to express my disappointment in the form of the oath administered to the Committee."[29]

Since the full committee seldom met face-to-face during the year it existed, and because telephone conferences were expensive and impractical, its executive secretary, Dr. Robert K. Carr, bore the brunt of responsibility for the committee's labor. A professor of government at Dartmouth University, Carr was primarily responsible for soliciting and cataloging all of the report's data and for managing all sixteen different personalities, which it turns out were not that diverse when it came to race. Of the sixteen PCCR members, only two were African American: the lawyer and civil rights advocate Mrs. Sadie T. Alexander and the religious youth worker Dr. Channing Tobias.

The constitutional responsibility and symbolic function of the federal government for all workers—both private and public—became dominant themes guiding the committee's work. Carr reminded every PCCR member that "in its race relations practices, Washington is almost a southern city . . . because it is a border city in which the patterns of the North and South meet, what finally emerges in Washington will be of major significance in any attempt to rebuild the structure of group relations throughout the nation." Carr thought it was "too obvious to require elaboration that the District of Columbia is the federal government's show case, both for Americans and for the representatives of the other countries of the world."[30]

Coincidentally, the National Committee on Segregation in the Nation's Capital (NCSNC, or National Committee), an independent local advocacy group, also formed in 1946 to study the prevalence of Jim Crow discrimination specifically in the postwar capital city. The NCSNC joined the PCCR in seeking and developing data about racial disparities roughly around the same time. The NCSNC was part of a growing liberal consensus that defined "rights" and "access" as new battlegrounds for social activists and was particularly inspired by other social scientists such as Gunnar Myrdal, who drew attention to stark racial disparities in the new postwar era. Serving on its executive committee were national luminaries such as Roosevelt's first "Black Cabinet member," Dr. Robert C. Weaver, NAACP lawyer Charles Hamilton Houston, and the renowned black sociologist E. Franklin Frazier. The chief architect of the National Committee was the white liberal philanthropist Edwin Embree. With additional funding from the Rosenwald Fund, Embree persuaded over a hundred leaders of national stature and diverse racial backgrounds to serve on the committee and conduct an exhaustive study on discrimination in the capital of American democracy.[31]

Both investigatory bodies issued seminal reports before they disbanded; the President's Committee released *To Secure These Rights* in December 1947, and the National Committee released its report on *Segregation in the Nation's Capital* a year later. Together, the reports helped flesh out the early nature and extent of racial discrimination in the federal government.

TO SECURE THESE RIGHTS

The President's Committee's report, *To Secure These Rights*, was broad in scope and touched on several key dimensions of race relations in the United States. The report is historically significant because it represents one of the first and most effective official government efforts to gather data about federal employment, pay, and race. Since then, the federal government and various agencies have cultivated protocols in gathering data and issuing reports. But at that time, *To Secure These Rights* was a breakthrough. As part of the process, the committee collected revealing data about black federal workers in DC. It found that although more blacks had obtained "good jobs" during wartime, such employment did little to reduce overall workplace discrimination in the postwar era. While the government provided a wider range of jobs and more white-collar positions than in the private sector, most black workers were still "ghettoized" within the federal workforce. Black-collar workers remained in the lowest pay grades, performed menial tasks, and advanced less frequently than their white colleagues.

Simultaneously, the NUL conducted an exhaustive 1946 study on race relations in the federal workplace, which came to conclusions similar to those found in the Truman report (e.g., "The Negro group is relegated to lower occupational levels and is concentrated largely in the unskilled labor groups, less technical jobs, and in minor clerical occupations").[32] Data acquired by the NUL mirrored data found by the PCCR, documenting that although the Veterans Administration increased its black hiring nearly fivefold to 2,907 by the end of the Second World War, "over 70% of the Negroes in the Veterans Administration were nonetheless in clerical jobs."[33] However, between the two groups, the PCCR had the inside track for greater potential political influence with its findings.

Accordingly, hoping to gain a large and receptive audience, the President's Committee issued a 178-page report that was quite conciliatory in tone and had the blessing of the White House.[34] For example, in noting that about a fourth of all FEPC complaints were against the federal government, the President's Committee merely questioned "the effectiveness of the Civil Service Commission rules against such discrimination" rather than outright condemning or criticizing the Civil Service Commission. While the NUL report received scant attention and the mainstream media largely ignored it, the incontrovertible data from these multiple sources demonstrated its influence on President Truman when he issued Executive Orders 9980 and 9981, which facilitated discrimination reviews and appeals in the federal workforce and equal treatment in the armed forces, respectively, in July 1948. While Executive Order 9981 did not specifically desegregate the armed forces, it was quite difficult to demonstrate equal treatment with completely segregated units and barracks based on race.

NATIONAL COMMITTEE ON SEGREGATION IN THE NATION'S CAPITAL

In contrast to the broader national scope of the President's Committee's report, the National Committee's report was more specific to Washington, DC. As an independent body, the National Committee had leeway to be more critical of the state of racial affairs in its stinging, 91-page report. It concluded, "The segregation of Negroes (in Washington) is worse than it was 60 years ago."[35] De-spite President Truman's demand that government agencies eliminate internal discrimination, inequities in the federal workplace persisted as the federal ide-al of workplace equity appeared very different when practiced locally and re-gionally.[36] As the NUL observed, "There are many [federal agencies] in which discrimination in the employment of Negroes is widely practiced, although . . . national policy distinctly forbids such discrimination."[37] In some cases, na-tional agencies deferred to local Jim Crow laws and customs, despite federal mandates that should have made such segregationist policies unenforceable. For instance, in 1947, the official Veterans Administration (VA) policy was "to hospitalize all veterans without discrimination in the same institutions. . . . The only exceptions made to this policy are dictated by the local custom of the community in which the hospital is located and from which it draws the larger part of its patients."[38] Unfortunately for many black veterans, states like Vir-ginia still held fast to segregationist customs, which in turn affected black em-ployees working at the VA desirous of nonsegregated work spaces.

Similarly, institutional discrimination at federal work sites such as the Washington National Airport continued to fly under the radar because of a 1945 District of Columbia–Virginia boundary bill subjecting the National Airport to Virginia's criminal code and, consequently, to Virginia's Jim Crow statutes.[39] Although black National Airport employees worked for the fed-eral government, as black-collar workers they also suffered the humiliation of having to use separate and inferior toilet facilities on their federal jobs. In addition, blacks working for the airport avoided patronizing the coffee shop or restaurant at the facility to shelter them from racial rebuke or abuse.[40] Rec-ognizing the gap between federal policy and local practice, Department of Commerce solicitor Harold Young lamented in 1945 that "we do not have the authority to compel the company operating the restaurants to ignore or vio-late the laws of the State of Virginia."[41]

Hence, the National Committee report had at least one clear success: just days after it was released in December 1948, the Civilian Aeronautics Admin-istration unexpectedly abandoned its strict segregationist policy at Washing-ton National Airport.[42] Discrimination observed at the National Airport was discontinued just days after the NCSNC released its stinging national report and, not coincidentally, just days before a segregation lawsuit was to be heard on the matter.

Furthermore, the National Committee outlined three levels of black em-ployment in the federal government based on models of *exclusion*, *segregation*, and *integration*.[43] The committee cited federal agencies such as the State De-partment, Justice Department, Bureau of the Budget, Federal Trade Commission, and Federal Reserve Board for consistent *exclusionary* tactics in which hired blacks obtained placement only in menial jobs that whites refused to accept.

The National Committee cited agencies such as the Census Bureau, the Government Printing Office, and the Bureau of Engraving and Printing for operating a *segregation* model that employed blacks but isolated them in separate units where they performed the most routine jobs. One noteworthy example of continued physical, racial separation included the discovery that in 1947 the VA had "segregated a number of colored employees on a floor below the sub-basement in its main Washington office where there is poor ventilation and trouble with rats."[44]

Lastly, the National Committee identified the Office of Price Administration and the National War Labor Board as having official *integrationist* policies that held jobs open to blacks at all levels on equal terms. But such agencies were extremely rare, and both were temporary wartime phenomena.[45] Furthermore, as chapter 1 made clear, the OPA still exhibited internal inconsistencies in the promotion and tenure of black federal employees, especially with job placements in the immediate aftermath of the war.

HOW THE COMMITTEES GATHERED DATA

Whereas the President's Committee consulted with numerous individuals and organizations nationwide, the National Committee had a narrower focus, drawing much of its information from local branches of the NAACP. The NAACP had actually done its own research, having canvassed two hundred federal agencies and having detailed thousands of individual cases, before beginning this cooperative relationship with the National Committee. But the NAACP research, like that of the 1946 NUL report, had failed to reach a wide audience even though consistent findings of discrimination were common in both reports. In other words, forward-thinking black advocates were actually a step ahead in diagnosing the problem that affected them directly.

In 1946, Joseph Young, a black *Washington Star* journalist, summarized the dilemma of being a black-collar worker in DC, during the postwar era. He wrote that federal wages stacked up poorly when comparing raises for upper-level professional positions in similar private sector jobs, and concluded that government employment made more economic sense for lower-level positions. Analyzing the relative growth in salary for federal employees in the lower brackets, Young found that if one was already at or near the bottom of existing income levels, government jobs likely provided "greater salaries than employes doing comparable work in private industry."[46] But upper-level private sector professional jobs, which had no caps or limits on potential income

and no transparent hiring practices or established antidiscrimination protocols, were more elusive to black workers. While it was often easier to get a career started in the federal government than in the private sector, it was harder
to end up wealthy. Ultimately, the federal government mirrored the private
sector by "ghettoizing," or limiting the majority of its black workers to low-
wage, mostly manual-labor positions.

Even though both the National Committee and the President's Committee
reports revealed that government action effectively reduced employment discrimination during wartime, by the end of the war, many black wartime gains
had eroded.[47] A staunch labor advocate, the NAACP labor secretary Clarence
Mitchell noted as much when he championed unsuccessfully in early 1947 for
a separate agency to prevent discrimination in federal employment. Mitchell explained to NAACP secretary Walter White: "Approximately 85% of all
colored workers in government during the war were employed by emergency agencies. This means that 73.1% of all colored workers in the CAF [Cleri-
cal, Administrative and Fiscal Service] classifications and 69% of all colored
professional workers were in this group. Even if there was no discrimination
against them because of race, curtailment of wartime activities would mean
that practically all of the [wartime] gains of colored workers in government
would be wiped out." The NAACP had also noted ominously, "Thousands of
[other discrimination cases] escaped attention because the bewildered victims
of discrimination do not know where to turn for assistance."[48]

One such harrowing example of discrimination came from the Navy Department. In 1946, a navy interviewer initially refused a black applicant because he "was told by the Navy interviewer that he had to be a permanent
status employee," as opposed to a contract or term worker without a full-time
job in hand. Undaunted, the applicant produced papers showing he had obtained permanent status, only to be told that "the job was for a veteran." After
the applicant indicated that he was a veteran, he "was told that disabled veterans were preferred." Finally, when the Navy Department applicant produced
"evidence of his status as a ten-point veteran, he was told that the Department
had enough applicants for the openings. A check with the Civil Service Commission several days later revealed that the orders were still open."[49] At every
step of the way, the candidate met the stated requirements, only to learn about
a "new" requirement that he failed to satisfy, similar to the accounting games-
manship that occurred with disadvantaged and illiterate black sharecroppers
who could never seem to turn a profit—even in profitable harvests. In these
small, underreported spaces, black-collar workers often paid a high price—
both economically and psychologically—for not correctly guessing what the
system desired of them next.

Typical of black-collar worker status, the navy veteran's story underscores how over time racist notions of black incompetence persisted, but the narrative, or description, of black inferiority merely shifted to fit new circumstances. Black-collar workers were continually at a disadvantage because they lacked the leverage to manipulate the so-called transparent merit and preference system in their favor. Despite the existence of the Veterans' Preference Act, this navy veteran's story is probably more typical than not, as countless other black veterans missed out not only on economically sustainable employment opportunities but also on financial benefits that they had "earned" through service (i.e., G.I. Bill).[50]

The President's Committee and the National Committee both asked federal agencies to voluntarily supply information on barriers to racial equality. The President's Committee yielded the highest response rate given their officially recognized capacity to acquire such information. But even the President's Committee quickly discovered how federal agencies responded differently to these formal information requests, with their reactions reflecting and revealing how much of a priority it truly was to pursue a policy of antidiscrimination. Only a few agencies, such as the left-leaning OPA, responded fully and self-critically. It was more common for agencies to avoid acknowledging racial disparities altogether.

In response to a query for statistical information by the President's Committee, F. J. Lawton, director of the Bureau of the Budget informed Carr of his desire to avoid racial conflict entirely. "The general pattern of the Bureau's work is not such as to bring its staff into direct contact with any of the problems which may have been encountered in carrying out policies concerning minority groups. Our experience, therefore, does not reveal any information which would be of value to the Committee."[51] Other groups claimed they did not even have "racialized" data to share; for example, the National Labor Relations Board claimed, "Our Agency does not keep a color line file." These responses illustrate how some agencies stonewalled the President's Committee, thereby frustrating the whole point of the enterprise.

The Department of State also minimized the extent of Jim Crow influence in its ranks and asserted to the President's Committee that "[w]e feel that we have met with more than an average amount of success in the realization of [nondiscrimination in] this program." State officials made this statement despite having subprofessional and professional blacks represent one-fifth of 1 percent of all positions (see table 2.1).[52] At the time, the Department of State was also one of the larger federal agencies, employing over 5,000 workers, but was fairly consistent with other sizable agencies having 5,000 or more employees. Professional blacks constituted only 1.1 percent of all Department of

Table 2.1. Postwar data responses to PCCR inquiry, 1947

Agency	Total	Negro (Percent of total)	Professional and subprofessional (Percent of Negro)
Department of Commerce	11,763	1,553 (13.2)	135 (8.6)
Department of Agriculture	8,440	695 (8.2)	9 (1.2)
Interstate Commerce Commission	1600	97 (6.0)	0 (0)
Department of the Interior	3,326	277 (8.3)	27 (9.7)
General Accounting Office	N/A	814 (N/A)	28 (3.4)
Navy	1,683	804 (47.7)	18 (2.2)
Departmental Service of the U.S. Tariff Commission	299	10 (3.3)	0 (0)
Civil Service Commission	1,901	422 (22.1)	5 (1.1)
National Labor Relations Board	349	69 (19.7)	2 (2.8)
Federal Security Agency	4,346	931 (21.4)	165 (17.7)
Executive Office of the President, Bureau of the Budget	540	25 (4.6)	0 (0)
U.S. Atomic Energy Commission	257	16 (6.2)	0 (0)
Department of State	5,202	552 (10.6)	10 (1.8)
Housing and Home Finance Agency	586	29 (4.9)	3 (10.3)
Office of Price Administration. (November 1945)	36,040	758 (2.1)	105 (13.8)

Notes: All jobs are Clerical, Administrative and Fiscal Service (CAF) or Crafts, Protective and Custodial Service (CPC) unless otherwise indicated as subprofessional or professional. The list is neither exhaustive nor comprehensive. Many notable and significant agencies such as the Treasury Department and the Post Office Department neglected to respond.

Source: Federal Housing Agency, "Response to Questionnaire Memorandum RE: 'Employment of Members of Minority Groups,'" May 16, 1947, Box 7, RPCCR.

Commerce workers (11,763 total), 0.1 percent of all Department of Agriculture positions (84,440 total), and .2 percent of all OPA workers (36,040 total).

Similarly, the VA responded to the President's Committee that if it had data regarding the "employment of Negroes, we would be glad to comply with your request. We, however, have had a long established policy of non-discrimination and no data of this kind are kept."[53] Such policies made it difficult for black employees and their allies to acquire concrete statistical evidence with which to back up the allegations of racism that they knew existed. Conversely, agencies may have failed to collect data on race to avoid reporting numbers on blacks because it was common for such information to be used to set discriminatory quotas. In other words, once the quota of black workers was reached, no efforts would be made to hire another black and add to the total number. Consequently, while some agencies may have hidden behind this fact as a convenient excuse not to collect data, the collection of these data for discriminatory purposes was a legitimate concern in this period.

Other agencies resisted responding to the inquiry of the President's Committee; for example, the Department of Labor withheld minority employee data, but provided copies of its employee relations' policies instead. Similarly, Keith Himebaugh of the United States Department of Agriculture (USDA), responding to a request for minority statistics, indicated: "As to your request for recommendations on use of our information programs for an educational campaign on civil rights . . . the Department of Agriculture, of course, is not charged with enforcement, has no powers other than those legally assigned to it, and therefore could not participate in a civil rights educational campaign unless a legal basis were provided." Himebaugh made a statistical inquiry a legal one, and equated Carr's intentions with an "educational campaign on civil rights."[54] Himebaugh further underscored the necessity for a centralized mechanism with enforcement power by essentially daring the President's Committee to force his agency to comply in the absence of "a legal basis."

Himebaugh's frosty response only validated the apprehensions of NAACP labor secretary Clarence Mitchell, who earlier in 1947, lamented to Civil Service commissioner Arthur Flemming, "I regret that, in far too many [racial grievance] cases, the heads of agencies are much more interested in explaining away discrimination than they are in correcting it."[55] And if Himebaugh were so defensive in response to a white official's request for mere *minority employment data*, black federal workers with *racial grievances* were equally as unlikely to gain Himebaugh's—or his agency's—sympathy.

In the end, the President's Committee established that federal agencies consistently ghettoized black federal employees in Washington, across agency lines, making their black-collar status nearly inescapable. The committee uncovered a systemic issue of institutional proportions that informed the very culture of federal employment (see table 2.1). The OPA director of personnel Everett W. Reimer echoed and affirmed the limited trajectory for black-collar workers when he responded to the President's Committee with a general pronouncement that "by the middle of '42 there were 250 Negroes on the Washington staff. With few exceptions, however, they were in clerical or laborer jobs." Reimer was forthright in describing his agency's segregation practices when he relayed that most blacks "were concentrated in a few organizational areas, many worked in all Negro units," and that "there were numerous large organization units with no Negroes." Reimer referenced the OPA's postwar progress, noting that there "had been a break in the dam, but non-discrimination had by no means been achieved."[56] While the OPA did lack a high overall percentage of black workers, it contained a higher percentage of black professionals in contrast to other federal agencies. Nonetheless, if the OPA was one of the most forthright and candid agencies in addressing the issue of discrimination in federal employment, the prospects for black federal workers in other "old-line" agencies were less encouraging.

The OPA was unusual in its stance and leadership, and the President's Committee was aware of this fact. Accordingly, Carr quoted a 1947 article in *Survey Graphic*, which explained that if one contrasted "the personnel practice of the Department of the Interior under Harold L. Ickes, or OPA under Leon Henderson and Chester Bowles, with the racialism of the tradition-bound Department of State, or with the paternalistic Department of Agriculture . . . you will find that a large area of administrative discretion actually exists."[57]

A few officials in other agencies did apologize for their low statistical showing, in part to avoid public exposure. President's Committee data gathering revealed that some agencies privately acknowledged inconsistencies between their actual personnel practices and the official, more egalitarian aims. For instance, Fletcher C. Waller, director of Organization and Personnel for the Atomic Energy Commission, confessed to Carr: "Our problem of staffing is peculiarly complex, and accordingly it is being resolved relatively slowly. . . . For this reason, we would prefer that you do not make it available to any other agency. The information does injustice to the non-discriminatory policies of the Atomic Energy Commission, and the increasing effectiveness with which they are being administered."[58] While Waller's request acknowledged that black-collar workers rarely secured professional positions, his wish to conceal unwelcome data only served the enduring myth of the nonexistence of real discrimination.

EXPLAINING THE GAP

LACK OF EDUCATION

Both reports from the two committees showed a paucity of black federal workers in higher-level positions. One real barrier to promotion was the lack of education. In 1945, on average, whites in the United States had three more years of schooling than did blacks.[59] As a result, although upper-level jobs required experience that many black workers possessed, without proper edu-

Table 2.2 Analyses of college graduates in DC federal employment, 1947

Employment ranking	Total white graduates	Percent white graduate distribution	Total Negro graduates	Percent Negro graduate distribution
	368	100	104	100
Professional	245	67	5	5
CAF 5–15 (mid-level)	69	19	6	6
CAF 2–4 (low-level)	34	9	86	82
CPC (custodial)	20	5	7	7

Notes: CAF 5–15 = supervisory and administrative; CAF 2–4 = rank-and-file clerks; CPC = unclassified; CAF = Clerical, Administrative and Fiscal Service; CPC = Crafts, Protective and Custodial Service.

Source: President's Committee on Civil Rights, "Memorandum from Staff of NCSNC to Members of the President's Committee on Civil Rights," June 23, 1947, Box 7, RPCCR.

cation, these workers frequently missed out on landing the jobs that provided the additional experience necessary for advancement.

Yet the black-collar worker dynamic still operated for that small group of black federal employees who had earned a college degree. As Thomas Richardson, international vice-president of United Public Workers of America observed: "The major sections of Government employment were lily-white, with the exception of custodial workers, many of whom were Negroes with Bachelor, Master and Ph.D. degrees."[60] While Richardson may have been somewhat exaggerating the problem, research from the National Committee demonstrated that inconsistent evaluation of black and white educational experiences was a bothersome issue. Table 2.2 shows that 86 percent of white college graduates worked at mid-level or professional grades. Conversely, 89 percent of black college graduates worked for the federal government in low-level or custodial grades.

The President's Committee demonstrated this pattern of discrimination in a survey of an unnamed federal agency. Out of about 3,000 employees, one-third were black and of the 472 college graduates, 104 were black. Yet 89 percent of all black college graduates worked at the clerical rank or lower in stark contrast to 86 percent of their white colleagues with college degrees who had slots in administrative, supervisory, or professional jobs. While the authors noted that they did not "take into consideration work performance," the numbers alone indicated "an unbalanced utilization in terms of educational qualifications."[61]

Another example from the State Department illustrates the "unbalanced utilization" of black-collar workers. Sensitive to criticism for its failure to employ Negroes, the department asked for a "highly qualified colored college graduate" for a "responsible" position. The position, it turned out, was only that of a low-level mimeograph operator with a rating of CAF-3.[62] Along these same lines, the State Department told a black applicant with a bachelor of science degree via telephone that she was "acceptable for a job as supervisor of a cafeteria in the Pentagon." When her employers met the applicant in person and discovered she was black, they told her it was "against policy" to hire her. The following day, she saw another advertisement in the *Washington Post* for the same job. While the position advertised was the same, the ad specifically requested a white candidate. The NAACP intervened, and the black college graduate finally landed the job for which she had originally applied. However, her "responsible" position consisted of being assigned to a snack bar "which had failed to pass War Department health inspection during [1946]."[63]

Moreover, her immediate supervisor "did not inform persons working under her that the new employee was a supervisor." At first, the white employees could not believe that "the newcomer had been hired for anything other than a counter job." While most college graduates benefited from a presumption of competency and capability, the frustrated black applicant mused that black employees were expressly instructed to call any white supervisor "Miss or Mrs., [while white employees] were told they could call the colored supervisor 'anything.'"[64] Hence, even for black college graduates, education in and of itself was an imperfect barrier to being treated as a black-collar worker.

To rectify the absence of black federal workers in higher-paying positions, agencies like the FHA took the proactive step of mailing weekly Personnel Division listings directly to local civic organizations such as the NAACP, the National Council of Negro Women, and the NUL. While these organizations never guaranteed results, government officials often saw the membership of a black worker in one of them as evidence of the personal stability required for a career as a federal professional.[65] In one instance, the FHA director or Personnel, Edward A. Macy lamented that of the four direct referrals received from the NAACP, three black candidates spurned federal offers to work for the private sector. While existing documents do not shed light on the precise reason for the job refusal, one can presume that if workers were marketable to the federal government, they were likely equally if not more marketable in the private sector. For those rare few blacks who pushed through to higher levels of education, a premium was often placed on their unique status and their exceptional credentials often shielded them from more common racist vitriol experienced toward the bottom of the totem pole.

LACK OF EXPERIENCE

The PCCR and NCSNC reports merely made tangible what many black federal workers had long experienced on the job. However, given the correlation between low levels of education and placement in lower-level positions, many black federal workers had the additional burden of working with less seniority and were thus commonly the first to lose their jobs.[66] Given the precarious financial state of many blacks before they had secured federal employment, such premature job loss was especially difficult to endure. Few agencies recognized this problem. In 1946, an administrative assistant at the Civilian Personnel Office's Employee Relations Section observed, "Most Negroes fall into the lower income levels, consequently many of their problems are of a financial nature, and that is why we have set up an Employe Relations Loan Fund."[67] This initiative, despite its noble intentions, still failed to address the question of why wage disparities existed in the first place.

Nonetheless, many black federal workers agreed that federal employment remained the best alternative to a Jim Crow, postwar private sector economy. Despite the attendant difficulties of federal employment, E. B. Henderson observed, "It is because private employment refuses to give Negroes jobs in many areas of work that causes them and some other minority groups to look for jobs under the Federal Government."[68] Ultimately, a job fraught with some racial difficulty was better than no job at all.

Even when black experience levels were comparable to those of their white coworkers, black federal workers still suffered from black-collar status and limited promotion trajectories. In one study, the National Committee analyzed a controlled pairing of forty workers matched by similar demographic variables (e.g., educational attainment, length of job tenure, age, sex, etc.) from a pool of 503 white and 292 black federal workers. Attesting to their parity, the average efficiency ratings for both the black and white federal workers were the same. But the committee found that whites received twelve grade promotions in total service of twenty-two years, which equated to an average of one promotion for every two years of service. In contrast, in their control group, black federal workers received only two grade promotions out of total service of twenty-eight years, which equated to one promotion for every fourteen years of service.[69] Black workers were simply unable to amass the necessary experience qualifying them for promotion at the same rate as their white colleagues.

Black stenographer Lula Fields exemplified how difficult it was to push such racial barriers aside, which often resulted in dire and direct economic consequences. In a 1948 letter to the *Washington Post*, Fields complained that "the Negro stenographers are given the most insignificant stenographic positions. They are mostly placed in stenographic pools; they are seldom placed in individual offices where they can have a chance for advancement." Her reference to "Negro stenographers" indicates awareness that the unseen obstacle between black federal stenographers and more substantive career assignments was racial discrimination.

Fields went on to report that when she did receive a job callback, it was only to be offered a lower-grade position as a typist, which was below her trained expertise as a stenographer. "In the agency in which I am employed there are white girls with just a clerk-typist status—who have never passed the stenographic test, but are working as grade 5 secretaries." Fields continued, "Also there are some who don't have any status but are working as grade 5 secretaries. Yet, Negro stenographers are told that they can't get a grade 4 stenographer job unless they have passed the Civil Service test as a stenographer."[70] Fields's knowledge of her white colleagues' inferior background and experience only exacerbated her frustration.

While the federal workplace provided a somewhat transparent and more level playing field than did the private sector, black workers nonetheless suffered the consequences of impoverished professional relationships. Segregation affected the lives of black workers since many blacks lacked casual and formal opportunities to make contact, network, and acquire information necessary for improved job performance and experience both inside and outside the workplace. Living in segregated neighborhoods also hampered the ability of black federal workers to further develop their professional relationships informally outside the workplace, thus preventing them from networking that could often lead to information about promotions. Black federal workers in ghettoized positions generally had fewer opportunities for casual contact with higher-ranking whites, and thus to manipulate strategic relationships that could lead to better job opportunities.[71]

Residential segregation could have a deleterious effect on black advancement in other ways as well. For example, in 1947, just before its demise, the Office of Price Administration tried to use a local school building at night for an in-service training session for its clerks. The District of Columbia Board of Education denied the request after learning that the training session included both blacks and whites in the same classroom space; such racial mixing violated segregationist policy. While white employees arguably were also denied training opportunities, their black coworkers had even fewer chances to improve their status.[72]

Undisturbed exclusionary patterns in the federal workforce held wide-ranging detrimental effects for black workers. Since black-collar workers were often systematically restricted from high-ranking administrative positions, their absence itself became "proof" that blacks were not deserving nor desirous of such positions. For instance, in 1947, the NAACP's Clarence Mitchell reported that "the State Department called [another federal agency] and asked for some person who could work on fiscal matters. The person calling specified that the individual should be white. I called the [State] Department personally, and talked with the individual who had given the order. It was said that the specifications were a mistake because 'one just didn't think of a colored person as being able to do that kind of work.'"[73] Mitchell's follow-up telephone call revealed that ignorant white attitudes about black competency had wide-ranging professional consequences. As evidence of the difficulty black-collar workers faced in dispelling the dominant disparaging narratives concerning the black image in white minds regarding value and worth in a racially hierarchical workplace, the State Department official also told Mitchell, conversely, that he did not think to ask for a black professional any "more than you would think of asking for a white janitor."[74]

REPORTED OUTCOMES

The reports issued by the President's Committee and the National Committee did help many white administrators understand the full scope of the discriminatory issues they faced. In so doing, they validated the experience of black employees and illuminated the pervasiveness of racial discrimination in the federal ranks. Moreover, the reports quietly alerted black federal workers to the ever-evolving nature of racial discrimination. New advocacy would have to confront new attempts to block the improvement of black status in the federal workforce. For if the past was any predictor, the reports showed that as new protocols emerged for mediating federal employment discrimination, new methodologies of black career blockage emerged as well. Quite simply, despite numerous policy and personnel changes in the federal government over time, what remained consistent was how employees' black-collar status and its resulting economic marginalization were merely reinscribed in new policy regimes over time.

For instance, in the fall of 1946, when the OPA underwent its largest reduction in force, OPA officials organized a final effort to find jobs for displaced employees. Virtually all 300 of the employees losing their jobs were black. The OPA was still highly regarded for its front-running, antidiscriminatory stance in contrast to other federal agencies despite its overall low rate of employment of black federal employees. In a separate article lauding the rare occurrence of high-placed black federal employees working in the Pentagon building, the same author noted: "Two important things were discovered as a result of making this tour. . . . Negro employes are perhaps better integrated in 'key' jobs in the Pentagon than they are elsewhere in the Federal service, OPA excepting."[75] Here, the OPA is noted for its unusual left-leaning stance.

Nonetheless, OPA administrator Everett Reimer tried unsuccessfully to find lateral placements in other federal agencies and grew exasperated by polite demurrals and deferrals, none of which explicitly referenced race. Over half a year later and still supremely bothered by a discriminatory practice with which he disagreed, Reimer vented his displeasure in an eleven-page memorandum to a receptive Carr amassing data for the President's Committee on Civil Rights report in May 1947. Reimer complained: "Few people admit prejudice themselves. Most discrimination is under the guise of protecting others or out of real or simulated fear of the reactions of others to minority group members. Chase the prejudiced person down and often you won't find him."[76] The inability of Reimer to find the "prejudiced person" highlighted the increasing subtlety with which systemic discrimination against black federal employees occurred.

Although the reports of both the President's Committee and the National Committee demonstrated continued discrimination by federal agencies against black employees, the methodology of racism was changing. Overt tactics, now increasingly frowned upon, gave way to more subtle methods. As newer agency protocols forbade blatant discrimination, more whites grew more nuanced in making the same discriminatory decisions that yielded the same discriminatory results. Over time, it became increasingly difficult to find blatant evidence of invidious racial discrimination against blacks.

Instead, a relatively quiet ideology of white privilege began to emerge under the guise of protests of "unfair treatment" for all employees wherever special considerations were given. If anything, helping blacks exclusively (without any reference to historical considerations precipitating such restorative justice tactics) gave way to mounting charges of "reverse discrimination" by whites as a way to protect a "zero-sum game" approach to resources in the workplace. In other words, a promotion with increased wages for a black employee was perceived as directly taking away resources from another capable white candidate.

For instance, Herman J. D. Carter, a DC Southeast resident and war veteran working in the War Department, provides a lucid example of the indignity of covert discrimination. Ever since he had started in his job in February 1941, Carter had consistently received reviews of either "Very Good" or "Excellent." Yet these ratings changed as Carter changed his disposition toward racial mistreatment on the job. In 1947, Carter first drew the ire of his supervisors when he "brought charges against a white guard who had thrown soup on a colored woman and man in the War Department cafeteria." Thanks to Carter's complaint, administrators compelled the guard to apologize and make financial restitution to the victim. However, Carter's supervisors terminated his employment soon after he reported the guard's attack. They contended they "had received frequent letters from his creditors asking for settlement of claims against him" and that such letters reflected poorly on his fitness to do his job. Carter felt blindsided by his termination since he knew he had satisfied his creditors over six years earlier.[77]

Carter's termination was likely in retribution for upsetting the informal and unspoken rules of racial etiquette that frowned upon the challenging of whites by blacks in positions of authority. Exemplifying the more nuanced discrimination tactics, Carter's supervisors clearly "punished" the offending white guard while focusing their attention on a seemingly unrelated personnel issue with Carter. From Carter's perspective, the contested personnel issue was untimely, personal, and irrelevant to his current job function. Carter's takeaway lesson was that after challenging authority to defend black dignity, the effect was the loss of his job. Conversely, while unable to hold on to his bowl of soup, the offending guard did manage to hold on to his job.

In addition, several agency heads felt that the emerging postwar focus on antidiscrimination was detrimental to an efficient workplace. In June 1947, the National Committee shared with the President's Committee an account of a frustrated federal administrator who complained, "Whenever we have an inefficient colored person and want to fire her there is a charge of race discrimination. Because race discrimination is charged whenever a Negro is inefficient, we have supervisors who tolerate Negro inefficiency. They have to prove it up to the hilt whenever they want to fire one."[78] While the sentiments are similar, the words employed had dramatically changed. Instead of a black slave laborer being "shiftless" on the job in the era of enslavement, black wage laborers were now merely "inefficient" on the job during the postwar era.

On one hand, some white employees felt that black allegations of racial discrimination often covered up and hid actual instances of black incompetence. On the other hand, the broader Jim Crow culture created conditions in which black employees suffered additional pressure, scrutiny, and higher expectations. For example, the National Committee discovered a federal practice of agencies "leaning over backwards in choosing our [Negro] supervisors; that is, we have insisted on an extra measure of ability and skill in a colored person before we have made him or her a supervisor simply because we did know that they were on the spot in a way that a white is not."[79] For the few blacks that made it into higher pay grades, their experiences loosely paralleled the pressure Jackie Robinson felt at the same time as the first black man to play Major League Baseball in the twentieth century.[80] The pressure was on the black federal pioneers to meet increased expectations without exhibiting signs of defensiveness or, worse, aggression.

Of course, as with any group of employees, some black workers failed to fulfill their job responsibilities. The President's Committee addressed this concern in its final report: "In presenting this evidence, the Committee is not ignoring the fact that an individual Negro worker may be less efficient than an individual white worker or vice versa. Nor does it suggest that wage differences, which reflect actual differences in the competence of workers, are unjustifiable."[81] Many blacks lacked the educational background and experience required for upper-level management positions. Race discrimination was still a major factor in persistent wage and rank gaps for blacks in black-collar employment compared to whites. As the President's Committee concluded, "What is indefensible is a wage discrimination based, not on the worker's ability, but on his race."[82] Here, the President's Committee intuitively diagnosed the condition of the black-collar worker.

A few white employees acknowledged the black-collar dynamic themselves. In a 1948 letter to the NAACP, a DC federal employee named Phyllis Zeughauser admitted that she was "annoyed with the goings on in my office" since a heavily credentialed and excellent black female operator filled the opening for a comptometer operator, but "because of her color, she was not hired." Two weeks later, a white woman was sent for the same position "and the supervisor in charge was told that the second person, a white girl, was not as good as the first one, but nevertheless, the [white girl] was hired for the position." Zeughauser revealed that incidents "similar to this one have been happening for quite sometime. In fact, out of at least 100 employees on my particular floor, there is only one Negro person employed." Yet, she was reluctant about sacrificing her own career for an anti-racist cause: "Naturally, because of my position here, I would rather that my name is not used."[83] Unfortunately, the archives contain only a handful of such confessions from white employees in contrast to abundant communications from defensive and/or complacent white agency officials.

Still, at the dawn of the postwar era, the federal government did take steps to show concern for the persistence of racial discrimination—prodded by left-wing public unions, Cold War pressures, and an evolving liberal agenda. When the President's Committee completed its work at the end of 1947, President Truman declared that it had "shown once and for all that it is possible to equalize job opportunity by governmental action, and thus eventually to eliminate the influence of prejudice in the field of employment."[84]

The declaration was welcome but premature. Although weak and inconsistent policies frustrated early attempts to combat discrimination, racial equity nonetheless remained on Truman's mind and would be the subject of further federal study on how best to secure these rights. Undoubtedly, black men and women had increased their numbers in the federal workforce, but the content, character, and quality of their jobs still lagged far behind the egalitarian ideal.

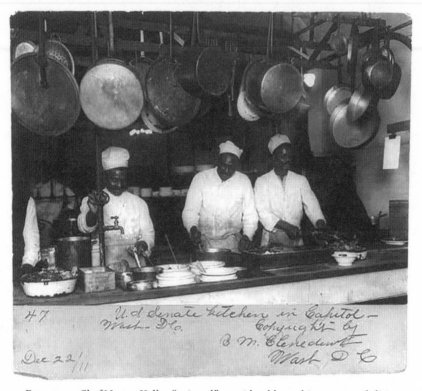

FIGURE 11. Chef Neaser Kelley "enjoyed" considerable cooking responsibilities, where as a black male chef, he oversaw a staff of thirty-one employees, similar to the ones depicted in this photo. Library of Congress.

CHAPTER 3

"THIS IS NOT WORKING"

WHITE RESISTANCE TO BLACK PERSISTENCE, 1948–1959

Around noon on a humid August day in 1948, Federal Security Agency (FSA) employee Neaser James Kelly was hard at work. As an official federal chef, Kelly was busy preparing cinnamon buns, hot rolls, cookies, fruit salad, and dessert ices in addition to tomato juice, coffee, tea, and milk for a business luncheon. Suddenly, federal investigators interrupted Kelly's lunchtime preparations and brusquely whisked him away from the FSA office building at 4th Street and Independence Avenue to a hearing of the Senate Appropriations Subcommittee on Labor and Federal Security inside the Capitol building.

Kelly, a rare, high-ranking black federal employee, was actually the head chef for the FSA, where he supervised a staff of thirty-one employees. But down at the Capitol, Kelly received few questions about the content of his menus, the quality of his cooking, or *how* he performed his work in general; the controversy concerned *where* Kelly was doing his work. Although investigators had found Kelly while he was cooking at FSA offices in downtown Washington, his regular post was at St. Elizabeth's Hospital—a federal mental institution under control of the FSA—roughly five miles away in the Southeast part of town.[1]

Federal investigators requested that Kelly explain his absence from the hospital and clarify how he could possibly fulfill his managerial obligations cooking for hundreds while simultaneously making a five-mile commute to prepare private lunches every day. Rather than doing the commute to earn extra pay, Kelly endured the arduous work schedule because his immediate supervisor, chief federal security administrator, Oscar R. Ewing, asked him to do so. Only after the federal investigation did Ewing learn that he could no longer use Kelly as his "personal servant" to prepare meals in Ewing's private office.[2]

Ewing openly admitted but defended the practice claiming it was more efficient to have food readily available than to lose time searching for lunch, adding that there was "nothing improper or illegal about it."[3] Ewing also reasoned that because lunch meetings occasionally involved both black and white attendees, government facilities were more hospitable than segregated facilities outside the office. Moreover, Ewing's boldest defense was that this protocol actually increased the *efficiency* of his agency by having a private dining room reserved for top aides who could still "conduct business" during luncheon conference meetings. Committee chairman Senator William F. Knowland (R-California) was not persuaded, stating that it was a bad practice "taking the head cook of a hospital responsible for feeding more than 2,000 persons, and putting him to work preparing luncheon for a handful of persons."[4] Knowland believed that Ewing just wanted have his own private chef at the workplace.

The FSA was a large, subcabinet agency encompassing various other agencies with wide-ranging responsibilities (e.g., the Social Security Administration, the Public Health Service, the Office of Education, and the U.S. Employment Service).[5] Despite his agency's high profile and Ewing's occasional meetings with President Harry Truman, his status was not high enough to merit around-the-clock personal servants. Yet his treatment of Kelly illustrates the blurred line between public service and *servitude* for black-collar workers, even those who held high-paying, managerial positions.

Despite working a full shift at St. Elizabeth's, Kelly had spent as many as five additional hours daily working for Ewing for the previous ten months. Kelly appeared not to mind the additional labor as he "told a reporter the luncheon duties do not interfere with his regular work at the hospital. He said his work at St. Elizabeth's is done at 10 a.m. and doesn't begin again until 4 a.m. He said his staff has its work laid out while he is absent." However, further underscoring Kelly's predicament as a black-collar worker, he received no additional financial compensation for such work, "other than bus tokens for his trips to and from the hospital."[6]

When the scandal broke, however, Ewing clarified that FSA administrative funds compensated St. Elizabeth's Hospital for "the part time use of its cook."[7]

Rather than find extra funds to compensate Kelly directly for his labor, Ewing instead found sufficient money to build a kitchen inside Ewing's office in order to "expedite" his lunch meetings. Kelly's unusual working arrangement and the reasoning behind it belies an undervaluation of black labor, ironically at the expense of overvaluing the worth of Ewing's time as a white male administrator. On the one hand, Kelly earned an annual salary of $3,225 and enjoyed managerial responsibility—both of which had been extremely rare for blacks a decade earlier.[8] To place Kelly's salary in perspective, in 1939, only ten male cooks in the entire city of Washington, commanded a salary in the $3,000 to $4,999 range.[9] Further, the median income for nonwhite families in 1950 was $2,190 with 72 percent making less than $3,000 annually.

On the other hand, Ewing exploited Kelly's culinary talents purely for personal satisfaction, illustrating Kelly's subjugated status as a black-collar employee. Kelly's high salary was an enormous departure from the status of the average black federal employee, but his treatment on the job was not. While Kelly's job was as a chef, Ewing's construction of a kitchen and imposition of additional working hours underscores his perception of black employees as individuals who were not present to serve their country, but existed to serve the capricious whims of white superiors. Adding to the idea that black laborers like Kelly were not valued as much as similarly situated white employees, NAACP labor secretary Clarence Mitchell confronted Ewing separately and directly about other FSA practices whereby some FSA employment service offices were "operated with backdoor entrances for colored people. In others, the offices for colored applicants are set up in unsanitary and outmoded buildings where those seeking employment must face extremely uncomfortable conditions."[10]

Ultimately, Ewing failed to recognize any wrongdoing—let alone any racial implications—of his actions when he casually defended himself by stating, "I intend to continue using him."[11] While it is unclear whether the Senate Appropriations Subcommittee levied any sanctions against Ewing, it is clear that the end result was not fatal to his career; Ewing retired from his position with the FSA several years later in 1953.[12] The hearings indirectly underscored the true level of federal concern about black dignity and respect in the workplace; the hearings were likely more a political technique to embarrass Ewing than a substantive technique to root out racial improprieties. After all, as the commanding supervisor, Ewing, and not the supervising chef, should have been hauled in front of the investigating committee himself. But ultimately, the urgent nature of the subcommittee meeting had less to do with Kelly and more to do with Ewing as Southern Democrats used such public, political fodder as ammunition to attack progressive New Deal agencies such as the FSA.[13]

Finally, it is unknown whether Kelly was any the wiser about the predicament. When interviewed by Knowland, Kelly remarked that preparing the additional meals for Ewing and his parties (attended by five to twenty people) was "all right," and he personally rationalized his role with the disclaimer, "We have not been serving cocktails," as if to suggest that Ewing and his colleagues had not truly exploited the situation because they had refused to cross the line of excess by excluding alcoholic beverages.

Or perhaps, Kelly was well aware of his predicament.

Similar to enslaved African Americans who feigned illness, stupidity, or slow wit as a strategic tactic to avoid scrutiny while playing into the egos of their white owners, Kelly, knowing full well the value of an above-average $3,225 annual salary (recall how Dorothy Boggess was doing quite well for herself, having started off at $1,440 annually), may have calculated that his economic bottom line was important enough for him to take on the extra work—with no *public* complaint. If Kelly were even a casual observer of history up until that point, he would likely know that any protest at that time was unlikely to bear fruit; thus, Ewing's "requests" for lunch were truly non-negotiable demands that were simply part of the "cost" of doing business with the federal government. Whether Kelly calculatedly took on the additional responsibility or he failed to notice that he was being shamelessly exploited, his high salary still came at the price of marginalization—at least relative to upper-level white workers' standards. The high salary did not protect Kelly because his black-collar worker status still rendered him vulnerable to economic exploitation.

SHIFT IN STANCE

A year and a half after Oscar Ewing received orders to stop taking Neaser Kelly away from his official post at St. Elizabeth's Hospital, his office was in the news again. Illustrative of the ambiguous role the government played in enabling versus eliminating discrimination, this time, the FSA was supporting the cause of equality rather than undermining it. In March 1950, the Washington Urban League held a daylong career conference at the FSA auditorium. That day, Ewing's black assistant, Anna Hedgeman, delivered a keynote message of optimism, boldly declaring, "We are no longer a problem." She went on to assert the centrality of black workers in the federal government, claiming, "American democracy is no better than what Negroes help America make it."[14]

Hedgeman took pride in having a federal job, even though her distinguished education certainly overqualified her for the clerical duties she performed for her boss. While holding the title "Assistant to the Administrator" at the FSA at the time, Hedgeman was an accomplished college graduate who

FIGURE 12. Anna Hedgeman (*right*) seen planning political activity with (*left to right*) labor leader A. Phillip Randolph and civic activist Roy Wilkins. Library of Congress.

had served as director of two different YWCA facilities and as executive director of the National Council for a Permanent Fair Employment Practices Commission *before* joining the FSA.[15] She was headstrong and confident as the first black student and graduate of Hamline University in Minnesota, having come from a household where her father was a college graduate as well.

Hedgeman saw the distinguished author and sociologist, W. E. B. DuBois speak publicly at her college graduation, and was instantly inspired to become an educator, having obtained a teaching position at Rust College in Mississippi. DuBois espoused a "talented tenth" philosophy that suggested African Americans should focus on developing elite, intellectual talent as the best strategy to attain economic and political power in America, rather than adopt a more practical, grassroots, "bottom-up" approach as espoused by his formidable contemporary, Booker T. Washington. Having been part of the only black family in Anoka, Minnesota, Hedgeman's ability to survive and adapt to carefully choreographed expressions of racism likely shielded her from the indignities that other blacks suffered in urban areas or the South, while simultaneously emboldening her to interact with whites, seeing them as competitive equals.

"We are America's greatest asset," Hedgeman continued in her keynote, "but we have to act like it."[16] Hedgeman's "encouraging admonition" was similar to the tone struck a few years earlier by another black federal worker, George Holland of the Veterans Administration. In 1946 Holland reminded unemployed black war veterans that work was readily available and that "you're just wasting your time if you don't do something about it."[17] Neither Hedgeman nor Holland acknowledged the degree to which many white workers opposed those same black federal workers who did try to "do something" by obtaining promotions, which they deserved based on experience and seniority, but often did not receive.

STORM WARNINGS FOR THE NEW RACIAL CLIMATE

COLD WAR FRONT

In the early stages of the postwar era, blacks' increased expectations of better treatment in society and the workplace were similarly reflected in the "Double V" campaign sponsored by several civil rights organizations and black newspapers both during and after the war. Double V symbolized victory against fascist enemies without and victory against racist enemies within. The Double V strategically leveraged the moral thrust of America's constitutional responsibility as the United States sought to win the global battle for political supremacy and convincingly illustrate the superiority of American democracy over communism. To this end, Truman issued Executive Order 9835, otherwise known as the "Loyalty Order," designed to root out communist influence in the federal government. An unfortunate by-product of this order was that many black government activist employees—in particular black postal workers in the National Alliance of Postal Employees (NAPE)—were targeted. Many federal administrators took advantage of the fearful political climate to further stifle criticism of the federal government, especially criticism involving socioeconomic disparities along racial lines.[18]

Government officials felt pressure to avoid hypocrisy by publicly opposing Jim Crow at home. This gave black federal workers an opportunity to challenge their second-class status on the job. Nonetheless, many of their white colleagues resisted such demands for equality. Ewing's treatment of Kelly, while possibly devoid of overt racial animus, nonetheless demonstrated that black-collar workers still had large hurdles to overcome with respect to blurring the line between dignity and duty on the job. Despite the federal government's official antidiscrimination stance, both white administrators and their employees continued to practice segregationist habits.

Furthermore, despite evidence of recalcitrance by upper-level administrators, President Harry Truman continued to lead the charge to make the federal workplace more accessible and hospitable to African Americans. He implored Congress to adopt the recommendations of *To Secure These Rights* in several candid speeches on the topic as he was confident that government action could equalize job opportunity and "eliminate the influence of prejudice in employment."[19] But most of the recommendations of the President's Committee on Civil Rights (PCCR) did not become law. Its own report suggested one reason for this: "In a world forever tottering on the brink of war, civil rights will be precarious at best. In a nation wracked by depression and widespread economic insecurity, the inclination to consider civil rights a luxury will be more easily accepted."[20] Yet Truman saw poor race relations at the federal level as something that the United States could not afford during the international Cold War; the president felt the federal government should embrace its constitutional responsibility and encourage democratic businesses in the private sector to follow its lead.[21]

The research staff of the National Committee on Segregation in the Nation's Capital exposed America's duplicity on the global stage when it cataloged the experiences of international visitors treated as racial inferiors in postwar America. In 1948, one visitor from India commented, "I would rather be an Untouchable in the Hindu caste system than a Negro in Washington." The historian Mary Dudziak observes that to avoid losing momentum in its quest for democratic supremacy during the Cold War, improving race relations became a part of diplomatic policy. Dudziak specifically notes: "The Ethiopian Minister to the United States was asked to change his seat in Constitution Hall during a meeting of the American Association for the Advancement of Science," and that this was "confusing" or "embarrassing" for American diplomatic hosts to run interference for international guests who "were not recognized." The federal government's focus on the external appearance of its domestic democratic practices, as Dudziak acknowledges, only confirmed the PCCR's prescient suggestion that an insincere motive to eradicate discrimination would result in inconsistent results. The National Committee further addressed the hypocritical image of American race relations when it reported that "four Negro students from the British West Indies sat at a downtown lunch counter. The waitress informed them they would have to stand to receive service. But when they produced their British diplomatic passes, she apologized, remarking she didn't realize they were 'not niggers.'"[22]

Widely circulated photographs of squalid living conditions within plain view of the Capitol embarrassed the government internationally. The *Washington Post* observed, "Pictures of putrid slums 'right in the very shadow of the Capitol' are no rarity."[23] This contrast prompted acting secretary of state Dean Acheson to confess in 1947: "The existence of discrimination against minority groups in the U.S. is a handicap in our relations with other countries."[24] However, the State Department's paucity of black subprofessional and professional workers (i.e., 10 out of 5,202) demonstrated its own failure to turn the administration's promises into reality.

SHORT REIGN OF THE FAIR EMPLOYMENT BOARD

Of concern to Truman was the President's Committee final damning and succinct proclamation that Washington, DC, was "a graphic illustration of a failure of democracy."[25] To rectify this embarrassing failure, Truman created the Fair Employment Board (FEB) with Executive Order (E.O.) 9980 in 1948, which made reports and recommendations to the Civil Service Commission about workplace inequities. In recommending general regulations governing fair employment practices for the federal workplace, E.O. 9980 stated that findings of discrimination against a designated federal employee were subject to direct appeal to the head of the department, whose decision on "appeal shall be subject to appeal to the Fair Employment Board of the Civil Service Commission, hereinafter provided for."[26]

In recognition of the problems "inherent in the collection of certain statistics . . . regarding informal complaints filed with the first-line supervisor," the Fair Employment Board changed its policy in early 1949. Originally, one's supervisor registered complaints.[27] In many instances, however, the supervisor was the direct source of the conduct complained about. While it lacked significant enforcement powers, the FEB did become an independent source to which black workers could now report their grievances.

Theoretical measures to help black federal workers were only as effective as the white administrators responsible for executing them. In 1948, black federal employee Alvin Webb complained that, despite Truman's request that agencies ensure fair employment opportunities and promotions for black workers, "agency heads have emasculated the Chief Executive's order by selecting, in most instances, the very personnel directors who are already guilty of discriminatory employment practices."[28]

Even when white administrators observed the recommended antidiscrimination protocols, they rarely admitted to finding discrimination under their supervision or on their watch. Moreover, they had little incentive to incriminate themselves or their agencies. The government therefore revised its protocol by requiring a third-party deputy officer at the FEB to receive and review initial complaints as well as appeals. This protected black victims from having to file a grievance with the very supervisor responsible for the alleged discrimination.[29] Nevertheless, according to the Fair Employment Board, "[D]uring the period, July 26, 1948 through December 31, 1953, there were 797 written complaints filed." Of the 797 complaints, aggrieved black workers successfully appealed only 13 percent of all cases to the board. The ultimate disposition of the 797 complaints was as follows: "52.3 per cent, no discrimination found; 32.2 per cent, withdrawn; and corrective action taken in 15.5 per cent of the cases. Most complaints, 87 per cent, were filed by Negroes."[30] Even though the federal government had taken the necessary step of recognizing and confronting discrimination, the implementation of its policies often fell short.

Superficial quantitative analysis sometimes allowed officials to believe in tangible progress in the fight against discrimination. For instance, in a 1950 memo addressed to President Truman, Donald S. Dawson, his administrative assistant, observed that the "record of Federal Civil Service on Fair Employment practices is extremely good" because "only 168 complaints were filed and a finding of discrimination was made by the top Board in only eleven cases." Dawson's memorandum reflected the assumption that the low number of discrimination findings was worthy of celebration, especially when "[n]ine of these cases arose out of a single incident in the Treasury Department."[31] Such reports still neglected the innumerable cases black employees chose not to report due to fear of reprisal, embarrassment, or ignorance about the grievance process. Nor did such reports measure investigators' inadequate training to detect all but the most overt forms of racial bias given the subjective and personal nature of communicating and comprehending racial discrimination.

Finally, in view of the infectious nature of Jim Crow politics freely pervading society at the time, such "extremely good" reports also did not account for the possibility that some findings of "no discrimination" were simply categorically inaccurate, dishonest, not thorough, and unfair.

WHITE WORKERS SLOW TO CHANGE

SEGREGATION BY A DIFFERENT NAME

Although it was once the rule, physical segregation in federal workspaces was quickly diminishing after the Second World War. In 1949, the NAACP's Labor Department reported that "efforts to end segregation in the cafeteria of the Government Printing Office were successful in Washington. Colored employees are no longer required to sit in a special area."[32] The line of separation between black and white workers was no longer overtly physical; the newer subtler form of separation was more functional in nature. In federal ranks at the time, only 5 percent of black male employees held professional, semiprofessional, proprietary, managerial, clerical, or sales jobs—compared with 30 percent of all white federal employees.

Furthermore, as segregation became more informal, it also became more difficult to prove. For the Fourth of July holiday in 1951, a federal announcement placed in the *Washington Post* invited all federal workers and their families to a cruise along the Potomac River with "a list of absolutely free, no-strings-attached things you, the Federal employe, can do on July 4." While the notice did not invite only *white* federal workers and their families to partake in the cruise, the implicit message of the cruise being a segregated affair was clear. In fact, the notice added information at the very bottom of the "black option" separate and apart from the mainstream white one: "Negro employes and their families are welcomed at an outdoor dance."[33]

Black federal workers often had to endure these smaller, insidious instances of racial animus, or microaggressions, as part of the normal, daily workplace order. In 1952, postal employee Violette Taylor wrote a letter to the *Washington Post* about the indignity of eating her food in a cafeteria directly adjacent to a "much larger and more attractive" cafeteria for white employees.[34] Such exclusions prevented black workers from acquiring the social capital necessary to advance their careers in a government bureaucracy dominated by whites. Having little contact with white superiors, few blacks had plausible prospects of improving their percentages for promotion given their limited access to the natural, informal exchanges of insightful, inside information they could possibly leverage on their behalf for new and different employment opportunities, whether they were lateral or vertical in nature.

OLDER HABITS DIE HARDEST

In the postwar era, many white federal employees had to alter their behavior to work in an increasingly integrated workplace. Once they stepped away from their jobs, however, they could still believe in and practice racial inequality. Within the federal workplace, new antidiscrimination rhetoric was bumping up against older discriminatory practices, when normal workplace routines dictated that black workers accept small humiliations without complaint. For example, late in 1950, a branch chief at the Office of the Quartermaster General was leaving to accept an overseas assignment. The quartermaster's black and white employees signed a scroll, paid $2 each to cover the cost of gifts, decorations, and refreshments as well as helped prepare the office for his going-away party. The white employees, however, excluded black employees from attending the very function the black employees had helped to plan, fund, and organize.[35]

Before the FEB's grievance process, there was virtually no recourse for routinely excluded black workers and no punishment for the excluding white workers. Such behavior was normal. It is unknown whether the blacks who were not invited to the party filed an official grievance. Even if the jilted black workers did file a grievance, it would be difficult to hold the employing agency responsible since the crux of their complaint revolves around the lack of comity and respect displayed by fellow workers for a non–work-related task, rather than management denying black employees their rights based on their professional obligation to the agency.

White workers found other ways to resist the new order of racial equality. In 1953, the U.S. Civil Service Commission's Fair Employment Board verified that some whites were still reluctant to work under blacks when it ruled in favor of a civilian naval employee, Elmer Harris. Washington, DC, legal representative Frank D. Reeves of the NAACP filed a formal FEB complaint on Harris's behalf asserting that, in addition to the navy maintaining segregated facilities, "there was an unwritten policy of refusing to promote Negroes to any position which requires supervision over white employees"—a key line segregationists wanted to defend since "Negro workers seldom hold jobs which require them to give orders to white workers."[36] The NAACP's investigation found that "only one black" obtained a promotion to the Wage Scale GS-4 classification of Storekeeper out of the previous twenty-one promotions to that position from GS-2 and GS-3 levels.[37]

The significance of the Storekeeper GS-4 position is that it carried supervisory responsibilities over other Storekeepers in GS-2 and GS-3 classifications as well as shipping, receiving, and stocking duties. Storekeepers performed a

variety of shipping, receiving, and stocking activities for government operations that sold directly to other businesses or individuals (e.g., sale of snacks
and other sundries inside the main office building). Although promoted, Harris initially lacked supervisory abilities over two white Storekeepers of lower
grade classifications. Harris sought the NAACP's help because after he initially made his grievance known internally, he was dissatisfied that only a
segregated "group of Negro Storekeepers were assigned to him from various
units."[38] Nameless white workers refused to work under Harris and no one
compelled them to do so—their discriminatory preferences remain forever
protected from exposure within the public record.[39] Harris's story is unfortunately not unique given the numerous examples of insubordinate acts of discrimination in the federal workplace as well. Dr. Robert Carr included in the
To Secure These Rights report of the PCCR an article reporting over fifty white
machine-card punchers in the Bureau of Internal Revenue, Statistical Section
who engaged in a work stoppage and left their jobs because a "Negro girl" was
moved to their section of the room in Washington on March 4, 1947.

But unlike the workers rejected from the party, Harris successfully pursued his grievance, and the FEB ruled in his favor. Acting chairman Fred C.
Croxton found that "there has been a reluctance on the part of some officials
and supervisors in the Ships Supply Depot to promote Negroes to positions
requiring supervision over white employees. This reluctance has resulted in
Negroes not receiving the same consideration as white employees for supervisory positions."[40] However, Harris's victory was a limited one. The FEB, whose
enforcement powers were limited, was unable to deliver an order capable of
being enforced and instead issued a recommendation that "the Navy Department take such steps as are necessary to insure that candidates for promotion,
particularly to supervisory positions, are accorded consideration with sole reference to merit and fitness."[41] Harris won his case, but failed to win relief. He
therefore lost an opportunity to stem the tide of events that ultimately tor-
pedoed his subordinated naval career, even if he was *Bound to Rise* (Horatio
Alger).

Rather than warn Harris's white supervisees against insubordination, the
navy decided to defer to the preferences of Harris's underlings and allow a
black supervisor to have only black trainees. At the same time, most blacks
had no choice but to work under whites at the Navy Department and other
federal agencies, and had to deal with daily indignities or risk appearing incompetent or incompatible. Economic historian William Sundstrom argues
that social norms in the form of a "racial etiquette" governed interracial interactions in the workplace, thereby undergirding segregation. Largely unquestioned racial norms about value, worth, and place prohibited black workers

from obtaining jobs superior to those of white workers or jobs that intimated increased social interactions with whites, thus dividing labor markets by function and occupation.[42]

UNEQUAL PAY FOR EQUAL WORK

While Truman was president, Congress reformed the federal workplace by passing the Classification Act of 1949 and enacting the General Schedule. The 1949 act replaced the Classification Act of 1923 and was designed to reduce and eliminate some of the pay rate inconsistencies experienced by federal workers across different agencies while establishing a consistent and transparent system of worker expectation and compensation. The 1923 act had only covered positions in the DC area; the 1949 act extended the new pay structure nationwide. Before 1949, four different service categories of federal workers had existed, each with different grades of responsibility, and each grade having up to seven promotional levels.[43] This wide latitude for classifying workers lent itself to vast disparities among workers' pay and the Classification Act of 1949 helped normalize salaries by simplifying the service, rank, and promotion categories in order to best equalize pay.

The Classification Act of 1949, while not expressly created to curb racial disparities in pay, did benefit many black federal workers because they now had a concrete tool to measure their market worth. The normed wage scale allowed black workers to assess their value relative to white workers performing similar tasks or working within the same pay grade. But the Government Wage Scale also underscored the marginalization plaguing black-collar workers in DC in the postwar era; whatever their education, placement, or rank, they still received less pay and fewer opportunities for advancement. From 1949 onward, the General Schedule or GS Scale (GS) became the standard for most federal employees, as it did not apply to postal employees. Jobs ranked GS 1–7 were entry level and generally more manual in scope; jobs ranked GS 8–12 were mid-range and supervisory in nature; and top-level positions ranked GS-13 and above were managerial and policymaking ones.[44] As of 1949, employees in GS-1 through GS-10 earned annual salaries between $2,200 and $5,000; those in higher grades earned roughly $1,000 more at each stage, up to $14,000 for a GS-18 (see table 3.1).[45]

There is no direct evidence linking the newly fashioned GS scale and race, but in keeping with the "cat and mouse game" of an ever-present narrative of black inferiority that shifted to meet new circumstances, the GS scale became an additional layer of protection and transparency for white administrators who used the new criteria to justify nonpromotions. The new system also meant that there were more bureaucratic hurdles for black-collar workers

Table 3.1. Step 1, effective for first pay period on or after October 28, 1949

Grade	Salary
GS-1	$2,200
GS-2	$2,450
GS-3	$2,650
GS-4	$2,875
GS-5	$3,100
GS-6	$3,450
GS-7	$3,825
GS-8	$4,200
GS-9	$4,600
GS-10	$5,000
GS-11	$5,400
GS-12	$6,400
GS-13	$7,600
GS-14	$8,800
GS-15	$10,000
GS-16	$11,200
GS-17	$12,200
GS-18	$14,000

Note: $2,200 (GS-1) in 1949 would be worth approximately $21,204 in 2012; likewise, $14,000 (GS-18) would be worth approximately $134,936 in 2012.

Source: Office of Personnel Management, "Rates of Pay under the General Schedule," accessed April 19, 2013, http://www.opm.gov/oca/pre1994/1949_GS.pdf.

to navigate than for their white peers when it came to obtaining promotions in reality.

The GS scale made it easier to chart the status of black employees and their rates of progression throughout the structured levels, as well as their career progression in comparison to their white counterparts. However, it did little to prevent black-collar workers from earning less and having fewer opportunities for advancement—irrespective of their education, placement, or rank. Although the new wage scale made it possible for the government to "offer a greater incentive to able young men and women considering whether to enter public service as a career," it was common for many blacks with low GS ratings to essentially "keep" their low GS ratings over the course of their careers.[46]

Public sector administrators, keenly aware of their obligation to appear accessible to the public, strove to remain accountable to notions of fair play during hiring and promotion—notions skirted more easily in private sector enterprise. Despite many federal agencies' shared ethos of transparency, opportunities to advance depended heavily on favorable performance evaluations, recommendations, advanced training, and higher education—all of which were variable elements in a subjective formula for promotion.[47] While it is possible to study aggregate numbers of blacks in lower GS pay grades, it is difficult to measure the number of black workers in lower GS grades who stopped working as hard, lost motivation, or quit in light of the ever-elusive climb toward higher-paying jobs and positions of power.

Careful analysis of the GS salary scale reveals that the overwhelming majority of black workers remained largely segregated to or trapped in inferior, entry-level positions in the GS 1–7 slots. These positions paid less in comparison to the higher-ranking slots and tended to be manual, monotonous labor. Further, such positions required little or no interaction with white coworkers, lacked managerial functions, and did not include supervisory powers over white employees. While designed to level the playing field, the GS scale ironically exposed the older, tenacious, discriminatory, and segregationist habits of white administrators and employees. While it is unclear whether one reason for the GS system's creation was the result of reformers' efforts to document discrimination, ultimately, the GS scale made even clearer what the President's Committee had already reported—economic inequities were still common.

CONFRONTING WHITE RESISTANCE

DEALING THROUGH ACTIVE AVOIDANCE

As racial tensions and discrimination persisted on the job—albeit less overtly than before—black federal workers debated whether, when, and how to address such tensions. One passive-aggressive strategy was to act as if such tensions did not exist. The FSA chef Neaser Kelly probably employed this strategy when he declined to protest the five hours a day he spent cooking meals for his department supervisor five miles away from his official job. Dating back to the Wilsonian segregationist era, Anna Hedgeman's inspiration, W. E. B. DuBois, counseled in 1913 that an African American "who would succeed cannot be frank and outspoken, honest and self-assertive, but rather he is daily tempted to be silent and wary, politic and sly; he must flatter and be pleasant, endure petty insults with a smile, shut his eyes to wrong; in too many cases he sees positive personal advantage in deception and lying."[48] Thus, black workers felt pressure to get along with their white bosses, who were the majority at nearly every agency.

Working alongside one another in office spaces required new levels of interracial interaction at meetings and more informal sharing of ideas. Thus, black employees routinely had to decide whether to openly advocate for racial justice or to quietly continue to work hard in hopes of earning a promotion. Take the case of black federal employee Jessica Valentine. After being called "nigger" several times publicly with her supervisor joining in group laughter, Jessica found her environment to be racially hostile, but she ultimately alienated herself further by pursuing her claim. Her internal inquiry came to a halt when the agency head suggested that Jessica could resign if she was being "too sensitive." According to Jessica's agency head, her options were either to leave or to keep working silently in response to racial epithets. Jessica chose a third option and appealed to the NAACP to intervene.[49]

Jessica's third alternative was to openly agitate for race-specific remedies. Still, many blacks found this delicate balance between free speech and career promotion difficult to maintain. After all, in 1948 several DC postal workers with at least fifteen years work experience lost their jobs over disloyalty charges merely because they also belonged to the NAACP. While the firings blatantly violated the First Amendment, thus indicating the devalued status of black-collar workers, little was made of this case and its disposition. A lone NAACP letter dated November 26, 1948, mentions the sudden discharge for disloyalty of postal workers holding NAACP memberships. The final disposition of an indefinite quantity of discharged black postal employees is not known.[50]

Many black federal workers restrained what they said on the job. As the historian Constance Green noted, "Colored civil service employees, fearful of losing their jobs, refused to lodge complaints, leaving NAACP officials without provable grounds for protest."[51] In 1947, the NAACP's labor secretary reported receiving a call "from a government employee who asked whether she should say that she is a member of the NAACP." But not all black workers were afraid to speak out. In 1947, the NAACP interviewed a postal official who welcomed discovery of his membership, declaring, "The present loyalty investigations were a good thing because now agencies could find out who these people are who go to outside organizations for assistance."[52]

The National Urban League (NUL) abetted the practice of self-censorship when recommending black candidates for federal jobs and echoed Branch Rickey's famous 1947 advice to Jackie Robinson to remain civil in the face of incivility when Robinson broke Major League Baseball's notorious color line after seventy-eight years of racial exclusion, or rather to learn "to take it without dishing it out."[53] Hence, the NUL suggested that job seekers tolerate some racial abuse in order to advance black progress over all. In placing a solicitation for potential federal employees, the NUL specified "'pilot placements' who can meet the demand in respect, not only to job competence, but to human relations in the position of the first Negro employed."[54] The league understood that black employees would likely suffer from unfair treatment at some point, but it counseled prospective employees to be "mature" enough not to respond in a manner that reflected poorly on the organization recommending them.

However, going along to get along was seldom a good way to advance to a better job. Take the example of Nina Hilburn, who, in 1954, was the black secretary to George W. Snowden, minority group housing adviser of the Federal Housing Authority. Hilburn's duties were typical for a secretary: "Taking and transcribing dictation—correspondence, conferences, long distance and other important telephone conversations . . . all office housekeeping procedures— organization and maintenance of files, keeping current mailing lists, binding and otherwise maintaining special reference books, etc."[55]

But Hilburn often acted as an office manager when Snowden was absent on field trips and believed she merited a promotion to that position, along with the higher salary that accompanied it. As she told the NUL, "I am required to have a working knowledge of the operations of each of the Departments under the Office of the Commissioner and the inter-relationship of those operations with the functions and operations of our own office and am responsible for knowledge and application of established office procedures, policies and regulations."[56] But Hilburn remained in her secretarial post.

TOO MUCH TRUTH TOO SOON

By the 1950s, an African American had finally landed an appointment to a high-status subcabinet position. When President Eisenhower appointed J. Ernest Wilkins assistant secretary of labor in 1954, he became the first black American to hold such a high government post.[57] Wilkins occasionally attended cabinet meetings at the White House when his superior, Labor Secretary James Mitchell, was away. In public statements, Wilkins declared that, when he appeared as the official American representative to the International Labor Organization, his presence "sort of destroyed the propaganda effect of Russian claims of discrimination here [in America]."[58]

Notwithstanding his visual value in selling America's message of inclusive democracy, Wilkins fell out of favor with the administration when he refused to confine himself to celebrating the status quo of moderate racial progress. While many black workers usually avoided protesting workplace inequality and other forms of racism out of concern about jeopardizing their job status, Wilkins when walking down the hallways, "noticed all-white sections and complained to personnel.[59] *Ebony* magazine's Washington Bureau Chief reflected, "As the first black sub-Cabineteer, Wilkins earned the ire of supervisors by approaching black workers in hallways and inquiring about their jobs, grades and advancement opportunities. He became a one man [Equal Employment Opportunity Commission] in the department and a miniature NAACP outside the building."[60]

Wilkins also had to weather the accusation that he failed to defend the United States adequately when attending an overseas meeting at which Soviet delegates lambasted his country for its poor record on civil rights. When Secretary Mitchell demanded to know why Wilkins did not counter the attacks, he flatly responded, "because [the Soviet delegates] were telling the truth."[61] Such blunt advocacy of racial equality led Eisenhower to dismiss Wilkins from his position at the Labor Department and to appoint him to a seat on the Civil Rights Commission, set up by the 1957 Civil Rights Act. While there is little public record on the matter, it was generally known that the position was targeted and would be filled by the man eventually replacing him, George Lodge, son of U.S. ambassador Henry Cabot Lodge.[62]

In a move that bespeaks either supreme professionalism, dedication to his political party (with an eye on an imminent and eventual appointment), or extreme internalization of his own oppression (i.e., passive-aggressive avoidance a la chef Neaser Kelly), Wilkins had declared upon leaving his position at the Labor Department that racial discrimination in "the theaters, the hotels and schools . . . all those things have been cleared up since the Eisenhower Administration came in."[63] But Wilkins's statement must be taken with a grain of salt; similar to FSA chef Kelly, such a statement might have been sincere, or it may have been a calculated political ploy to "save face" to maintain his continued employability and ability to generate income in the public sector.

As a hint that Wilkins's initial ameliorative statement was merely placating in nature, he ultimately changed his mind, protested his public demotion, and asked to state his case to President Eisenhower directly. Fighting rumors that he was ill and unfit to perform his duties, Wilkins tearfully pleaded with the president to be able to retain his subcabinet job.[64] But Eisenhower held firm; Wilkins died, in 1959, less than a year later, but remained a black-collar worker until the very end.

LIKE IKE

Despite a sparse track record of landmark civil rights advancements, President Eisenhower did take one important step to advance the government's com-

FIGURE 13. President Dwight D. Eisenhower intuitively understood and articulated the federal government's constitutional responsibility to serve as an example of equity-based practices for the private sector. Posing from left to right, Channing Tobias, Arthur Spingarn, Dwight D. Eisenhower, Clarence Mitchell, Walter White, and Theodore Spaulding. Library of Congress.

mitment to civil rights in the federal workplace. In August 1953, the president issued Executive Order 10479, which promised "successful execution of, the equal employment opportunity program of the United States Government" through the creation of the President's Committee on Government Contract Compliance (PCGCC). Under the terms of the order, the head of each contracting agency had to report whether firms doing business with the federal government complied with existing antidiscrimination regulations. In issuing an executive order, Eisenhower repeated the pattern set by Franklin Roosevelt and Harry Truman. Like them, he avoided proposing a civil rights bill that required a difficult and lengthy legislative process potentially ending in failure. However, the trade-off was a unilateral executorial move that lacked political buy-in and consequently lacked rigorous enforcement power.

Under President Eisenhower, a civil rights bill, the Civil Rights Act of 1957 focused on voting rights, did gain passage after lengthy debate, but only after the Supreme Court initiated desegregation dismantling "with all deliberate speed" in its landmark 1954 *Brown v. Board of Education* school case. Eisenhower enacted E.O. 10479 before the political tide had turned in favor of public desegregation and was unlikely to garner sufficient political support necessary to make antidiscrimination efforts in government contracts equal to the force of law. Fittingly, the historian Thomas Sugrue characterizes the PCGCC as a "largely do-nothing body that gathered information on race in government contracting but did little to enforce antidiscrimination measures."[65]

Eisenhower did, however, recognize that because of America's constitutional responsibility federal antidiscrimination efforts were now obligatory. At the first meeting of the PCGCC in 1953, he declared, "On no level of our national existence can inequality be justified. Within the Federal Government itself, however, tolerance of inequality would be odious. What we cherish as an ideal for our nation as a whole must today be honestly exemplified by the Federal establishment."[66] That November, when Secretary of Labor Mitchell announced that federal jobs were available to all "qualified persons," the federal government finally eliminated any remaining doubt that it had repealed Woodrow Wilson's 1913 decree of segregation.[67] Mitchell's declaration signaled the federal government's continued progression away from blatant and overt discrimination—a significant step that the private sector had yet to take, let alone take *voluntarily*.

In 1955, Eisenhower issued Executive Order 10590, which established the President's Committee on Government Employment Policy (PCGEP) with the power to prevent discrimination against members of minority groups. The PCGEP differed from its predecessor, the Fair Employment Board, in that it called for departments to author regulations ensuring a compliance mechanism for hearing and resolution in accordance with its ambitious mission of stopping all discrimination in all federal employment. The PCGEP improved upon the Fair Employment Board, because it involved federal agencies more fully in the government's push for antidiscrimination. Initially, the FEB only made reports and recommendations to the Civil Service Commission about federal agencies' behavior while the PCGEP required that individual agencies take stock of their own disparities (if any) and create a protocol for addressing them. The PCGEP's process did not ensure agency compliance with antidiscrimination, but such requested regulations attempted to share the responsibility for discouraging discrimination outside of a lone federal department head.

Although the PCGEP represented the administration's concerted attempt to make nondiscrimination an extension of federal policy, its recommendations for action were merely "advisory in nature." The PCGEP conducted its own data analysis and an initial survey showed that although 24.4 percent of black federal employees (numbering 48,536) worked in Washington, DC, in 1956, 85 percent of blacks were still concentrated in GS-1 through GS-4.[68]

While black federal employees continued to draw benefits from federal employment, in contrast to existing private sector alternatives, many still had to contend with the deeply ingrained and habitual practice of racial harassment by white colleagues and administrators on the job. In the absence of overtly egregious and blatantly personal attacks, more subtle racial discrimination was difficult to detect systematically given the federal government's decentralized agency model and widespread nature. Further, to the extent that the government had early mechanisms to ferret out inequities at the workplace, white administrators found few instances of "official" racial discrimination.

Long before the federal government developed an investigative arm that had the ability to issue findings containing economic consequences like those from the impending Equal Employment Opportunity Commission, it was quite difficult for antidiscrimination committees to identify larger patterns of *institutional* workplace bias. It was far easier to isolate a bigoted, renegade employee maltreating a black employee than it was to castigate an entire department of mostly white directors, managers, supervisors, and mid-level managers for consistently passing over qualified blacks for promotions over a prolonged period. As white resistance evolved and changed, so did the need for black federal workers to revise how they fought for equal treatment on the job.

In essence, the struggle of black federal workers for increased dignity and respect highlights another tension between actual and relative progress. Official pronouncements from high-ranking federal officials and new commission formations signaled to international observers abroad and black workers at home that the government was serious and actually committed to the successful practice of democracy. Yet, as antidiscrimination efforts adapted and improved, so did white resistance. Discrimination became less overt and increasingly covert and difficult to trace or detect. Only with comprehensive statistical data were discriminatory patterns more apparent suggesting a more complicated reading of black progress. However, data sets were still early in their formation after the PCCR started the process of collecting racial data in 1947. While actual gains for black-collar workers remained precarious relative to white institutional responses, the struggle for the American Dream, dignity and respect included, remained constant.

CHAPTER FOUR

"RATS! DISCRIMINATED AGAIN"

JULIUS HOBSON AND THE RISING CIVIL RIGHTS MOVEMENT, 1960–1969

On a humid morning in August 1964, a tall, swarthy black male wearing a fedora and smoking a pipe, drove a station wagon slowly through the streets of Georgetown—an upper-class residential enclave in Northwest Washington, DC. The driver was taxiing his cargo from one side of town to another, careful not to upset the occupants with any heavy handling of the brake pedals. To the driver's delight, onlookers stared with horror, wondering whether he would ever let his passengers out as he wound his way to his destination: a Rat Relocation Rally.

The driver's name was Julius Hobson, a former economic researcher for the Library of Congress who also worked for the federal government as a statistical analyst with the Social Security Administration. Even though the day was Saturday, Hobson, was nonetheless still at work, exhorting the city of Washington, to treat its black citizens with more dignity and respect. Hobson's "passengers" were rats that he had collected using rat traps he bought at a Sears department store.[1] Before the Rat Relocation Rally was conceived, city officials for years had conveniently ignored complaints of rat infestation in the Northeast and Southeast neighborhoods where working-class blacks lived. In contrast, exclusively white and wealthy neighborhoods like Georgetown were rat-free—at least until Hobson had something to say about it.

Figure 14. Julius Hobson was simply unafraid to speak the truth, or his truth—in either instance, he made his voice known. Courtesy of Hobson Papers, DC Community Archives, Washingtoniana Division.

Convinced of the notion that "a DC problem usually is not a problem until it is a *white* problem,"[2] Hobson used his ingenuity to make the blacks' rat problem a *white* problem as well. In grandstanding fashion, he invited the press to follow him as he planned to "share" the rat problem with affluent white DC residents at a "Rat Relocation Rally." Hobson packed up rats from the poor black sections of DC and drove to the more affluent parts of the city, threatening to release the rats into the streets of the "rich neighborhoods." Hobson claimed to have "chicken coops" full of rats hidden in the city, and using his federal training as a researcher, had discerned that he had no legal obligation to keep the rats and could not be prosecuted if he turned them loose. Within days, city leaders instituted new sanitation and pest control policies, quickly implementing rat extermination programs in *all* parts of the city.

In actuality, Hobson did not have hundreds of rats but more likely ten or twelve. While they were large in size, it was the press that sensationalized the matter and made the rats even larger in the fearful minds of wealthy whites. The savvy Hobson leveraged extensive media coverage, a few rats, and few hundred fearful white residents in causing the city to change its policies and spending habits with immediate results. Like a hunk of government cheese, Hobson states "and of course the press just really ate up the rat thing."[3] Hobson never intended to turn the rats loose on the streets, but rather dumped them and drowned them in a Georgetown sewer late at night after the rally.[4] But perhaps Hobson really was keen on carrying out his plan, as he remarked "and I was going to turn these rats loose on Georgetown. The fact of the matter is it was hell to catch those damn rats."[5]

By the time the 1960s arrived, it was still black federal workers who were catching hell on the job and still finding it exceedingly difficult to catch a break with respect to black-collar conditions of lower wages and slower raises. Hobson knew this firsthand as a former federal employee who left his daytime job to engage in full-time activism. Despite his extensive training and experience, the ever-clever Hobson would nonetheless find himself at his wits' end in creating effective advocacy for black-collar workers.

NEITHER AFRAID TO WORK NOR FIGHT

Two decades after entering the federal workforce en masse, black federal workers were an indelible part of it by the 1960s. What had begun as a temporary arrangement largely based on need had now changed. Many black workers, like many other workers, were no longer content with merely being employed, but instead sought satisfaction from a job that reflected their ability to contribute. But this was not new. Ever since the outbreak of the Second World War, black employees had always advocated for improved conditions. Tactics included joining unions, local civic organizations, and other national groups, or leveraging media (especially black newspapers) that had been organizing around individual cases and groups of employees with grievances.[6]

Nonetheless, during the 1960s, black federal workers slowly shifted to a more aggressive stance in voicing their concerns. Because it was so difficult for black-collar workers to confront their supervisors directly, many ended up doing so primarily through organizations and advocates outside the workplace itself. Blacks also demonstrated agency through lobbied congressional hearings, staged rallies at local churches, organized protests, picket lines, and public demonstrations, as well as studies and debates in the media about this topic—all of which laid the groundwork for subsequent workplace initiatives.

As the burgeoning civil rights movement continued to grow during the late 1950s and early 1960s, it attracted the attention of many black federal workers. As the labor historian Robert Zieger put it, "It was a short step from demanding equal rights in schools, restaurants, and voting booths to demanding higher wages, improved working conditions, and fair treatment" on the job.[7] The larger social environment of activism was infectious, and served as a source of support to black federal workers who tried directly harnessing its momentum to advance their own opportunities and status on the job.

One of the aspects of federal employment that came under repeated scrutiny was the seemingly intractable status of black-collar workers who routinely suffered from systemic racial discrimination consistently resulting in lower wages and slower raises.[8] For example, in one grievance of unequal pay, 101 black workers cited data showing average black salaries in the General Services Administration (GSA) Procurement Division of $6,442 in contrast to average white salaries of $10,028 for 357 white employees in similar GS grades.[9] Such incontrovertible data made clear what black-collar employees knew all along—that there was a cost to them on the job based on their racial identity.

The stubborn pattern of labor discrimination had crippling, cumulative economic effects over time since "not only are Negroes at the bottom of the job ladder, but they receive less pay than whites for the same work."[10] For many black federal workers, the direct and immediate financial consequences of such economic restriction meant fewer retirement benefits, lower life insurance values, lower-quality health insurance, poorer living conditions, inferior educational opportunities, and even access to lower-quality food. In recognition of this puzzling dynamic—one that appeared to be without solution—Sterling Tucker, executive director of the Washington Urban League exasperatedly stated in 1963, "The Negro in Washington—and everywhere else—is expected to live as well, eat as well, dress as well, educate his children as well and have a nice home on less money than whites . . . and even Negroes aren't that smart."[11]

Compounding these economic frustrations was the collective political impotence of black-collar workers on the job. Although more blacks held more federal jobs than two decades prior, few had obtained positions in upper management to facilitate or broker better working conditions on the job. At the beginning of the 1960s, African Americans held only 1.3 percent of all upper-level GS positions (i.e., GS 12–16).[12] Still mired in the lowest pay grades, nearly 64 percent of all black federal employees in the district occupied the bottom GS grades, 1–4.[13] Despite the overall growth of black employment, the percentage of blacks in upper-level management positions had changed little since the 1940s when segregation was the rule. Out of 82,257 federal workers in Washington, DC, in 1940 (excluding postal and defense workers), only two-tenths of 1 percent of black workers held professional or semiprofessional positions.[14] While the increase of professional black federal workers did grow from 0.2 percent to 1.3 percent over two decades, such growth is still small against the background of sweeping administrative changes that no longer formally acknowledged racial segregation in the federal workplace.

Despite the formal elimination of federally segregated spaces, many black federal workers still felt uncomfortable initiating racial grievance procedures directly on the job. A *Washington Post* columnist pointed out that "proving discrimination in Government is a difficult task. Negroes point out that complaints in the Federal Government are often reviewed within the department by the supervisors who may be the source of the discrimination in the first place."[15] Agency grievance procedures typically started with one's own supervisor, thereby creating a major disincentive for individuals willing to bring forth a complaint. Hence, the stress of working under fear of retribution or risk of a punitive performance review made self-advocacy difficult especially for any worker whose effectiveness depended upon shared group feeling, comity, and support. Unsurprisingly, many black federal workers looked to a variety of sources outside of the workplace for assistance. During the hotbed of social activism that characterized the 1960s, many civic groups were overwhelmed with requests for help from scores of black men and women with additional equity concerns besides fair employment. Fortunately, local black federal workers could still rely upon Julius Hobson.

ACTIVIST FOR HIRE

MEET JULIUS HOBSON: ACTIVIST-AT-LARGE

Julius Hobson was the perfect advocate for black federal workers, if only because the federal government was entirely responsible for his career. Born in 1922 to a Pullman porter and an Alabama schoolteacher, Hobson grew up in a hostile Jim Crow South that his mother taught him to confront head-on through education—he was christened in the same 16th Street Baptist Church that the Ku Klux Klan viciously bombed in 1963, claiming the lives of four little black girls. Later in life Hobson used the confidence he had gained from education to confront the political establishment over its inconsistent and discriminatory policies.

After finishing high school, Hobson worked as an electrician for the Birmingham Paper Company until he lost his job in 1941 due to a racial confrontation. After a coworker called him "nigger," Hobson retaliated by punching the coworker, ending the verbal assault, but also ending his career with the paper company.[16] Hobson then joined the wartime Army Air Force. He took part in thirty-five flight missions as an artillery-spotter and earned distinction upon discharge. After discharge, Hobson remained steadfast to his mother's teachings about the value of leveraging education in pursuit of the American Dream and decided to attend Howard University in Washington, DC, on the G.I. Bill for his bachelor's degree. As for many, college was a transformative period for Hobson, who was first introduced and attracted to Marxism after hearing and making friends with the German émigré left-wing economist Otto Nathan. Hobson decided to continue his education, pursuing a master's degree after graduation. Much to the chagrin of his master's thesis adviser, Hobson used Marxism to deepen his understanding of the relationship between capitalism and racism, the powerful and the oppressed.

Despite his collegiate pedigree, Hobson entered the federal workforce in 1948 only as an entry-level desk attendant at the Library of Congress. He worked his way up, eventually landing a position as a statistician and economist with the Social Security Administration where he worked for two decades starting in 1950. In 1953, Hobson began a long career of civil rights advocacy when he sought a better elementary school education for his son. In walking his son to a segregated, overcrowded, all-black school, Hobson became increasingly infuriated as he passed by a better-manicured, all-white school closer to his home. His son's school, Lucy D. Slowe Elementary, had the same name as one of the segregated dormitories the federal government built for Negro G-girls during the Second World War. Dissatisfied with the response he received from school officials, Hobson pressed the city's Board of Education, which denied his request for equal spending per pupil at his child's segregated school. While it appeared that Hobson was stymied, he had just begun to fight.

Hobson became best known for a school desegregation case, *Hobson v. Hansen*, inspired by his concern for his children's education.[17] In the 1967 U.S. District of Columbia federal case, Hobson demonstrated that despite landmark changes in civil rights law, statistical data strongly suggested that there had been less than progress. Disparities persisted in the per pupil spending rates for black and white students, with black students receiving significantly less than their white peers, even when it was documented that both sets of students came from the same neighborhood.

Convinced that no jury could find fault with sound statistical data, the famed, radical white lawyer William Kunstler agreed to argue the case while Hobson paid Kunstler's expenses and assembled all the research. Hobson's successful triumph resulted in the district's abolishing the different tracking, or separate and unequal curricular planning systems, it had in fact been using for both black and white students. Hobson's lengthy life of public service concluded with his successful election and service as an at-large member on the Council of the District of Columbia from 1974 until his death in 1977.

HOBSON'S BRAND OF ACTIVISM

By 1964, Hobson had become one of the leading activists in DC. He had organized more than 80 picket lines against job discrimination at about 120 downtown retail stores, which won jobs for some 5,000 blacks. He also initiated campaigns that resulted in DC Transit's hiring its first black bus drivers as well as the hiring of the first black auto salesmen and dairy company employees in the district. Hobson's creative thinking set him apart from many other activists at the time. While known for his wit and irascibility, Hobson also skillfully used the media to create negative publicity campaigns and leveraged the resulting social pressure to achieve his results. Accordingly, Hobson summarized his proactive political philosophy quite succinctly when he stated: "My experience leads me to the conclusion that discussion is not as effective as direct action."[18]

In 1964, for example, Hobson created a "Cop Watching Wagon." This tactic employed a parabolic microphone attached to his station wagon to surreptitiously record officers using abusive language and abusive tactics against black citizens as he rode slowly through the town. Hobson then falsely advertised rallies featuring prominent activists like Stokely Carmichael to generate crowds and media interest, only to play the inflammatory recordings for the extra police who showed up for security detail.[19] Hobson considered Carmichael his adopted son ever since the two had worked together in the Congress of Racial Equality (CORE) in Washington, and young Carmichael was often seen babysitting for Hobson's young child. Hobson thus used his personal relationship with Carmichael to expose law enforcement's inappropriate and inconsistent behavior. These public victories garnered Hobson considerable local respect as an independent activist in need of only "six men and a phone booth" to implement his agenda.[20]

Hobson's advocacy, while largely individualistic, marked a change from methods employed by established local southern civil rights groups like CORE and Student Non-Violent Coordinating Committee (SNCC), which relied more on moral suasion to heighten awareness and pressure institutions and businesses to change outside of any extralegal means to force the issue. Further, organizations such as the NUL and NAACP sought to build new "partnerships" with federal agencies for the future benefit of present members in hopes of obtaining gainful employment for members. In contrast, Hobson, as a lone individual beholden to no particular federal agency, preferred the impersonal legal system, relying on statistical evidence to support his claims and force changes in behavior. If anything, Hobson gained the confidence to take on the federal government through training he acquired while employed doing data accumulation and synthesis.

His political opponents criticized Hobson for being ornery, which damaged his relationship with the local chapter of CORE. Hobson chaired the local DC chapter of CORE for over three years, but the national board voted him out in 1963 due to philosophical differences—despite having successfully led the local chapter on numerous marches, sit-ins, and demonstrations.[21] Hobson came to see CORE's emphasis on nonviolent tactics as too restrictive for his creative and freethinking tastes. He said, "I'm nonviolent. . . . It's just not a religion with me."[22] Ironically, while Hobson felt CORE's national leadership was too restrictive, national leadership expelled him from the organization in December 1964 for "undemocratic procedures" in running the local DC chapter autocratically.[23] Shortly after expulsion, Hobson formed his own organization, Associated Community Teams (ACT), which he led until his death in 1977.

But ACT was an organization in name only. It had no members, other than Hobson himself, and a small group of loyal allies. In addition to lobbying federal agencies directly, through ACT, Hobson put pressure on local companies doing business with federal agencies to engage in equitable practices. It was during Hobson's tenure with ACT that he received most of his requests to advocate for black federal workers.

Many black employees, frustrated by the complexities and long duration of the more developed federal grievance process, authorized Hobson to represent them. The form they used stated that they authorized "Mr. Julius W. Hobson to speak for, represent, and act for me in regard to my grievance and claim against the U.S. government in regard to racial (and sex) discrimination in employment."[24] Although no law expressly allowed Hobson to adopt this intermediary role, the desire of black government workers to seek independent, grassroots assistance gave him that opportunity. An open question is how different agencies within the federal bureaucracy accepted Hobson in his advocate role given the scant evidence of major results. While little available evidence expounds on agency feeling, the volume of letters aggrieved black workers sent to Hobson along with his invitation to testify at informal congressional hearings about federal discrimination against black employees suggest Hobson was effective in generating a modicum of recognition as a trusted advocate.[25]

THE GOVERNMENT EMBRACES CIVIL RIGHTS

KEY LABOR DEVELOPMENTS IN THE EARLY 1960S

As a young Democratic president who narrowly defeated his Republican opponent in Richard M. Nixon, John F. Kennedy initially moved cautiously on the civil rights agenda as Cold War issues dominated his attention. At first, he entirely avoided agitating the fractious Southern base of his party, whom Nixon would skillfully recruit with his effective "Southern Strategy" a few years later. As the historian Daniel Stevens writes, "Despite his campaign promises of vigorous executive action, the first two years of [Kennedy's] administration were characterized by mostly symbolic actions and the strenuous avoidance of association with initiatives to introduce legislation to Congress."[26]

Nonetheless, Kennedy made a few decisions about American labor that significantly affected black federal workers. One was the signing of Executive Order 10925 on March 6, 1961, which required the government and government contractors to practice nondiscrimination in their hiring practices. The individual responsible for executing the order, Secretary of Labor Arthur Goldberg, a former union lawyer who had negotiated the merger between the American Federation of Labor (AFL) and the Congress of Industrial Organizations (CIO), was a devout liberal and strong supporter of civil rights. Goldberg used the order to finally abolish segregated facilities, which still existed in some government offices, namely the U.S. Employment Services, the federal apprenticeship and training program, and public sector unions in addition to the Department of Labor.

Goldberg, as a hard-line negotiator, was largely unmoved and unimpressed by new data from numerous federal agencies claiming and proclaiming racial progress when he had failed to see such results manifest in his own department. Goldberg stated when installed in his position, "I was not satisfied with a quantitative analysis, so I went around and had a survey made of the grades and classifications encompassed in this area." Goldberg also astutely noted the black-collar worker phenomenon of black workers confined to lower-level jobs: "I find, those of us in government, and I am sure the same thing is characteristic of private industry, that the concentration of [black] employment is in the lower grades, messengers, other production people, people who load on the working platform, and clerks."[27]

To interrupt this pattern of black-collar employment, on at least one occasion, Goldberg leveraged his sphere of influence to unilaterally appoint a black employee to a deputy director position at the Department of Labor. Prompting Goldberg into action was the inexplicable ranking of the black male applicant lower than two white applicants. While the two white applicants had a high school diploma and a fourth grade education, respectively, the black male had compiled an excellent service record as a Cornell University Ivy League graduate.[28] In actuality, however, this case was not unusual in the sense that a black college graduate was initially denied an opportunity to advance despite having superior credentials. On the other hand, the case was unusual in that highly qualified and deserving black candidates were not always given the benefit of the doubt by the reigning secretary of labor who was willing to intervene on their behalf. Thus, scores of black-collar workers suffered from a constant devaluation of their efforts and contributions, and paid the price directly through chronically lower wages and promotion rates.

Table 4.1 President-led initiatives to reduce discrimination

Administration	Year Began	Year Concluded
ROOSEVELT (1933–1945)		
President's Committee on Fair Employment Practice	1941 (E.O. 8802)	1946
Note: E.O. 8802 issued in response to A. Phillip Randolph march, prohibited racial discrimination in national defense industry and federal civil service.		
War Manpower Commission	1942	
Fair Employment Practice Committee	1943 (E.O. 9346)	
Note: Enlarged committee's staff and strengthened directive to employers		
TRUMAN (1945–1953)		
President's Committee on Civil Rights	1946 (E.O. 9808)	1947
Note: Disbanded after delivering 1947 report		
Desegregation of Armed Forces	1948 (E.O. 9981)	
Note: Prohibited racial, religious, and ethnic discrimination in the armed forces		
Fair Employment Board	1948 (E.O. 9980)	1955
Note: Allowed for inaction and omissions in grievances		
EISENHOWER (1953–1961)		
President's Committee on Government Contract Compliance	1953 (E.O. 10308)	1961
Note: Sought to ensure nondiscrimination in companies having governmental contracts		
President's Committee on Nondiscrimination in Government Contracts	1953 (E.O. 10479)	
President's Committee on Government Employment Policy	1955 (E.O. 10590)	1961
Note: Replaced Fair Employment Board		
KENNEDY (1961–1963)		
President's Committee on Equal Employment Opportunity	1961 (E.O. 10925)	
Note: Became Equal Employment Opportunity Commission via Civil Rights Act of 1964		
PCEEO has powers expanded	1963 (E.O. 11114)	1964

Much like Chester Bowles's tenure with the Office of Price Administration, Goldberg was only one left-leaning cabinet secretary. The question remained how to compel the remaining overwhelming majority of federal agencies to eschew discriminatory practices and habits detrimental to black workers, without liberal leadership leading the charge for increased equity. In 1961, E.O. 10925 established the President's Committee on Equal Employment Opportunity (PCEEO), which monitored nondiscrimination on government contracts. E.O. 10925 distinguished itself from previous executive orders designed to eradicate discrimination by endowing the PCEEO with expansive policymaking powers.

Rather than focus purely on responses to individual worker complaints, the PCEEO also requested that employers complete and file compliance reports as part of the bidding process for government contracts. In selected cases, this new measure prompted behavioral changes; some government contractors and subcontractors hired more black workers motivated by the fear of losing a lucrative federal contract. Accordingly, new measures like E.O. 10925 fostered much optimism and enthusiasm among federal officials who wanted to theoretically stop discrimination on the job. For instance, in March 1963, President Kennedy gushed that the President's Committee on Equal Employment Opportunity "received over 1,300 complaints in two years . . . and has achieved corrective action on 72% of the cases handled—a heartening and unprecedented record."[29]

Another key labor decision Kennedy made came nearly a year later on January 17, 1962, when he issued Executive Order 10988, authorizing, for the first time, limited collective bargaining rights for federal employees. Labeled "Employee-Management Cooperation in the Federal Sector," E.O. 10988 helped federal employee union membership skyrocket and triple from 10.8 percent in 1960 to 32 percent by the end of the decade.[30] On June 22, 1963, Kennedy also issued Executive Order 11114, which expanded the authority of the President's Committee on Equal Employment Opportunity to govern nondiscrimination in government contracts and in contracts financed with federal assistance. The foregoing executive orders certainly helped narrow racial disparities in federal employment (see table 4.1), but they failed to address underlying racial tensions in the federal workplace between black workers and their white colleagues or with white supervisors over disparate pay and promotions.

KENNEDY'S SHIFT

By 1963, President Kennedy admitted that, because of pressure from a growing civil rights movement, his executive orders had not solved the problem. In June of that year, speaking to a conference of mayors, President Kennedy

FIGURE 15. In discussing the site of Dr. Martin Luther King's legendary "I Have a Dream" speech, many often refer to the gathering in Washington, DC, simply as the "March on Washington." The organizers Bayard Rustin and Cleveland Robinson remind us that the event was indeed a march for jobs *and* freedom.

acknowledged the black-collar worker phenomenon when he observed that, although "we have undertaken to eliminate segregation and discrimination in Federal employment . . . in our cafeterias and other facilities," the "proportion of Negroes holding Federal jobs in many areas is still distressingly low—particularly in the higher-grade jobs."[31] Still, Kennedy offered only vague, aspirational statements (e.g., "but we aim to change this as quickly as possible") rather than specific, substantive solutions or demanding certain results within a finite timeline, the way he had with man's mission to the moon.[32] In August of that same year, a Baptist preacher from Georgia named Dr. Martin Luther King Jr. helped organize a mass demonstration in the nation's capital to raise awareness about the essentiality of economic freedoms in a capitalistic society. Officially titled, "March on Washington for Jobs *and* Freedom," the gathering shows how black organizers banked on the practical idea that continued segregation of blacks from higher-grade jobs would frustrate the liberty to pursue happiness that was promised and sold as the American Dream. This event is best remembered for Dr. King's inspirational "I Have a Dream" speech.

Whereas many black employees shared ambitions similar to those of their white colleagues to work hard, improve, and advance in rank, their careers differed from their white coworkers in that they still received less pay and fewer promotions over time. More costly than the immediate loss of pay however, was the long-term opportunity cost to black-collar workers; many saw years pass as they tried to navigate the latest antidiscrimination mechanism installed by the government. But as the federal government's efforts against discrimination were the culmination of trial and error, a certain amount of time had to pass before the government accumulated enough feedback to assess an initiative's effectiveness. The "correction lag," or time that elapsed between the implementation of a new antidiscrimination measure or policy and the response time to correct it could often take years—precious years that an individual black employee often could neither afford nor absorb. Hence, as correction lags grew longer, more black workers risked stagnation in their careers, which prompted many to call upon grassroots advocates like Julius Hobson to intervene.

JOHNSON'S TREATMENT

When Lyndon Johnson became United States president in November 1963 after the sudden and shocking assassination of John F. Kennedy, he quickly made plans to enact the civil rights legislation proposed by his slain predecessor earlier that year. The Civil Rights Act (CRA) of 1964 was a high-water mark in the history of antidiscrimination on the job (and in American society as a whole) in that it declared equal access to existing jobs as its domain and provided legal courses of action in instances where such access was wrongfully denied in the past. Thus, the historian Nancy MacLean correctly identifies the 1964 CRA as symbolizing a new brand of inclusive politics since Congress designed the new law to provide unprecedented economic opportunities to (white) women and Latinos in addition to blacks. More important for black federal workers, though, was their inability to take advantage of the remarkable protections contained in the 1964 Civil Rights Act. Unquestionably, when Title VII created the Equal Employment Opportunity Commission (EEOC), unlike past impotent iterations of the FEPC or FEB, for the first time ever in American history, a federal investigative body had the unprecedented power to adjudicate disputes, file lawsuits, and enforce monetary penalties for racially discriminatory behavior in the workplace—that is, in private workplaces.

Unfortunately for black-collar workers with specific grievances, federal workers were initially exempted from the EEOC's purview. While the establishment of the EEOC signaled that the federal government was committed to improving working conditions for all employees and would no longer tolerate willful discrimination against black rights, this commitment did not initially extend to the federal workplace itself for nearly another decade.

The 1964 CRA's passage after surviving numerous revisions and after surviving the longest continuous debate in U.S. Senate history symbolizes the triumph of high-stakes, political compromise and deserves attention as a keystone victory for civil rights.[33] As part of such compromise, the CRA's provisions were neither sweeping nor immediate. Under the 1964 act, only private employers with one hundred or more employees were within the EEOC's jurisdiction. This number decreased annually until July 2, 1968, when it was twenty-five.[34] The federal government only tangentially started to police itself when President Johnson released Executive Order 11246 in September 1965, which created the Office of Federal Contract Compliance Programs as an enforcement mechanism to ensure compliance with federal mandates of vendors doing business with the federal government not to discriminate along the parameters outlined in Title VII. The newly created office could terminate government contracts awarded to firms that failed to practice affirmative action in employment.

Not until 1972, nearly a decade after the CRA's passage, was Title VII amended through the Equal Employment Opportunity Act of 1972 to include state, local, and federal government actors and their employees within its purview.[35] The 1972 amendment also allowed the EEOC litigation authority to initiate lawsuits on behalf of a complainant against nongovernmental actors. Thus, while rightfully trumpeted as a breakthrough in American labor relations, an unfortunate by-product of the act's compromise was that it initially exempted a significant number of employees from its protections. But not standing idly by, many National Association of Postal and Federal Employees (the NAPE changed its name in 1965) members served as some of the first government Equal Employment Opportunity specialists in the mid- to late 1960s, several years before the 1972 EEOC Act formally brought federal government workers under the purview of the 1964 CRA's Title VII.

Nonetheless, the "cat and mouse" game ensued once again. A nationwide policy was created that purported to be promising in its potentially wide scope, but was severely limited in its application. Why even create a policy that applies to only a quarter of the nation's employees? A trend that has remained relatively unchanged is the fat-tailed distribution of businesses that have significant numbers of employees. Studies show that 90 percent of U.S. companies have fewer than twenty employees.[36] All public sector employees and all private businesses with up to twenty-five workers were excluded from the 1964 act's provisions. Although the 1972 Title VII amendment lowered the CRA's eligibility cutoff from twenty-five to fifteen employees, a large number of American enterprises conducted business as usual, safe from having to comply with the CRA's new enforcement provisions. As late as 1979, only 1.4 percent of the nation's businesses had one hundred or more employees.[37] Thus, one effect of the EEOC for black federal workers was similar to the placebo effect experienced with the FEPC in 1941—it had a symbolic function, but offered no practical, substantive change to the institutional discrimination that was normalized in the workplace. At a minimum, the symbolic function of the EEOC was further evidence of America's tendency to extend constitutional responsibility toward the private sector.

It is therefore unsurprising that the 1960s was a period of economic stagnation for black federal workers in DC—even well after the CRA took effect. As the economist Andrea Beller observed, "Title VII's enforcement had no significant overall effect on the earnings of black males relative to those of white males through 1969." Beller's study concluded that the "enforcement of Title VII as a means to combat racial discrimination must be characterized as unsuccessful during the sixties for the combined effect of its provisions was to reduce, albeit insignificantly, relative [disparities in] black employment and wages."[38] Beller's research is part of a larger consensus shared by many scholars who believe the Civil Rights Act had a marginal economic influence on black workers' incomes.[39] Hence, in the wake of the changed rhetoric of government disapproval of discrimination, individual activists like Hobson played an instrumental role in continuing to publicize the gaps between the acceptable rhetoric and the unacceptable, inequitable results.

PARADOXES OF THE EEOC

Nonetheless, the EEOC represented the federal government's most conscientious attempt since the end of the Second World War to directly address workplace discrimination. No longer did agency heads have to stress compliance or go out of their way to observe federal inclusion initiatives. If an individual employee had a grievance, they now had an official, independent federal outlet at their disposal that did not draw upon existing employees' resources during work time. Unsurprisingly, the EEOC soon became inundated with formal complaints. But while the EEOC provided formal recourse for aggrieved workers, it also elevated routine complaints to the commission level and weakened efforts at informal resolution at the agency level because many agencies now took the position that they were relieved of the responsibility to seek equity since a separate government arm was also to do so. Ironically, the creation of the EEOC contributed to the very inefficiency it tried to eliminate.

In its first year of existence, the EEOC received over two hundred complaints a week and had a backlog of three thousand cases—although none directly involved federal actors or agencies. Furthermore, only five conciliators were on staff to render decisions. By August 1968, the average case took sixteen months to complete.[40] By 1969, the backlog had grown to nearly two years.[41] Since few black complainants found new jobs while awaiting final disposition, obtaining confirmation of past discriminatory actions on the job was of little consolation. The government still lacked the ability to compensate employees retroactively for time lost while waiting patiently for a more just and prosperous future. The *Harvard Law Review Association* noted in 1971 that "to require a destitute or unemployed plaintiff for whom speed is essential to wait out this period is tantamount to denying him an effective judicial remedy."[42] The civil rights movement advocate and icon Dr. Martin Luther King Jr. also famously expressed similar sentiments scrawled in the margins of a newspaper from the confines of a Birmingham, Alabama, jail in 1963, writing: "For years now, I have heard the word 'Wait!' . . . This 'Wait' has almost always meant 'Never.' We must come to see, with one of our distinguished jurists, that 'justice too long delayed is justice denied.'"[43]

Many black men and women had endured years of working for the federal government without ever having an honest chance to get ahead or advance their careers and economic standing. For example, the *Washington Post* reported in 1963 that a black federal employee "recently retired as a Grade 5 after nearly thirty years' service as Government clerk. He, too, trained whites, which rose to Grades 14 and 15. He is a bitter man."[44] Time was of the essence for many black-collar workers pursuing promotion or career advancement cases, and few individuals had three decades to spare. Black workers often spent a good deal of time seeking to obtain the lost pay and promotions that their experiences should have granted them. As James Farmer, the head of CORE once observed, "Before an aggrieved person can get a remedy [from the EEOC], he may have found another job or starved to death."[45]

In such cases, individual activists like Julius Hobson became all the more crucial to helping black federal workers combat institutionalized, systematic discrimination. The Civil Rights Act and the EEOC reinforced the need for sustained advocacy; the new legislation fell short of its idealized purpose and increased black activism was an immediate response to a well-intentioned federal government that was ill-equipped to make a rapid response. Hobson used his own frustration with racist practices to galvanize supporters. He often narrated the plight of his mother as moral motivation; a local white hospital in Mississippi turned her away when she was pregnant with him and his twin brother after she had already begun delivering them both. She developed complications en route to the "colored hospital," which was farther away, and his twin did not survive. Hobson claimed his mother was never "right" after that. Neither was Hobson—he used this pain as incentive to right the wrongs he saw.[46]

EQUAL RIGHTS IN NO TIME

As the federal merit system of advancement developed, more black workers grew exasperated over the amount of time it took to get the new protocols functioning efficiently. For example, in 1966, the Pentagon mailed eight hundred questionnaires to a cross-section of approximately four thousand civil service employees at United States Air Force Headquarters in DC. Respondents marked their race and provided open-ended comments assessing the Merit Promotion program's efficiency.

Most black respondents were pessimistic about the benefits of the Merit Promotion program. "Personal favoritism plays an important part in promotion policies in HQ USAF," claimed one worker. Many comments were quite dismissive: "Merit Promotion Program is a farce"; "I have found the merit promotion program to be practically a joke"; "they should do away with this program as it is absolutely a waste of time." One black respondent wondered sarcastically: "USAF Merit Promotion Program—What is it?—Where is it?" A black employee revealed the favoritism behind many promotion decisions. "Merit Promotion in our Directorate is a joke!" she wrote, "Every time a career civilian transfers, retires, or drops dead, particularly at the GS-12 level, and up, the General sends over the name of a retired buddy of his as a suggested applicant. Usually the 'suggested applicant' is the selectee over any other civilian. I have been a GS-11 for 9 years."[47]

Secretary of Labor W. Willard Wirtz also recognized this frustration. Wirtz positioned himself as a conscious white ally when he addressed the Convocation of the NAACP Legal Defense and Education Fund on May 18, 1966, saying, "I am sick and tired, furthermore, of the false piety of those who answer inquiries about the racial aspects of their employment or membership practices with the bland, smug answer that: 'We don't know because of course we wouldn't keep records on anything like that.'"[48] Nonresponsive survey entries merely underscored that some antidiscrimination measures were only as effective as the varying interest levels of different agencies.

UPPER-LEVEL RESISTANCE

Still, according to many white federal administrators, the presence of antidiscrimination protocols was itself almost proof that discrimination did not exist. In a 1966 letter to Julius Hobson, Civil Service Commission (CSC) chairman John W. Macy Jr. bristled about Hobson's criticism of the CSC's poor record of handling black workers' grievances. In defending his approach to equality in the workplace, Macy detailed the protocols he expected all managers to enforce, although he declined to state whether the managers actually enforced them. He said the CSC "looks for agencies" to: (1) perform self-analysis of their "equal employment opportunity situation" and identify problems, (2) then develop a plan of action with "specific and realistic goals for achieving definite and measurable results," (3) delegate responsibilities, (4) enlist "understanding and support of all employees," and finally (5) constantly "evaluate progress in relation to program goals."[49] On paper, Macy's protocols seemed simple enough to execute. But he overlooked the bureaucratic barriers that made it difficult to rectify a history of inequitable pay and unfair promotion procedures. Hobson was quite critical of such barriers, angrily stating, "I'm not going to argue that the [Civil Service] Commission is racist by design. but if it isn't, then the so-called merit system was designed by an idiot."[50]

White federal administrators had considerable leeway in making subjective decisions about employee advancement. Antidiscrimination became an increasingly sensitive issue for them as white workers grew apprehensive that an emphasis on equity for blacks would slant the norms unfairly against whites. In a 1968 report, the Civil Service Commission acknowledged this white concern, branding it "tyranny of color," where an "incompetent manages to hold onto his job only because of his race. This form of blackmail cannot be tolerated. Equal opportunity to be hired implies an equal opportunity to be fired."[51] Many white administrators thus worried about being unable to offer legitimate criticism to black colleagues fearing that their feedback would always appear to be discrimination in the eyes of the recipient.

That same year, disparate treatment in at least one major federal agency—the United States Department of Agriculture (USDA)—prompted the *Washington Examiner* to call it "the last citadel of Southern racism in the Federal Government . . . run by the large Southern white farmers, and Southern committee chairmen in Congress."[52] Regardless of any assessments involving competency, white federal workers at the USDA resisted the idea of having black employees altogether. Such exclusionists had the support of the high-ranking senator Sam J. Ervin from North Carolina, who protested that many black workers were "brainwashed" into taking up social causes that had nothing to do with their jobs, while they sought ill-deserved protection from workplace discrimination.[53]

Individuals who were farthest removed from the problem often trumpeted modest gains made in the workplace most loudly. This partially explains why, in 1968, several Democratic congressmen (both black and white) observed that the heads of few federal agencies found fault with themselves, since "findings of discrimination by the [Civil Service] Commission are extremely infrequent," and "not one contract has ever been cancelled for non-compliance."[54]

The 1964 Civil Rights Act was simply not designed to protect all black federal workers from lower wage and slower promotion rates—barriers that kept blacks "segregated" or ghettoized in lower-grade positions and away from higher-paying ones. While lack of education and experience were becoming increasingly legitimate rationales to explain disparities in black promotion, some protocols still lent themselves to racial abuse, among which were the grievance procedures themselves. The more such standard bureaucratic procedures incorporated new complaint mechanisms, the more encumbered such processes became. For instance, one reason that blacks with grievances had to wait before obtaining their day in court was because EEOC regulations required a complainant to first file with the EEOC, and then wait sixty days for all parties to go through the conciliation process.[55] While the architects of the CRA intended to avoid backlogs in the courts by encouraging informal resolutions of workers' claims, the EEOC was not a binding authority and a decision in favor of or against a complainant still did not preclude the worker or the alleged perpetrator from their day in court. Hence, the sixty-day wait rule usually amounted to at least a two-month delay since the vast majority of EEOC cases went forward with the legal process before achieving resolution using more informal means. Conversely, many workers were willing to wait for an initial EEOC determination, strategically thinking that a preliminary finding in their favor would bolster their legal case.

Just because a process for adjudicating discrimination complaints existed did not mean the process was always effective, fair, or timely. Aggrieved workers now had to record their experiences on paper so that an impartial individual (other than their supervisor) could review the case. While a detailed recording of racial discrimination charges makes sense in maintaining transparency and consistency in adjudicating disputes, the task proved difficult for many black complainants. In completing such paperwork, the victim had to recall specific past scenarios that appeared insignificant at the time, but combined with other microaggressions persuasively established a larger pattern of mistreatment. In the name of due process, the assumption was that no one was *intentionally* or *purposely* discriminated against based on race. Thus all complainants had the burden of "proving" their case. Given the historical data and impetus for creating the grievance procedures in the first place, it would have been interesting to see an approach that assumed discrimination based on pervasive statistical evidence of discriminatory patterns.

In late 1968, Hobson complained to Representative William F. Ryan (D-NY) at an unofficial congressional hearing that "grievance procedures now available to Negro victims of discrimination are useless and intimidating and need to be revised."[56] Ryan held the informal hearing after repeated attempts to hold formal hearings failed due to a lack of support from several congressional committees. At Ryan's hearing, Michael Ambrose, a white ally, related that due to personal frustration with the low priority given to antidiscrimination efforts he had resigned from the Civil Service Commission where he helped administer the EEOC. Ambrose testified, "The grievance system does not work and only jeopardizes careers of employes who resort to it."[57]

White administrators often explained that their failure to hire black workers in high-status, well-paying jobs was due to the technical nature of the available positions. In the fall of 1968, John Macy told Representative Ryan why only four of the 180 employees in the laboratory of the National Institutes of Health (NIH) were black. According to Macy, black candidates were culturally deprived: "the reason for this ratio is allied to the fact that the acoustics and the underwater acoustics field is relatively new and demands a high degree of technical training. There is a scarcity of trained personnel in this field, in general, and more so from the Negro race."[58] For Julius Hobson, such rationales by Macy constituted an attack on black intellect, professional competency, and the capacity to compete. The NIH's reluctance to hire blacks reminded him of those government officials during the Second World War who argued that blacks like the Tuskegee Airmen could not be fighter pilots because they were believed to be incapable of handling expensive machinery that required a high degree of technical training. In response to such specious but alluring arguments, Hobson huffed, "Culturally deprived is just another word for nigger."[59]

LIFE AFTER MLK

After the assassination of Dr. Martin Luther King, Jr. in April 1968, Hobson began a new, aggressive campaign to mobilize black federal workers. After all, the country and Washington, DC, had changed. Many citizens were confused

FIGURE 16. Riots ravaged much of black DC, paving the way for gentrification in subsequent decades. Library of Congress.

and concerned, frustrated and crestfallen by the news of King's death. In DC, as in other urban areas at the time, black citizens mobilized in the streets and one of the nation's worst riots broke out; several thousand people were arrested and injured and millions of dollars' worth of damage was done to hundreds of buildings. Given the high concentration of black federal workers in DC at the time, at least a couple of dozen federal workers were arrested for their participation. One black female government employee with a master's degree was arrested, but was discharged after only six hours when the police sergeant was moved by her story. She rode to 14th Street just to "see what was going on" with two male companions when one suddenly jumped out of the car and returned with four bottles of liquor. This black-collar employee recalled how "for those ten seconds after we got the liquor, I felt the System had finally given me something for nothing. White people do not realize the mixed emotions that an educated Negro feels every day. They tell you to go to school and get educated and then they give you some penny-ante job and expect you to feel like the world has been so gracious."[60] This black-collar employee's experience clearly relays a larger source of deep-abiding frustration that found an outlet in the calamitous aftermath of the King assassination.

Immediately after the riots died down, in May 1968, a Southern Christian Leadership Conference Poor People's Campaign called for two thousand demonstrators to settle into a shantytown called Resurrection City on the National Mall in DC. For more than a month participants marched daily to various, nearby federal offices and took part in a mass demonstration on June 19, 1968. While Hobson did not pitch a tent on the National Mall, through his Associated Community Teams, he circulated a petition claiming that King "endorsed the fight against racism in Federal employment as a part of his Poor People's Campaign." It is unclear exactly how many signatures Hobson collected or what eventual impact they had, but Hobson informed the *Washington Post* that he had received more than three thousand letters from frustrated black federal workers by June 1968.[61] Notably, the petition solicited signatures on two points:

> I (we) agree in principle that available official data on Federal employment of minority groups do not fully reveal Federal discriminatory practices.
> I (we) agree in principle that the grievance machinery designed to deal with individual discrimination is inadequate and intimidating.[62]

In an important shift, the petition made clear that discrimination no longer meant, as it had before and during the Second World War, the outright refusal to hire blacks for powerful, high-paying jobs. Now, black-collar treatment meant that blacks were included in the hiring process, but were subject to selective hiring in "ghettoized" areas, commonly separated from whites who routinely landed all ranges of positions. Many of the antidiscrimination mechanisms became limited in their actual function due to the lack of diverse people and perspectives operating them at the upper-administrative levels. One method that attempted to rectify this issue was through the hiring of different candidates for these upper levels. But the irony was that due to their black-collar status, many workers could not get high-placed jobs that would position them to better ensure that other blacks could be hired, promoted, or treated fairly. Here, Hobson's language was uncharacteristically passive, perhaps revealing a desire to avoid offending potential white allies as a potential strategy to gain better access to those upper-level positions.

MANAGING MICROAGGRESSIONS

Over time, discrimination cases became increasingly difficult and complex to resolve. In the absence of a direct racial epithet or a clear attempt to separate workers according to race, the victim had to prove an abstract feeling. It was difficult to provide proof of numerous microaggressions—the routine, seemingly insignificant instances of racial insensitivity, the cumulative effect of which created an overall feeling of rejection in the workplace. Disparaging jokes, hostile facial expressions, and antagonistic tones of voice could all make a black federal worker feel put down even if a supervisor did not explicitly communicate that sentiment.

Knowing it was nearly impossible to establish a discrimination case based on feelings alone, Hobson used disparate pay and promotion rates as evidence of racial disparities. For example, in 1968, he wrote an article for the *Saturday Evening Post* that markedly increased his visibility as an advocate for black government workers. In "Uncle Sam Is a Bigot," he criticized the federal government for being slow to improve black representation in the higher ranks, citing statistical data from a 1966 Civil Service Commission Study.[63] Soon more black employees than ever before contacted Hobson with tales of how they had been blocked or delayed from federal promotions.

One of these workers was Brad Johnson, who wrote to Hobson two months after the *Post* article had appeared. Omitting the name of his agency, probably out of self-protection, Johnson noted that he worked "in the mail room as a GS-2 Messigner [*sic*], and I have not been able to advance any further than a Messigner since 1960."[64] Johnson mentioned that he had earned a bachelor of arts degree in business administration with a minor in economics and had managed to obtain a real estate broker's license in his spare time. He was also a veteran of the Second World War. While Johnson did not mention where he obtained his college degree, it is likely indicative of a disadvantaged educational background that Johnson was unable to correctly spell the title of his own occupation. Nonetheless, in reflecting on his stalled career, Johnson lamented: "I have a family to support and educate, my children like to wear nice clothes and have some of the things in life for enjoyment like all red-blooded Americans."[65]

In 1969, Malissa J. Bozman, a black procurement clerk for the Defense Construction Supply Company, also contacted Hobson for help. Bozman reported, "I have been employed in Federal Service for the past 19 years and in my present grade for the past 6 years." The six years of career stagnation for Bozman exceeded the five-year average for other black federal workers and was a source of confusion to her. Bozman confided that her "201 [personnel] file according to performance ratings does not show poor Potentials, Initiative, or lack of Experience but after 19 years I'm only a GS-4."[66] She reported to work for years knowing that her chances of upward advancement were slim.

Julius Hobson made it his personal mission to find data to support the complaints of federal workers like Johnson and Bozman. At a 1969 hearing before the Senate Subcommittee on Labor and Public Welfare, he quoted a survey by the Library of Congress, which found that 6 percent and 5 percent of the white and black employees, respectively, had college and postgraduate

FIGURE 17. Here, these unnamed, everyday activists suggest that the path to one's American Dream necessarily marries the two concepts of civil rights *plus* full employment; in other words, both political and economic freedoms are key to unlocking the American Dream. Library of Congress.

degrees. But blacks obtained promotions once every five years, while whites in the same department landed promotions once every fifteen months.[67]

The stories told to Hobson demonstrated that change for black-collar workers remained elusive, even after passage of the momentous Civil Rights Act. What mostly changed over time was the style, method, and manner in which discrimination took place. As Arthur Fletcher, the former assistant secretary of labor remarked: "I received the shock of my life to discover that in 1969 the Department of Labor (DOL) was looked upon as a bastion of liberalism and considered one of the best departments in government with reference to black and brown employment." In reflecting on the small number of blacks in upper-level positions at the DOL despite significant efforts to increase black participation, Fletcher continued, "I remember saying to myself, 'If this represents liberalism, then Lord save us from the liberals.'"[68]

REFLECTING ON CIVIL RIGHTS PROGRESS

MORE THAN EXCLUSION

Implementing antidiscrimination measures was a far more complex task than creating them. Whereas the president of the United States could unilaterally issue an executive order calling for a new study, it proved more challenging to coordinate the efforts of thousands of individuals in the federal workforce to implement the study's recommendations. Many white supervisors and colleagues of black employees, some through intentional acts, some unwittingly through "bad habits," continued daily practices that contributed to the devaluation of blacks as well as hyper-scrutiny of black job performance, which resulted in more incidents of discipline and punishment. Despite increasing official support for equity through grievance mechanisms and data collection, numerous instances of racial discrimination persisted. Overt discrimination gave way to covert marginalization (see table 4.2).

A common justification for the marginalized roles of black-collar employees was that they lacked formal experience. Julius Hobson fought to open opportunities for blacks that led to valuable experience. He inquired into the availability of federal summer jobs (e.g., in the U.S. Senate) for black students, which traditionally had gone to whites and were often associated with a lawmaker or official. "The problem," he charged, "is not overt discrimination in present employment practices but rather the failure to use affirmative recruiting procedures which might result in attracting Negro college students."[69]

Even though Congress initially excluded the federal government from the 1964 Civil Rights Act, the struggles that black federal workers endured on the job were relatively tolerable in relation to the less transparent and openly

Table 4.2. Black-collar workers discrimination chart

Overt discrimination	Covert marginalization
Dirtiest and most dangerous jobs	Lowest-paid jobs, jobs with lowest GS rating
Limited access to any job	Limited access to upper-level jobs
Enforced physical segregation	Encouraged integration of non-white-collar, manual spaces (e.g., gardening)

Note: Here, 1965 is the date of definitive transition from segregation to marginalization. Signed in 1965, the Voting Rights Act was preceded by the Civil Rights Act the year before. Together these acts represent the high–water mark in the civil rights movement, which greatly influenced the public perception of discrimination.

hostile private sector.[70] But that only made continued discrimination in the public sector harder to bear. As Kent Corey, the director of manpower and training for an unnamed federal agency asked Hobson in 1968, "How can we point the finger of blame at private industry for discriminatory employment practices when our own government not only condones but encourages discrimination?"[71]

During the late 1960s, most black federal workers continued to experience slower promotion rates and lower pay, despite stated policies that should have narrowed or eliminated such disparities. Advocating for black workers was easier said than done given the increased social pressure to acknowledge unprecedented social progress and new civil rights measures. While the unavoidable inconsistencies gave advocates like Hobson an opportunity to point out the gap between rhetoric and action, many agencies avoided disclosing statistics on their poor progress in ending discrimination to avoid embarrassment or reprimand. In one case, Theodore S. Hesburgh, president of the University of Notre Dame and chairman of the U.S. Civil Rights Commission, alleged that the White House tried to delay the publication of an October 1970 report charging the federal government with violating its own antidiscrimination policies in the hiring, promotion, and tenure of blacks until after the November 3 election. The White House alleged that the report, although eighteen months in the making, would be "harmful" and expressed concern about the timing of the report's release, to which Hesburgh responded: "We didn't share their concern."[72]

Accordingly, the Civil Service Commission in late 1969 authorized a controversial method for keeping racial data because of the difficulty associated with having federal agencies voluntarily maintain accurate demographic records for racial analysis. To prevent agency "flip-flops trying to determine the race of workers," employees would revive racial coding upon sight when hired (e.g., "Negro" = Code 1, "Spanish American" = Code 2, etc.). The CSC admitted that the sight observations by federal administrators "are necessarily broad and therefore not anthropologically precise," but nonetheless felt that the new program was "adequate to meet program needs."[73]

MORE THAN MONEY

The federal grievance system, despite the best intentions of its architects, lacked designs to make victims whole in the present moment; it relied on paying monetary damages for past discrimination. For black federal workers themselves, however, the money could not remedy the cumulative effects of innumerable social slights—both perceived and real—suffered over a long period. For example, Charles E. Shipp, a plasterer for the General Services Administration (GSA), was disciplined in early 1969 for complaining about the GSA's delay in promoting him. Shipp was a college graduate with twenty-one years of government service, but never received a promotion during his tenure with the federal government.[74]

For educated workers like Shipp performing their jobs amid expectations of advancing their careers, it was virtually impossible to determine when a negative performance evaluation that blocked advancement was truly constructive criticism or something more pernicious. In documenting and reporting every microaggression or small instance of possible racial hostility, black employees like Shipp risked appearing petty. To add insult to injury, once Shipp formally complained, a formal letter of reprimand was placed in his file.

Similarly, in 1968 federal employee John Craven contacted Julius Hobson and described his frustration: "I am speaking from 23 years of federal service. The average unsuspecting black is . . . brain washed into believing the system is fair because it represents the federal government."[75] Craven's term "brain washed" implies that in return for secure employment, the government was "buying" silence or cooperation from those black employees fortunate enough to have jobs. When Craven said, "brain washed," perhaps he was referring to a mindset that eschewed direct critique and activism in exchange for political favor. Craven elaborated that in the absence of brainwashing, the average black federal employee "becomes so completely disgusted and frustrated he gives up, or he decides to fight and is finally trapped in a mase [sic] of ambigous [sic] never ending red tape and ultimately he becomes the victim of unwarranted reprisals and variour [sic] other forms of mental torture with no hope of justice and redress of his grievance."[76] Here, Craven describes the psychological costs of submerging himself in a system intolerant of his presence.

As the postwar era progressed, discrimination took a larger toll on black federal workers beyond their devalued paychecks. Life as a black-collar employee was taxing in innumerable ways.

Julius Hobson's long career as a federal employee and fierce advocate provided a public referendum on the changing but still taxing relationship between black federal workers and the federal government. During the Second World War, the federal government adopted a passive stance against discrimination in the workplace. A few left-leaning agencies like the Office of Price Administration addressed racial disparities but had only limited success applying them in the absence of civil rights laws. Immediately after the war, federal commissions like the President's Committee on Civil Rights produced data backing up the grievances of black workers and called for action to remedy them. But well into the 1960s, despite passage of the right legislation, many white federal workers and administrators resisted black advancement. Many workers still observed racial customs and traditions outside the workplace, making the transition to a bias-free workplace difficult. Activists like Hobson pushed back against this persistent reality. When Hobson died in 1973, the *Washington Post* eulogized him as a man who "made a career of impatience, of speaking out when other men held back." The obituary concluded, "He was outrageous, inflammatory, melodramatic, insulting. A lot of the time, he also was right."[77]

CHAPTER FIVE

"I WAS HURTING"

BLACKS IN GOVERNMENT ON THE MEND, 1970–1981

One dramatic scene that had ominous overtones for black federal workers in the post–civil rights era was a contentious exchange that took place on March 27, 1970, at the Sonesta Hotel in Washington, DC, just a couple of days after a national postal wildcat strike ended. The chaotic scene at the Sonesta involved the failed attempt of the National Alliance of Postal and Federal Employees (NAPFE), an independent union of African American workers, seeking inclusion in the final resolution negotiations. NAPFE leadership was pushed away from the meeting room entrance as captured in photographs published in the *National Alliance* publication.[1] At the hotel, the only unions invited to negotiate with the government to bring about an amicable solution were craft unions that were also part of the AFL-CIO. Secretary of Labor George Schultz was conducting a meeting with the leaders of postal unions in order to negotiate a resolution to the nation's first major postal strike. However, only those seven unions "officially" recognized by the government were allowed to collectively bargain and represent the interests of their constituents. The confrontation at the beginning of this meeting revolved around NAPFE leadership seeking inclusion in the larger talks with the other unions.

An event several months later on Labor Day 1970 clearly illustrates this muddied picture of black federal employee marginalization. President Nix-

FIGURE 18. The 1970 national wildcat Postal Strike led directly to the reorganization of the Post Office Department as the current United States Postal Service. The grassroots movement would have been impossible to execute without the input from black federal workers, who are conspicuously absent from this 1971 photograph of postal union and postal service negotiations. Library of Congress.

on hosted a dinner attended by seventy top national labor leaders and their wives—but NAPFE president and DC resident Robert White was not among those invited. The NAPFE interpreted the noninvitation as another slight to a union that numbered more than 40,000 black postal members, more than any federal union in the country at the time.[2] "[W]e cannot help but wonder Mr. President," White remarked in frustration, "is it because we're black?"[3]

In the following summer of 1971, Congress ultimately reorganized the Post Office Department as a semipublic corporation and renamed it the United States Postal Service (USPS). Some government officials publicly complained about this move, believing it would do little to improve efficiency. Postmaster Lawrence O'Brien quipped, "The Post Office Department, as presently constituted, reminds me of the classic definition of an elephant—a mouse built to government specifications." O'Brien also stated that the Post Office Department "should cease to be part of the President's Cabinet" and "should become a nonprofit government corporation, rendering essential public service."[4]

O'Brien's comments reflect the growing fatigue felt in Washington over governmental spending and agencies that were increasingly viewed as bloated, unnecessary, and inefficient. While the government was the solution after the Depression and during the nascent stages of the postwar era, the government was now seen as the problem hindering the country from unbridled success as the "city on the hill" during the globally competitive Cold War. Reorganization of the Post Office Department was just the latest maneuver by the government to centralize operations and make them more operationally effective and economically efficient. To carry out this ambitious task, the federal government took the unprecedented step of collective bargaining with several postal unions after some 200,000 postal employees held the nation hostage in a "wildcat strike" in the spring of 1970.

The only problem was that the NAPFE did not receive an invitation to the bargaining table. Originally founded in 1913 when President Woodrow Wilson and Postmaster Alfred Burleson put their heads together to segregate black and white postal workers, the NAPFE formed a solid track record of representing black employees who were often maltreated by both majority white unions and majority white management teams on the job. Their cause six decades later was no different. Even as postal workers nationwide were seeking a unified front to better leverage better wages and working conditions in dilapidated buildings nationwide, white-led unions still enforced a racial hierarchy and turned deaf ears to NAPFE entreaties to work together.

Unlike other existing postal unions that were skill- and craft-specific (e.g., Railway Mail Clerks, Postal Letter Carriers), NAPFE organized itself as an industrial union. NAPFE leadership, concerned about creating solidarity among all black postal workers, opted for an organizing model that alleviated the need for black workers to choose affiliations based on their specific skills. The consequence of this strategy meant that the NAPFE was not granted recognition by the federal government when it outlined the rules of engagement with President John F. Kennedy's Executive Order 10988. Despite having a robust and significant membership that peaked around 50,000 in the 1960s (a number higher than membership in some smaller white-led unions that joined the merger, such as the National Postal Union's 25,000 members), NAPFE members had the disadvantage of maintaining dual membership with their specific craft unions that negotiated the large mergers (e.g., American Postal Workers Union) sufficient to collectively bargain with the federal government.

In effect, while the broader industrial foundation enabled NAPFE to maintain (chiefly racial) solidarity among black postal workers, its abstract structure hindered its ability to win specific recognition from the federal government during union elections. As the historian Phillip Rubio observes, the "Alliance's decades-old identity conundrum between labor union and civil rights organization had essentially been resolved for them over their objections. Without collective bargaining or grievance representation rights in the post office, they literally became the *civil rights union.*"[5] NAPFE members, in other words, were excluded from formal, serious negotiations, only because of the alliance's history of helping black postal workers who were excluded from formal, serious negotiations. The penalty for such advocacy was marginalization. Black postal workers received higher wages, as did white postal workers after the USPS reorganization, but the upward trajectory of NAPFE as a union was negatively impacted and it would never recover its national prominence or relevance.

While postal worker (and Defense Department) data are typically classified separately from other federal departments due to having the status of an independent agency, the story is nonetheless instructive of how black-collar workers were generally regarded and how they could expect to be treated. The USPS has been home to scores of black employees who joined the agency for economically strategic reasons similar to those of other black federal workers, as the odds are low of a postal career being the result of specific and targeted training when one is an undergraduate student in college. In the decade following the turbulent and activist 1960s, new legislation and policies courtesy of the 1964 Civil Rights Act logically should have emboldened black federal workers about being able to stake their economic claim to the American Dream with much less racial friction than in previous decades. Nevertheless, a significant number of black postal employees were marginalized due to their overall black-collar status, which was an ominous sign of what was to come for black federal workers in other agencies.

WE'VE ONLY JUST BEGUN

Since joining the federal rolls in large numbers during and after the Second World War, black federal workers continuously struggled against their perception by white colleagues and administrators as not being up to the demands of their jobs. In other words, black-collar workers were still presumed to be incompetent. Even a full three decades after the war, this pervasive, yet presumptive prejudice still helped justify lower GS ratings (i.e., wages) and slower promotion rates for black workers. As black federal workers from the National Institutes of Health (NIH) expressed cynicism over their black-collar status: "There is slow, slow progress in equality of opportunity for jobs outside of the laundry and housekeeping unit; there is the almost non-existent chance to break the GS13/14 barrier, unless you happen to be 'super nigger.'"[6]

How and why this damaging narrative continued to persist is perplexing. On one hand, in numerous instances the federal government had taken the lead and projected a more progressive approach to transparent hiring and grievance procedures than the private sector. Not until the passage of the 1964 Civil Rights Act with the creation of Title VII legal remedies did the private sector really start to pay attention to best practices on how to reduce racial friction on the job between fellow employees. If anything, the federal government was consistent in exhorting its agencies to show cause, issue reports, and comply with broad-based policies that comported with its constitutional responsibility, or general ideological principles consistent with a democratic republic.

On the other hand, as a demographic unit, black government workers were not able to buck the trend of lower wages and slower raises experienced by black-collar workers. Notwithstanding individual cases of success, black workers en masse still disproportionately occupied the lowest pay grades, and once there, remained there considerably longer than similarly situated white colleagues before being promoted, if they were promoted at all. By the beginning of the 1970s, it was becoming apparent to many black federal employees that federal employment was no perfect citadel protecting them from racial discrimination. Discriminatory patterns seen in the private sector were merely adapted and duplicated in the public sector. Much the way water adapts to the shape of its container, racism fluidly adapted to the African American working environment. Even for black federal employees working for an equal opportunity employer in urban metropolises outside of the South, racism still found them on the job. Black federal employees were neither tree loggers nor glassblowers. They were individuals working directly and expressly for the world's leading economy at the time, which was also highly influential in selling its message of democracy domestically and abroad.

By logical extension, the jobs of black federal employees were all rooted in the ideology that their tasks contributed to the continued propagation of democratic principles. American democracy stands for freedom—freedom to embrace life, liberty, and the pursuit of happiness. But perhaps the obvious but unacknowledged barrier for black-collar workers who continued to suffer a lack of democratic treatment—even when working directly for what was billed as one of the greatest democratic republics in the world at the time—was that ultimately, they were not American. Blacks were not seen or treated as fully American. They were African American.

The fact that blacks were presumed to be incompetent was nothing new; this narrative stretched back to the era of enslavement and was reinforced in popular writings during the Reconstruction Era. Perhaps what was changing over time was the manner in which this consistent narrative was stylized. Whites traditionally had more of a choice in how they would leverage their presumptive power over the average black worker they encountered in life.

The failed Reconstruction period bled directly into the Jim Crow era, which until the 1960s weathered solid legal and social challenges to its institutional structure. In other words, the narrative of black incompetence required little explanation or justification in the private sector. In the public sector, however, principles of constitutional responsibility provided new pressure.

It is accurate to say that this new pressure was not overwhelming, dispositive, or all-encompassing. A confluence of factors including the very public civil rights movement, the temporal strengthening of public sector unionism, and the overarching Cold War and its battle for the supremacy of American democracy over foreign communism nevertheless all contributed toward a scenario in which the federal government indeed felt pressure. The nation had emerged from the war primarily as the victor and in order to maintain its place as the global leader, it made sense to make a respectable local effort to honor global democratic principles. With respect to effort however, in 1971, President Richard Nixon declared, "With blacks [on the job], you can usually settle for an incompetent, because there are just not enough competent ones, and so you put incompetents in and get along with them, because the symbolism is vitally important. You have to show you care."[7]

Here, Nixon's unfortunate comments do two things. First, they explicitly acknowledge the perceived importance of symbolism. In the global fight for democratic influence, Nixon thought it was important for the United States at least to "show" that it cared about the fundamental principles it espoused as being so dear. These comments are not automatically representative of an entire nation, but as the elected president of the United States of America and the federal government's chief executive officer, Nixon's comments take on a representative nature. In other words, Nixon's comments, in casually referring to blacks as "incompetents," reflect the fact that even after the civil rights movement, ambivalence or indifference to true substantive equality was not uncommon. Nixon was generally agitated by what he perceived to be a public sector economy that had low motivation for performance and accountability. Complaining about how the bureaucracy of public sector job protections made it difficult to terminate an employee "at will" was not new or unique to Nixon. Thomas Jefferson once famously wondered, "How are vacancies to be obtained? Those by death are few; by resignation, none."[8] What was new was Nixon's general conflation of incompetence with blackness.

Second, Nixon implicitly acknowledged the pressure wrought by constitutional responsibility. When he states that "the symbolism is vitally important," the symbolism he refers to is the image of one nation united under general democratic ideologies that comprise the American idea. African Americans did not conceive or establish the ideological base on which the country stands insofar as they contributed very little to its formal creation. Their mere presence nevertheless forced a reconsideration of how such ideologies would be applied. The existence of both blacks and whites under a system originally created by and for whites tested the truth of the democratic principles that acknowledged every individual's investment in the republic founded on basic principles of citizenship and humanity. But just as individual boats continue to rise as the overall water level rises during high tide, Nixon implied that white ambivalence always rose above the next highest level of black protest. "You have to show you care" does not suggest that substantive sincerity is behind the action; when it came to black-collar workers, perhaps the appearance (if not illusion) of democracy was enough.

FEDERAL WHITE FLIGHT

Just as more blacks were moving in to federal jobs, whites in many agencies decided that they had had enough and opted for greener pastures, or rather, whiter suburbs outside of the "Chocolate City" of Washington, DC.[9] The musician George Clinton is credited as one of the first to nickname the nation's capital in response to statistical data that confirmed what was already manifest simply in walking down any street in the district—that Washington was inhabited by mostly black residents—71.1 percent. African Americans reached this population peak in 1971.[10]

Whether it was congestion, limited space and rising real estate prices, or sheer wariness of the city center in the aftermath of the 1968 riots, it was also around the early 1970s that many agencies decided to physically move their locations and operations to the outlying suburbs of DC. Why many of the same agencies did not decide to do the same during the height of the Second World War, when thousands of new workers arrived weekly is unclear. Maybe it was coincidence. Or perhaps it was just the so-called luck of the black-collar worker.

Many government officials explained that such moves had nothing to do with race and everything to do with "the high cost of land for plant operations in the central cities."[11] Not all black employees were convinced by this logic, however. Unlike several poor, illiterate, and disenfranchised blacks who encountered difficulty in officially challenging the dominant political structure in the South, many workers in the North adopted a different stance. In 1970, several black Health, Education, and Welfare (HEW) employees filed lawsuits to prevent their agency from moving more than twenty miles outside of the capital city's limits to the Maryland suburbs of Rockville.[12] This lawsuit is telling for two reasons: first, the black employees felt enough ownership and fealty to their jobs that they felt compelled to pursue legal action to keep their employment arrangement from being altered significantly. Many disenfranchised Southern workers holding down agricultural and domestic positions may not have had the same sense of place that accrues to an employee who perceives more stability on the job. Second, the black federal employees were in a social and financial position to file a lawsuit. The suit was privately financed because neither the NAACP Legal Defense Fund nor any other civic organization was involved. The middle-class status afforded black workers through their federal employment also provided them with the additional resources required to self-advocate and protect their jobs, which despite their imperfections, were still viewed as worth fighting for on some level.

The legal actions argued that the move should be enjoined as it imposed disproportionate hardships on black workers, many of whom did not own cars and would have to spend more on child care and transportation expenses out of lower salaries compared to what most of their white colleagues received.[13] For these federal "working poor," an additional $350 estimated in annual bus fare and a doubling of commuting time to five or six hours, round-trip, made the move to Rockville hard to bear, especially given the less developed state of Washington, DC's Metro system in the early 1970s. While a Rockville subway stop now exists on the DC Metro's Red Line, it was not constructed until 1984, which made commuting a distance of twenty miles a much larger task than what it appeared to be on paper.

This trend of federal agencies moving to the suburbs was so noticeable and widespread that the U.S. Commission on Civil Rights conducted an investigation and produced a report entitled *Equal Opportunity in Suburbia* in 1974. In compiling the report, the commission gathered testimony from more than 150 witnesses in public hearings held in St. Louis, Baltimore, and Washington, DC, between January 1970 and June 1971. One unidentified black federal employee testified to the DC Advisory Committee to the U.S. Commission on Civil Rights that, at the new suburban facility "we see our [black] men there, and most of our men we see are either in the mail rooms, they are messengers, or they are working machines. This makes us know that they are in [GS] grades 1 through 5. Then they're telling us about how their families are breaking up [from tough commutes]. I'm real concerned."[14]

By the early 1970s, at least forty-two different departments from eighteen different federal agencies employing over fourteen thousand workers had moved away from Washington.[15] Several reasons influenced moving decisions: (1) the higher costs associated with a more densely populated area, (2) the perception that inner-city DC, had become more dangerous and unattractive—especially after the 1968 riots, and (3) the constant growth of black population made an escape to the predominantly white suburbs a natural fit.[16]

Unlike the ignorance professed by white officials at HEW, many white federal administrators were well aware of the effect these relocations would have on their black federal workers. In 1971, for example, the executive assistant to the postmaster general noted that his agency's move to the suburbs "also means we are moving away from the urban centers where most of our black employees live. Blacks have expressed concern about this. They see the Postal Service moving to the suburbs moving without them, like the whites have done."[17] In the same memorandum under the subtitle "Possible Courses of Action," the memo suggested: "We should develop some kind of response to the concerns of the blacks in those cities where we are moving the facilities to the suburbs. It might be possible to develop a program for busing black employees from the cities to the new plants." This shows that USPS officials acknowledged the differing impacts of moving on different groups of employees.

The suburbanization trend was challenging for many blacks who were unable to find low-to moderate-cost housing or reliable transportation to their new job locations.[18] Before a District of Columbia Advisory Committee to the U.S. Commission on Civil Rights in May 1970, DC resident Charles Mahone testified that in Montgomery County, Maryland—site of the new headquarters for federal agencies such as the NIH, HEW, and Atomic Energy Commission—affordable housing "is almost non-existent for the black people who work for the Federal Government because, by and large, those people who work for the Federal Government are the lower paid employees." Mahone went on to report that newly constructed homes were selling for "$40,000, and anyone that earns $15,000 or less cannot afford to buy a house today in Montgomery County.[19] And I know very, very few black people who earn $15,000 a year."[20]

In contrast to the affluent Montgomery County located right over the border of Northwest Washington, blacks more heavily populated the neighboring Maryland suburb of Prince George's County, bordering Northeast and Southeast DC, or the two areas of the nation's capital with the highest concentrations of working-class and poor blacks. From 1960 to 1970, the population of Prince George's County grew 84.8 percent to 661,719 and was 15 percent black. In contrast, Montgomery County, which borders the outgrowth of the majority-white, more affluent Northwest DC neighborhoods, grew 53.8 percent in population size from 1960 to 1970 to 522,809, but only 5.5 percent of its residents were black. From 1970 to 1990, because of accelerated white flight, new civil rights and fair housing laws, and stable salaries from sources such as the federal government, the black population in Prince George's County mushroomed from 15 percent to over 60 percent.

Even before the issuance of its 1974 report, *Equal Opportunity in Suburbia*, in 1970 the U.S. Commission on Civil Rights condemned the racial impact of what appeared to be the mass exodus of federal agencies to the suburbs and exurbs. Although "equal employment opportunity and equal housing opportunity are cornerstones of national policy," the commission found that "the Federal Government has been inadequately concerned with the impact of its site selection policy in achieving these related goals."[21] Many federal agencies, such as the General Services Administration (GSA), routinely disregarded explicit directives to avoid harmful moves to suburban locations. The U.S. Commission on Civil Rights report thus concluded that if black federal workers "are to keep their jobs, black employees of federal agencies moving to the suburbs will face increasing housing and transportation difficulties."[22]

In efforts to encourage the efficiency and centralization of federal affairs, President Nixon issued Executive Order 11512 in early 1970, which also put pressure on federal agencies to find new locations that would not cause hardship for employees with lower pay grades.[23] The order, Planning, Acquisition, and Management of Federal Space, called for heads of executive agencies to consider "the need for development and redevelopment of areas and the development of new communities, and the impact a selection will have on improving social and economic conditions in the area" in addition to weighing the "availability of adequate low and moderate income housing," and "adequate access from other areas of the urban center."[24] But black federal employees were often dissatisfied with the government's reluctance to state the racial implications of suburban moves. In 1974, HEW employee William Jenkins complained, "If I am an employee of . . . HEW which supposedly is the watchdog of the nation's social conscience, and I am a participant to or an observer of my agency's indiscriminate, inconsiderate, ill-planned moves to the suburbs . . . I think that's a violation of my civil rights."[25]

A seemingly benign tactical move, the lawsuit to move HEW back to DC, made in the interest of efficiency actually underscored the fragile bonds between white administrators and black-collar workers. Suing to move the HEW facility back to DC undoubtedly would have been a challenging case to make persuasively in court. However, the lawsuit encapsulated the efforts of black employees to assert their existence in a space within which they felt they were rendered "invisible," despite sharing physical attributes or cultural markers that make them quite visible in their white colleagues' eyes. Above all, many black HEW employees saw the lawsuit as an expression of their disgust and mistrust, having learned about the agency's move three years after administrators had made the decision and more than a year after the agency had leased the new building.[26] Based on principles of transparency and constitutional responsibility, the presumption was that the decision to relocate to the suburbs was not *racist per se*, although the decision had undeniable *effects* along racial lines.[27] Chief among them was the inability of black-collar workers to find adequate and affordable housing. John M. Smith, a thirty-four-year-old chemist who worked for the U.S. Navy's Propellant Plant applied to twenty or more apartments during his first month in the DC area from Little Rock, Arkansas. Smith pointedly remarked, "I was a little surprised to find the Washington suburbs more segregated than Little Rock."[28] Civil lawsuits and injunction requests were largely unsuccessful, but HEW officials admitted they had not previously considered the difficulties caused by the move for black employees from DC. However, this late admission did little to remove the concerns of black HEW employees about their black-collar status moving forward.

GO FIGURE: MEASURING RACIAL PROGRESS

By the early 1970s, while black workers struggled against the new trend of federal offices moving to suburban locations, they also continued to cope with their black-collar status on the job. Despite the existence of civil rights laws and agencies to enforce them, 80 percent of blacks were still entrenched at the GS-8 grade or below. Moreover, it was still rare to find a top-level black manager or administrator in the federal ranks.[29]

Despite being compensated less than white federal employees, black government employees, on average, were better off financially than many African Americans working in the private sector. The 1970 median household income for black families was only $6,279 in contrast to the GS 5–8 salaries that ranged from $7,178 to $10,987. Thus, any black federal employee compensated in grades GS 5–8 was either close to or slightly above the national median of $9,867, while being as high as 50 percent above the black national median.[30]

Nonetheless, for a federal system premised on color-blind merit, whereby all employees of an established rank, level, and experience received standardized pay, black federal workers still earned significantly less than their white colleagues. Most blacks in the government made less than the 1970 white national median of $10,236. In contrast, white federal workers dominated positions in grades GS-9 and above, and the highest salaries in GS-18 were nearly nine times the black national average.[31] Meanwhile, Washington's black population grew to a peak of 71.1 percent (537,712) of the city's population in 1970, up from 28.2 percent (187,266) in 1940.[32] The number of black federal workers in DC grew apace: of the 360,058 blacks working in the city, 101,923 (28.3 percent) were working for the federal government in 1970.[33] Yet only 2 percent of all black workers employed in the District of Columbia commanded salaries of $15,000 or more.[34]

The subjective evaluation standards that black federal workers had to meet contributed to their difficulties in advancing their careers. In 1971, HEW commissioned a report by the Urban Institute to analyze whether federal testing had a discriminatory impact on potential new hires. Ultimately, the report recommended suspension of the Federal Service Entrance Examination (FSEE) as only 8.6 percent of black applicants passed the exam in contrast to 42.1 percent of white students because FSEE results were a key determinant in deciding an applicant's eligibility into the middle pay grades (e.g., GS 5–9). The Urban Institute concluded its report stating, "That the use of the FSEE is unfairly discriminatory to many black applicants seems unavoidable. It is unfortunate that this test has been used extensively for so many years."[35]

These disparate results were also corroborated in the Federal Court of Appeals case *Douglas v. Hampton* in 1971, in which eight black interns filed for an injunction to prevent further use of the FSEE after failing to pass with marks high enough for permanent placement. While the Civil Service Commission (which administered the FSEE) did not maintain pass/fail data according to race, it did maintain records according to the racial makeup of applicants' schools; schools with predominantly white populations (i.e., more than 99 percent) had a passing rate of 57.8 percent whereas majority black schools had passing rates of 11.5 percent.[36] Although the court did not cite specific evidence showing how the test content was discriminatory, it observed that once it finds that a test has a racially discriminatory impact, the burden then shifts to the employer to demonstrate that the test is germane to predicting successful performance on the associated job. The court determined that the FSEE had an effect equivalent to an "intelligence test" since the government administered the FSEE broadly to approximately 150,000 applicants yearly, using it to fill roughly 10,000 positions in over 200 federal job categories.

The injunction was later ruled moot since a new exam, the Professional and Administrative Career Examination (PACE), soon replaced the discontinued FSEE. A constructive proof of successful black advocacy through legal pressure is illustrated in the statement of a Civil Service Commission spokesman that "the PACE test was created in response to criticism of the FSEE, largely along the lines of alleged racial bias." Such criticism was undoubtedly heightened as a result of the public lawsuit along with the legal process that forced the CSC to demonstrate the legitimacy of the FSEE and defend it.[37]

THE BLACK-COLLAR STRUGGLE CONTINUES

A year after the 1971 *Douglas v. Hampton* case, in 1972 Arthur Parks, a lab technician at the National Institutes of Health told a Civil Service Commission hearing board that most of the NIH's three thousand black employees were "suffocating in thankless, low-paying, dead-end jobs, without any real prospects of meaningful advancement."[38] Unfortunately, Parks's pronouncement was not limited to the NIH. Of all black federal employees on the General Schedule or GS wage system in 1972, 81 percent held rankings of GS-8 or lower. For the USPS's separate but similar wage system, 87.4 percent of all black workers were ghettoized, or slotted at level 5 or below whereas only three-tenths of 1 percent were at level 13 or above.[39]

These trends reflected in statistical data were not lost on black federal workers. Exacerbating the troubling trends of lower wages and slower raises, were the conflicting and inconsistent messages black federal employees received from white administrators about addressing such disparities. New laws, procedures, and jobs intended to dismantle discrimination in the workplace often failed to produce the desired result and, moreover, produced the opposite in many cases.[40] The experiences of black federal employees Ruth B. Harris and John E. Womack painfully demonstrate this problem.

LOST IN SPACE: THEORY VERSUS PRACTICE

In the early 1970s, the National Aeronautics and Space Administration (NASA) hired a specialist to improve black employment at the higher-grade levels. In all of NASA at the time, there was just "one minority person at the GS 16–18 level, out of 640 positions."[41] That "one minority person," Ruth Bates Harris, was also one of the few black female employees at NASA. But Harris's unique status was short-lived: she lost her job after submitting a report pointing out the failure of the agency to adhere to equal employment goals, even though she was merely producing a report that NASA had asked her to complete.[42] Perhaps Harris's termination was for not providing the right *type* of report that NASA sought.

In 1971, NASA hired Harris as NASA's first woman deputy assistant administrator for Equal Opportunity. Ominously, her bosses at NASA had demoted her before she had even begun her job. One week after announcing her hire, and before she had officially left her previous position as director of human relations with Montgomery County Public Schools, NASA administrator Dr. James C. Fletcher actually hired her as an *assistant deputy director* rather than in the promised post as *director* of the department. Harris started her new job that October and immediately encountered resistance from white colleagues who viewed her pejoratively as a civil rights activist with a political agenda.

NASA administrators were well aware that their hiring rate for blacks was low. Although NASA felt it did as well as the private sector in hiring only 3.5 percent of minorities in similar technical positions, it lacked an effective

FIGURE 19. On April 27, 1971, James Fletcher was sworn in as the head of NASA. While he made the groundbreaking move to hire Ruth Bates Harris six months later, he also decided not to support her for doing her job, which was to report on the lack of diversity in NASA. Rather than fuss about dispiriting diversity data that were already public information, Fletcher thought that Harris should devote her time to "more positive kinds of things." Library of Congress.

answer for why it hired only 6 percent of minorities in all nontechnical positions. Administrators were quick to blame poor education for the gap. Education was not the issue for Harris, who was an honors graduate of Florida
A&M University and "a self described 'Harlem Princess' whose first marriage
had been to a [former] Tuskegee Airman." Harris went on to earn a masters
in business administration from prestigious New York University, and at the
time of her dismissal, she was NASA's highest-ranking black female, earning
an annual salary of $32,000.[43] Furthermore, during the mid-1970s, the pro-
portion of blacks and whites attending college was roughly equal, although
the total number of students was not.[44]

In 1973, two years after Harris had been involved in endless conflict with
administrators, NASA terminated her. Yet, ironically, Harris's termination
occurred around the same time that blacks started receiving political encour-
agement locally. Late in the year, Congress had passed the District of Columbia Home Rule Act, which paved the way for Walter Edward Washington to
become Washington's first publicly elected mayor, which began an uninter-
rupted string of eight consecutive elected mayors of African American de-
scent. Immediately preceding Harris's final departure, she and two aides had
issued a hard-hitting, forty-page report entitled "NASA's Equal Opportunity Program Is a Near-Total Failure." The report detailed how the agency was
"dragging its feet in hiring minority and women workers."[45] Other agencies
were equally at fault. At the Government Printing Office (GPO) in Washington, in 1973, only 23 percent of skilled workers employed were black, compared to 95 percent of unskilled workers.[46]

Almost reflexively, NASA administrator James Fletcher claimed that Harris was "not dismissed because of the critical report." He insisted that since
most of the data cited were already in the public record, "the time [Harris and
her aides] spent preparing it should have been devoted to more positive kinds
of things."[47] Another NASA spokesman said that the agency's termination decision was free from racial motivation since the agency official who had recommended Harris's dismissal was himself black—in fact, "physically blacker"
than Harris.[48]

Harris was seemingly punished for publicizing the facts surrounding low
minority participation. Her firing symbolized the varied frustrations that
black federal workers endured while working for the space agency. Black
workers accused the agency of blatant racism in both hiring and promotion
methods, and in protest formed MEAN, or Minority Employees at NASA. Although MEAN sent its first formal communication to NASA chief Fletcher in
the spring of 1974, the Harris firing in the previous fall had probably pushed
the workers into action. The complaints MEAN raised in its letter to Fletcher

formed the basis of a class action lawsuit filed that same year—part of a grow-ing trend among black federal workers seeking redress in the courts. After several lengthy appeals, the last of the MEAN plaintiffs finally obtained a set-tlement for their demands nearly a decade later in 1983.[49]

Harris quickly appealed her firing to the local district court as well. "I'm never just talking about people being nice to each other," she explained. "I'm talking about changing the system. We ought to have one big coalition" of blacks and "all our minorities" (including women) with which "we could change anything in this system."[50] The NAACP Legal Defense Fund took up her case and almost immediately had her salary reinstated while her status was under review. The main legal question concerned whether she was a po-litical appointee eligible for firing at will. Meanwhile, NASA administrators, hoping to rebut the negative publicity they were receiving, searched in vain for evidence that Harris was a radical who intended to disrupt daily operations. The historian Kim McQuaid observes that "*The New York Times, The Wash-ington Post*, three Senate committees, major African American newspapers, and local Washington radio and TV stations all featured the Ruth Bates Har-ris story shortly after Fletcher fired her. NASA blithely walked into a journal-istic tree-shredder."[51] By filing her suit and garnering press attention, Harris and her lawyers successfully highlighted how few female and male blacks par-ticipated in the space program.

Eight months after her initial dismissal, NAACP lawyers sat down with NASA attorneys to negotiate a settlement. NASA administrators conceded the need for additional hiring of minorities and better anti-bias training of current employees, but they resisted centralizing this oversight, claiming that the agency operated more efficiently without it. As with other national fund-ing programs that disbursed funds locally, decentralization allowed southern NASA regional centers to continue racist practices.

Harris returned to NASA in August 1974 as the deputy assistant admin-istrator of public affairs for community and human relations, although it was short-lived. The agency's newsletter, the *Astrogram*, made no mention of the circumstances surrounding her initial departure and only hinted at her qual-ifications for her new role, "Mrs. Harris has an extensive background in hu-man relations and equal employment opportunity positions."[52] In her new job, Harris made recruiting visits to black colleges such as Bowie State Uni-versity to talk frankly with students—"NASA has acknowledged its regret that up to and including the time of the Apollo program, very little has been done to encourage minorities and women to come to the agency"—and to persuade them to apply for a job at the agency.[53]

However, similar to other isolated black predecessors like Dr. Robert C.

Weaver, J. Ernest Wilkins, or even Julius Hobson, Dr. Ruth Bates Harris was still just a solitary actor with limited power and resources to alter institutionalized hiring patterns and practices on a systemic level. Harris's own resource limitations, her legal fight, and the continued frustrations of her job caused her much psychological pain. In 1976, she suffered a nervous breakdown caused by the cumulative effect of these pressures and dealing with a failed marriage while caring for a morbidly ill son. Harris permanently left her job at NASA soon after.[54] The inability of lone, talented, highly educated black-collar workers like Harris to "fight the system" prompted many black federal employees to strategize about a model that collectively supported individual achievement.

RIGHT RESULT, WRONG REMEDY

During the 1970s, other black federal workers also took their grievances to external outlets after exhausting internal protocols for resolving them. In 1972, the Equal Employment Opportunity Act finally brought federal employers and government agencies under Title VII of the 1964 Civil Rights Act. This action gave black federal workers additional options to reduce the waiting time for a final resolution of their grievances. For example, in 1974 after a lengthy but successful fight for a promotion, black federal employee John E. Womack's legal case was finally on a fast track toward financial resolution.

Again.

Womack, a black employee at the central office of the Federal Housing Administration (FHA) in DC, had fought for six years to rectify racial discrimination on the job in his division at the Department of Housing and Urban Development (HUD). After clearing a series of administrative hurdles, Womack won a challenge in the United States Court of Appeals, District of Columbia Circuit. Instead of dismissal, the appeals court remanded Womack's case to Federal District Court for a new trial.[55] Meanwhile, the financial relief for which he sued had to wait while the judicial process took its course.

Womack's main legal fight centered on his recompense for racial discrimination suffered while on the job, rather than proving the racial discrimination itself. Womack's saga began in 1968 when a white coworker with a lower pay grade and less experience obtained a supervisory position over him—a position for which Womack had also applied. In response, he pursued a grievance through the proper channels with both his governing department at HUD and with the Civil Service Commission. To Womack's relief, a hearing officer substantiated his claims early in the process and found that his supervisors had wrongfully passed over him in violation of President Lyndon Johnson's E.O. 11246, which prohibited discrimination by federal contractors.

In 1969, the assistant secretary for Equal Employment Opportunity at the Department of Housing and Urban Development, Samuel J. Simmons, ordered Womack's promotion. Simmons, however, declined to award him the seniority he should have accrued or the back pay he should have received.[56] Womack then decided to take his case to court. In the five years preceding the 1974 appellate court's decision to remand his case and start anew, Womack's documented racial discrimination at the federal workplace was never in dispute. The only subject at issue was the adequacy of the remedy for the acknowledged discrimination.

In 1970, HUD only made very slight concessions to Womack on the issues of back pay and the denial of seniority. When Womack appealed, the Civil Service Commission's Board of Appeals and Review denied him again. The following year in 1971, he filed suit in Federal District Court under a creative cocktail of several different federal laws. In 1972, when the Equal Employment Opportunity Act gave federal workers the right to sue the government for Title VII violations, Womack tried to revise his pending action. The District Court rejected Womack's revision request outright and dismissed his case that same day.

Although Womack's 1974 appeal was successful, the extent of his award was still undetermined. The court ruled in Womack's favor, finding that the FHA had wrongfully passed over him for white employee with less experience. Nonetheless he waited years for an increase in salary as he allowed the official grievance process to "take its course." His difficulty was in knowing what else to do. Now, in starting a new trial, he had to prove his case yet again. Finally in 1978, or a decade after first lodging his complaint in 1968, Womack emerged victorious—with an award of $100,000.[57]

This long, frustrating, grueling, exhausting narrative demonstrates the importance of time in judging whether a racial grievance succeeds or fails. During the ten years he pursued his case, Womack remained stuck in the same job and pay grade. His story demonstrates that under federal antidiscrimination policy, it was the responsibility of each individual to prove his or her case—the federal government was in no rush to indict itself—especially when large sums of money were at stake.

COURTING CLASS ACTION

Class action lawsuits, while attractive as a way to win redress for large groups instead of individuals—could take just as long to be resolved. For example, simmering tensions over the systemic denials of promotions due to race led to a large class-action lawsuit involving over two thousand plaintiffs at the Library of Congress, *Cook v. Billington et al.* Initial concerns prompted more than one hundred black federal employees at the Library of Congress to stage a sit-in protest in the main reading room in June 1971. An inadequate response by the agency then led to a 1975 Equal Employment Opportunity claim of discrimination. While the case was ultimately decided in favor of the black employees, the Library of Congress did not begin disbursing payments until 1996.[58] The $8.5 million judgment was the largest ever made by the federal government to settle a lawsuit against a federal agency at that time. However, the time gap between complaint and resolution may have been even more costly.

Similarly, by the 1970s, black employees of the Government Printing Office had long protested the practice of supervisors who strategically fired blacks to create job openings for whites.[59] In 1972, 326 black GPO workers sued the government, resulting in the case of *McKenzie v. McCormick*.[60] The suit arose from former Tuskegee Airman Alfred U. McKenzie's boiling frustrations when the GPO repeatedly passed over him and other black employees for promotions. McKenzie served as a faithful press operator for twenty-eight years, but never saw a promotion during his tenure despite receiving favorable performance reviews and after training numerous white former underlings who rose to supervisory positions. The court readily identified the stubborn persistence of the black-collar worker condition in clear and convincing fashion three decades after the release of *To Secure These Rights*, observing: "For the period 1971–73, blacks comprised roughly one-half of the employees of the [Offset Press Section] but no black held a supervisory position such as Foreman, Assistant Foreman or Group Chief. In those three years, well over 80% of the Uprate Pressmen were white, whereas the Printing Plant Workers, the lowest ranked employees, were over 90% black."[61]

With the aid of more than twenty attorneys from the Coalition of Minority Workers and the Washington Lawyers' Committee for Civil Rights, McKenzie endured and navigated the lengthy appeals process.[62] Finally, in 1977, U.S. District Judge Barrington D. Parker found a "lingering policy of racism" within the federal government in deciding for the black plaintiffs in *McKenzie*. Specifically, in the GPO, Judge Parker observed, "without remarkable exception, the higher-ranking better-paying positions in the section are held by whites, while blacks are clustered around the lower ranking and poorer-paying jobs." While the GPO argued that available data did not necessarily reflect racial bias, Judge Parker found that "in view of the record, the court is not convinced that there has been a radical departure from the past within the offset press section and that racial discrimination has been abated to any appreciable degree."[63]

McKenzie's tenacious background as a Tuskegee Airman prepared him for the ensuing dogfight, since victory had only partially been achieved. McKenzie himself retired in 1973, but he steadfastly persisted not only in obtaining justice but also in securing *economic justice*. After a lengthy appeals process, McKenzie's victory was upheld and the court finally approved a $2.4 million settlement for back pay in May 1987.[64] McKenzie personally received only a few thousand dollars since he was retired by the time of the award. In other words, after fifteen years spanning the Nixon and Reagan administrations, McKenzie had still never received the promotion for which he originally sued.[65]

Technically, he "won" the legal battle, but his victory is qualified by the immeasurable opportunity costs and lost economic opportunities that he sustained. If anything, the GPO won on a subtle, but significant issue. After twenty-eight years of employment and fifteen years of litigation, they fought to hold their line and not to concede McKenzie his promotion. For a decade and a half, the federal government fought for the right not to promote this lone, retired black-collar worker who did nothing but serve his country—both in war and in peace. The federal government had made its point about keeping this particular black man in his place.

McKenzie was nonetheless at peace with the result—was satisfied with the moral victory he had obtained. While moral victories are difficult to cash at a local bank, McKenzie took solace in having actively interrupted the suppressive cycle that had suffocated too many black federal workers' careers. Altruistically, he wanted his colleagues to have a better second chance than he, and was willing to sacrifice for the future of others. Perhaps when the settlement came down a decade and a half after the case was initiated, McKenzie's optimistic and conciliatory tone had been softened by age—he was nearly seventy years old when the settlement was announced. Or maybe he was distracted by other fortuitous events occurring in his life as he too looked forward to a better second chance. Less than a month after receiving the final judgment, Alfred McKenzie exchanged wedding vows for the second time, marrying a person with whom he had something intimately in common: McKenzie was a surviving and scarred former black-collar employee just like his new bride— former NASA administrator Ruth Bates Harris.[66]

WAITING TO EXHALE

In 1977, the same year the *McKenzie* class action suit achieved an important legal victory, an NIH gardener, Hoover Rowel, obtained resolution of an antidiscrimination case he had initiated some time before. While Alfred McKenzie privately celebrated victory with his new bride, Rowel celebrated his victory publicly, among such dignitaries as Senator Edward Kennedy, Congressman Don Edwards, and the civil rights activities Walter E. Fauntroy, as the American Civil Liberties Union honored his remarkable patience and persistence.

Patience was key for Rowel as he eventually settled his discrimination case out of court for $170,000.[67] But since it was a class action case, he, twelve additional men, and the widows of three others received individual checks of less than $10,000 apiece.[68] This was a paltry sum in view of the thousands of dollars Rowel had missed by not having received timely and consistent promotions from GS-3 over the previous two decades. He pursued a twenty-one-year-long legal fight to be rightfully promoted above his GS-3 pay grade. The award amount equates to less than $500 for every year of racial discrimination endured.

During his lawsuit, Rowel testified about the roadblocks and harrassment he faced in obtaining promotions: "In order to really advance at NIH you either have to know someone or you just didn't make it. It was just impossible for a black man to get a promotion. The jobs were not posted, it wasn't posted on the bulletin board and although we knew that the job was available through the grapevine, as they say, we would go and apply for the job and the job was either taken or it wasn't available."[69] Further, Rowel's supervisors denied him access to operating certain equipment that would have offered additional chances for advancement.[70]

In another instance where black promotion was stymied, a white WB-5 (Wage Board) employee was boosted to WB-7 after just one year on the job, but Rowel was a WB-5 for four of his twelve years at the NIH. Another white male was hired as a WB-7 even though testimony revealed that he was unfamiliar with the names or functions of a number of pavement repair tools necessary for the specific job title of "pavement repairer." Management responded by saying that this white male "displayed a lot more initiative" by staying late after work to read and study technical manuals. Not only did the white male not know his job, but he also testified that he had to wait an additional hour after work for his car pool to pick him up. This display of initiative quickly evaporated once he obtained his own car.

Rowel's case exposes a major flaw in federal antidiscrimination efforts— although the system discriminates against individuals, individuals cannot indemnify the entire "system" when proving their own cases. Individual grievances were handled on a "case-by-case" basis, thereby isolating the grievant and lessening his or her chances of success. Rowel persisted and persevered after twenty-one years, but it begs the question as to how many other nameless, faceless black employees endured similar or worse scenarios, only to be punished for not agreeing to wait out a long-suffering trial of humiliation and indignity.

FIGURE 20. National Institutes of Health (NIH) employee Hoover Rowel finally received a settlement check of $12,479 as compensation for failing to obtain a promotion for nearly two decades. Rowel served as a gardener mowing the lush and expansive NIH grounds in the exclusive suburbs of Bethesda, Maryland. Library of Congress.

Despite such blatant roadblocks, the NIH gardener stubbornly fought for ways to preserve his dignity on the job. Rowel recalled, "I remember once they put out a rule that if a heavy equipment operator wanted to go to the bathroom, he had to get permission from a supervisor. If there was no supervisor around, he had to leave a note on the machine indicating where he was gone and why." That rule was changed after "word got around that [Rowel] intended to park his machine right in front of the administration building with a huge cardboard sign saying: 'GONE TO S—.'"[71]

Flush with frustration, Rowel eventually filed a lawsuit after attempting to resolve matters via "the system." The NIH previously conceded that discrimination had occurred, but said it had no authority to order effective remedies. More specifically, back pay was the issue on which the NIH was unwilling to budge. One supervisor admitted that, based on his industriousness and craftsmanship, Rowel had qualified for a GS-9 promotion as early as 1958 but this would have meant moving up six slots at once from his GS-3 grade and was disallowed.[72] As Pulitzer Prize–winning columnist William Raspberry of the *Washington Post* put it, Rowel "couldn't be promoted because he hadn't been promoted."[73] Since Rowel began his quest for justice in 1956, seven plaintiffs had either retired or resigned and three had passed away. Undeterred, Rowel declared: "Frankly, I'm not a well-educated person, but I know what's right and what's wrong, and if I see something wrong, I'll speak up about it."[74] The twenty-one years he spent seeking justice did take a toll on him, however: "Everyone comes to me and says, 'you never got angry.' Believe me, I was angry . . . I was hurting."[75]

A PROFESSIONAL ORGANIZATION IS BORN

BLACK EMPLOYEES WORK TOGETHER

Frustration among black federal employees was mounting in the 1970s. If dutiful employees like Womack and Rowel had to fight for decades to receive promotions from low-level GS rankings, then black employees with their sights on the highest double-digit rankings clearly had a severe challenge on their hands. In 1973, the U.S. Commission on Civil Rights released a report entitled *The Federal Civil Rights Enforcement Effort, A Reassessment*. It reported that "minorities at the highest policy levels (GS 16–18) remain below 3%. Many agencies, including CSC (Civil Service Commission) have no minorities in such positions. None of the regulatory agencies have any minorities among their 418 GS 16–18 positions." The report also noted: "Minorities held less than 1% of the 982 such positions in the Department of Defense. The Atomic Energy Commission and the National Aeronautics and Space Administration (NASA) each have one minority person at the GS 16–18 level, out of 640 positions."[76] Accordingly, as the Marxist economist Victor Perlo observed, the more politically powerful the agency, the less likely blacks were to be integrated, while "less powerful agencies . . . by and large, have a less discriminatory hiring policy."[77]

Some black federal workers, concerned that meaningful change was growing more elusive, decided to take action. As the luster of the previous decade's highly heralded civil rights legislation began to fade, black collective action was one of the only options left since federal protocols in place to address workplace discrimination were still evolving and had to date often proved inefficient and ineffective. Since the NAACP and the NUL were also spread thin helping workers in the private sector, black government workers needed a vehicle that addressed their specific problems.

The same year that Walter E. Washington became the first black elected mayor of DC, five black employees of the Health, Education, and Welfare department in Rockville, Maryland, took the initiative to form Blacks In Government (BIG) as a professional support group with the express mission of enabling members to develop their careers, contribute to their country, and support their families in 1975.[78] The group began as a nonprofit organization that met only in private spaces out of fear of retaliation by management. Early BIG meetings also remained private to protect the group from criticism of being racially exclusive.[79] Its mission was to force the consistent application of civil rights laws, while urging black federal workers to support one another as members of an oppressed racial group.

The embers of such activism had been smoldering for some time now. Fueling their discontent was, in part, the HEW's decision to move from downtown DC to the nearly all-white suburb almost a decade earlier. BIG was not the only black advocacy group for federal employees, nor was it the first. For instance, the NAPFE labor union started in 1913 and continued to advocate for black postal (and federal) workers even though the post office reorganization to form the United States Postal Service in 1971 severely weakened the group's status, profile, and power. However, BIG's modus operandi differed from the NAPFE labor union in that individual success in one's career was of paramount concern. Whereas the NAPFE fought vigorously for better wages and working conditions for all black postal workers collectively, BIG emphasized education and empowerment of the individual so that he or she could accomplish personal goals, whatever those were in the federal workplace. BIG was never designed to make political incursions similar to a union.

Of the small group of frustrated black federal HEW employees, a major figure in BIG from the start was James Pat Daugherty. Similar to Alfred McKenzie of the GPO, Daughtery was "seasoned." Daughtery was a Second World War veteran of the army's predominately black 92nd Infantry Division—nicknamed the Buffalo Soldiers.[80] Like Julius Hobson, Daughtery was unafraid of confrontation, stating unabashedly, "How dare they draft me and force me to go into a war when I was living in D.C. and had to go to segregated schools . . . I was fighting two evils, the Nazis in Germany and my own country that was doing the same kind of things."[81] Similar to Hobson, in 1970, Daugherty moved on to elected office as the first African American member of the Board of Education for the affluent Montgomery County Public Schools.

Daugherty had joined HEW in 1966 as an administrator of the United States Public Health Service (USPHS), and stayed with that agency until his retirement in 1994. While there, he worked to increase access to health care for the poor and underserved, of whom many were black. In recognition of his stellar service, the USPHS subsequently honored Daugherty with its Administrator's Award for Excellence for servicing rural and urban poor communities alike, as well as coal miners, migrant workers, and men and women in prison.[82]

Despite Daugherty's positive contributions, his negative experiences at the USPHS also inspired him to help start Blacks In Government, and he served as BIG's first chairman until a membership election took place on June 1, 1977. One of the goals of the new organization was to organize BIG chapters in the Washington, DC, area and then to do so in federal agencies nationwide. Just as Edward Embree, the founder of the National Committee on Segregation in the Nation's Capital, had declared at his group's founding in 1946, "The symbolic significance of the Nation's Capital [is] the repository of the American Creed,"[83] BIG founders similarly saw federal agencies in Washington as vital spaces and places from which to advance their cause.[84]

The founders of Blacks In Government made a powerful statement by creating this grassroots organization in the wake of the civil rights movement. They were not content to wait for "the system" to adjust itself, nor were they satisfied with any extended correction lag between refurbished polices and rehashed results. They had read the Civil Service Commission report, released earlier in 1975, which analyzed federal employment data and synthesized its findings under the title, *To Eliminate Employment Discrimination*. Although delivered almost three decades after the President's Committee on Civil Rights report under Truman, *To Secure These Rights*, *To Eliminate Employment Discrimination* was remarkably and distressingly similar, in both its tone and findings.

To Eliminate Employment Discrimination provided a candid assessment of the government's inability to end racial inequities in the wake of the new civil rights legislation passed a decade earlier. The report concluded that "although there has been progress in the last decade," federal antidiscrimination efforts in the federal workplace were "fundamentally inadequate."[85] One of the sticking points was the diffusion of antidiscrimination responsibilities to several different agencies.

The 1975 report, while far less known than *To Secure These Rights*, was no more reassuring to black federal employees. Although perhaps few expected the new 1964 Civil Rights Act legislation to provide instantaneous results, black federal workers reasonably expected greater improvement more than a decade later. In the absence of formal barriers to progress, the continued pattern of "black-collar worker" status for black employees prompted black federal workers like James Daughtery to take a proactive stance and start a new pattern.

NO SMALL TASK

Initially, BIG members met privately during their lunch break mostly as a "crisis-oriented" group, providing emotional support for employees experiencing discrimination and offering informal career counseling. But the need was so enormous and commonplace, local BIG chapters quickly sprang up in various regions, with the majority located in urban centers. As BIG gained a reputation as a knowledgeable, problem-solving organization for black civil servants, membership quickly reached four thousand spread across eighty-seven chapters by 1981.[86] Incidentally, BIG adopted an organizational structure with which many black workers were already familiar, with chapters located in eleven regions throughout the country, based on the branch structure of the Federal Reserve System.

BIG representatives used both their professional and personal relationships to schedule meetings with department heads and White House officials. Common topics included the disproportionate impact of reduction-in-force moves on black workers, equal employment opportunities, performance appraisals, and employee rights and protections. In 1976, BIG also became an active participant in "Operation BIG Vote," a nationwide campaign to educate blacks and other Americans about their rights and responsibilities in the electoral process.[87]

BIG members were diverse in their backgrounds, interests, and occupations. They included executives, managers, supervisors, administrative assistants, secretaries, police officers, city managers, council members, state legislators, military personnel, and rank-and-file government workers of all kinds. This breadth and range gave BIG an advantage over the NAPFE, which was primarily concerned with the rights of postal workers despite its late efforts to expand its base in the early 1970s. As a labor union, the NAPFE was often in conflict with management, but BIG positioned itself as an ally to management that merely sought to improve worker productivity and social relations on the job. In this capacity it worked with similarly organized groups such as Federally Employed Women and the Federal Asian Pacific American Council.

SELF-SUFFICIENCY THROUGH SELF-ADVOCACY

Rather than rely on aid from external civil rights organizations, BIG members wanted to address the specific needs of black government workers themselves. For instance, in a March 1977 letter addressed to the administrators of HEW, BIG chairman Daugherty complained that "despite high quality educational and professional accomplishments and previous government positions of authority," black workers at the department were subject to "some unwritten rule against appointing blacks to executive and management positions; certainly—except occasional tokenism—to positions of power."[88] BIG specifically objected to the trend to "take career employees with authority to manage programs . . . and reduce them to 'special assistant to' positions of power, without the staffs, authority or budgets to justify their grades."[89]

Such tailored advocacy demonstrates an advantage BIG had over existing antidiscrimination groups. Whereas the EEOC had to investigate every complaint, Daugherty could quickly synthesize the experiences of his fellow black-collar workers and take them to the authorities. One example of BIG's influence was that HEW's assistant acting secretary Thomas McFee personally responded just two weeks later to Daugherty's 1977 letter stating, "I have decided to meet with you . . . to discuss those concerns."[90]

CONCRETE TOOLS

BIG chapters based at federal agencies primarily met at the workplace, making it relatively easy for members to participate. In keeping with their practical mission, BIG organizers designed a curriculum to assist members with their career development. An eighteen-page, typed booklet, the BIG "Winning Ways Employee Development Kit" was a key part of that project. The kit contained specific advice on how blacks could challenge discrimination on the job that prevented them from advancing their careers. Specific advice under the section "Documenting Your EEO Complaint" included, but was not limited to:[91]

Keep a diary of events
Generate responses in writing
Respond to disputes in writing

BIG organizers keenly understood that discrimination was a very personal experience; it was conceivable that not only might it take time to realize that one was the victim of racially motivated treatment, but also that one might react emotionally upon making such a discovery. Hence, the suggestions listed in "Documenting Your EEO Complaint" helped position the black federal worker to better articulate and advance his or her cause. More blacks were pursuing higher education, but overall, black employees still failed to benefit financially from their degrees. A 1979 study about income inequality within the federal government showed that blacks still received a lower return on their education than whites.[92] Thus, the "Winning Ways Kit" dispensed collective wisdom resulting from the sum total of shared black employees' experiences.

The advice in the "Winning Ways Kit" also underscored a troubling trend facing black federal employees: more developed institutional antidiscrimination measures meant more work for the individual victim to prove discrimination. Advice to keep a journal and to document and respond in writing alerted black workers to maintain a heightened awareness and sensitivity level in the event that isolated negative incidents became part of a larger pattern. Such thinking puts the black federal worker in the difficult position of having to choose loyalties; the black federal worker must trust and communicate with the other members of his or her team while maintaining a healthy skepticism about the sincerity of a (white) colleague's actions.

BIG's national leadership also included in the "Winning Ways Kit" documents such as "Coping with Discrimination in the Federal Workplace," offering members specific advice on how to spot discrimination outside of the garden-variety epithets that any employee would easily recognize. For instance, under the heading "Recognizing Discrimination," BIG leadership provides four different examples: disparate treatment (when a black employee is treated less favorably than another similarly situated employee), adverse impact (where business policies and practices adversely impact blacks and are not justified by business necessity), reprisal/retaliation (where black employees are punished after voicing grievances or concerns), and perpetuation of past discrimination (where past discrimination is maintained through the present operation of a seemingly neutral employment practice). BIG leadership buttressed each discrimination strand with scenario examples and case law where applicable. BIG educated its members so that if and when they interacted with the bureaucracy, they were more likely to be efficient in resolving their disputes as they would have more clarity about what was happening to them and what case law could resolve it.

Other documents included in the kit were "How to Get a Government Job," "How to Complete a Federal Job Application Form," and "Making Your [Job] Appraisal Work for You." Management notified employees about the increasing use of Performance Improvement Plans as a tool to raise an employee's performance to a satisfactory level. Performance Improvement Plans represented the first step in initiating streamlined terminations in federal agencies. Here, BIG chiefly advocated high performance as the best defense against an unwanted Improvement Plan, but also provided concrete tips on how to document, follow through, and clarify new expectations for job performance to improve black employees' chances of keeping their jobs.

The effectiveness of the "Winning Ways Kit" came from the ability of black federal workers to reduce victimization through isolation. By pooling resources and sharing information, black federal workers no longer felt alone in singlehandedly tackling overwhelming administrative processes. Said BIG national president Rubye Fields in the 1979 "Winning Ways" explanation letter, "The advice does not represent short cuts, but they are 'sure things.' That is, they work for other blacks and they will work for you."[93]

PREPARING BLACK WORKERS FOR FUTURE BATTLES

Hiring a lawyer was a strategy financially available only to some, not all black federal workers. While attorney fees were recoverable in some instances, as

articulated in Title VII for certain civil rights cases, not all firms took employment discrimination cases on contingency in what was still a new area of the
law. Black federal employees therefore required training in becoming more
adept at reading and interpreting social scenarios as they developed. To avoid
another grueling twenty-year saga like Hoover Rowel's, the chief way in which
Blacks In Government prepared its members and other black federal employees for the increasingly sophisticated fight for civil rights was through its National Training Conference.

The first of these nationwide conferences took place October 18–20, 1979,
at the Shoreham Hotel in Washington, DC. For the event, BIG billed itself as
"a nonprofit organization concerned with the professional and cultural development" of black government employees, and the training conference was
pitched as "designed for individuals at all levels of government service."[94] Yet
many of the black federal workers who attended felt pressure to remain in the
good graces of their white managers. Many black workers wanted to be careful to avoid stigmatizing labels as militants or separatists, despite exercising
their free speech to attend the Training Conference. The *BIG News* reported
that a "substantial number of conferees used their annual leave and funds to
attend," while only a few black employees obtained agency sponsorship for
their training.[95]

It was nevertheless an impressive and well-attended event. More than 2,200
registrants heard keynote speeches by EEOC chairwoman Eleanor Holmes
Norton and Representative Parren J. Mitchell, a Democrat from Baltimore,
and were also treated to a speech by First Lady Rosalynn Carter. Motivated
attendees took part in seventeen workshop sessions focused on three themes:
"Blacks and the 1978 Civil Service Reform Act," "Employee Problem Clin-
ics," and "Strategies for Black Survival."[96] Organizers reported that employees
were from twenty-eight states, as well as Guam and Puerto Rico. Employees
from twenty-five different federal agencies attended; the largest cohorts came
from HEW, the Department of Labor, and the Department of Commerce.[97]

If acceptance by the political establishment was BIG's goal, the conference
certainly achieved it. It received pledges of support from the NAACP, the National Urban League, and from unapologetically black Washington mayor
Marion Barry. President Jimmy Carter also sent a welcome letter to conference attendees. Not missing an opportunity to establish rapport with voters,
the president declared: "I applaud and fully support the provision in the recently enacted civil service reform law which directs new efforts to eliminate
the underrepresentation of minority groups in the Federal work force."[98]

Such mainstream political support from President Carter and his wife illustrated the successful evolution of a collective strategy. Much like the Na-

tional Alliance of Postal and Federal Employees or Julius Hobson had wanted, Blacks In Government sought to eradicate disparities in rank and pay for black workers. By the end of the 1970s, in packaging the same thrust for black empowerment in a voluntary professional organization that catered to the specific needs of black federal workers, BIG successfully obtained mainstream support for its cause without unduly compromising its mission to advocate for blacks. Rather than be seen as an all-black pressure group with militant aims, Blacks In Government appealed to the American Dream narrative that emphasized self-improvement as the primary path to career advancement. In this respect, in a stroke of ingenious strategy, BIG successfully positioned itself as a *partner* with the federal government in seeking to develop maximum human potential in its members, and therefore would require access and information to facilitate upward career trajectories.

NEW JOBS, SAME ISSUES

But one conference alone could not win full equality for blacks in the federal government. By the 1980s, although the numbers of senior black administrators had grown, it was still uncommon for them to supervise large numbers of white workers. In 1978, President Carter had signed a Civil Service Reform Act (CSRA) that created a new classification of higher-paying pay grades—the Senior Executive Service (SES)—to recognize valuable, high-ranking employees (i.e., policymaking or managerial) and dissuade them from pursuing higher salaries in the private sector. The CSRA also reaffirmed that merit was to be the cornerstone of federal civil service employment. In recognition of the federal government's constitutional responsibility, federal employees were to be selected and advanced solely on the basis of relative ability, knowledge, and skills. Here, the government underlined its commitment to antidiscrimination, as race should not serve as a dispositive barrier to career advancement.

Accordingly, starting in July 1979, the SES effectively eliminated the "super grades" of GS-16, GS-17, and GS-18. When given the option, more than 98.5 percent of eligible managers converted to the SES pay grade system from the GS super grades, creating an SES corps of roughly seven thousand.[99] SES salary inducements notwithstanding, black federal workers still viewed public sector employment favorably as a career.[100] As competition continued to increase in the private sector, the federal government was one of the few sectors where black employees could routinely gain good white-collar jobs without having to earn a college degree. For example, in 1975 federal employees without college degrees occupied nearly two-thirds of all administrative positions.[101] Federal mid-level administrative pay ranged from $8,000 to $12,000 (i.e., GS-4 to GS-8), whereas the national median income for black Americans in 1980 was \$12,674.[102]

In 1978, the proportion of black federal workers slotted in GS-8 positions or below still held steady at 74 percent (down from 81 percent in 1972), which meant that three out of every four black workers was removed from an upper-level, supervisory position. In contrast, in 1978 all minorities combined still occupied less than 5 percent of the highest GS rankings of GS 16–18 (with blacks weighing in at 3.5 percent), which maintains the overarching historical narrative of whites dominating the most powerful and prestigious positions in the federal power structure.[103]

Such hegemonic socioeconomic narratives seemed woven into the fabric of federal government identity. After decades of negotiation, struggle, and resistance, black federal workers only slowly saw their legal relationship with the federal government change, and through grassroots advocacy, they in turn influenced the federal government workplace for the better. Changes came about slowly because while the innovative Equal Employment Opportunity Commission provided aggrieved employees with a concrete means to seek restorative justice for racial indignities endured while on the job, it did very little to serve as a deterrent to discriminatory behavior. While flagrantly offensive behavior was becoming less socially acceptable as the 1980s approached, data demonstrated that stubborn patterns of racial segregation nonetheless persisted.

More important, the *perception* of racial progress made continued advocacy for black federal workers challenging. In 1981, Blacks In Government publicly condemned a proposal published quietly in the *Federal Register* to exempt nearly three-quarters of all 200,000 business firms with government contracts from complying with regulations requiring preparation of written affirmative action programs.[104] BIG president Lonis C. Ballard declared that the reduction proposal to exempt federal contractors "sends out a signal . . . that there will be an easing up with regard to the gains we have made in the last two decades."[105] The reduction maneuver reflected growing sentiment as articulated by the U.S. Chamber of Commerce that "equal employment opportunity should not be paved with new varieties of discrimination against other groups."[106] In other words, in the vein of zero-sum game theory, more inroads for black employees are tolerable as long as they do not reverse discriminate, or take away from otherwise deserving white employees. Fairness after all, must be observed. Thus, politically speaking, there was only so much justice that blacks could afford to gain. After so many documented gains "made in the last two decades," advocating that blacks had good government jobs, but still *could have better government jobs*, was a tough argument for many outside the black-collar worker paradigm to understand and accept.

While racial discrimination and segregation were well-practiced social conventions in America's history before the Second World War, innovative postwar interventions suffered from inconsistency since they were unprecedented and untested. The Civil Rights Act and other subsequent legislation were thus no immediate panacea for black federal workers. The EEOC was inconsistent and understaffed, and legal cases often took a long time, which even further delayed or denied relief for plaintiffs. Although potentially more rewarding, fighting discrimination cases through the court system usually cost black federal workers more time than the final judgments were worth financially. By August 1968, the average EEOC case was taking sixteen months to complete with some taking as long as two years. In 1977, just half a decade after the law changed to expand Title VII to include federal government employees, there was a backlog of nearly 100,000 cases with the average processing time of two and a half years.[107] The EEOC was arguably the federal government's most revolutionary and radical instrument designed to acknowledge, address, and abolish racial discrimination in the workplace. Yet by the end of the 1970s, the EEOC was not only exposed as imperfect, but impaired. Black-collar workers still had to ask themselves what to do when the federal government's sharpest antidiscrimination tool goes dull.

Black federal workers answered the question of how to confront continued workplace discrimination in an officially "nonracist environment" by forming professional grassroots organizations like Blacks In Government. All the while, they remained committed to the goals of a federal government labor structure that was still learning how to reciprocate these black-collar workers' ungrudging efforts. BIG's mission and its evolving agenda thus provide insight on how federal workplace discrimination against blacks stubbornly persisted despite ongoing improvements and changes in the federal workplace. Moreover, the history behind BIG is just as important. Why it was necessary to create a nationwide grassroots organization like BIG more than three decades after the Second World War and a decade after the most revolutionary antidiscrimination measure the United States government has ever created is still at issue.

A MOVING PICTURE OF
BLACK WORKERS, 1980–1981

ALL IN THE FAMILY

Family Guy is a popular American television sitcom created by Seth McFarlane in 2002, more than half a century after the conclusion of the Second World War. While all the characters are represented by animated, cartoon drawings, the show is targeted toward an adult audience and draws on contemporary and controversial themes. Thus, many of the gags are deliberately designed to toe the line of politically correct humor. During the twenty-seventh episode of its fourth season, the white, male, oblivious and blunt New Englander protagonist, Peter Griffin, finds himself in yet another outlandish scenario; the family is trapped inside their own panic room after robbers have broken into their main house.

To pass the time while trapped, Peter tells a fantastical "family history" whereby his ancestor, Nate Griffin, was an enslaved black male who eventually escaped to the North with his family. After boarding a chariot led by a galloping "white bronco" horse driven by a man named "Al Collins," the family successfully eludes would-be slave catchers and makes it to the "promised land." Peter then explains that after safely escaping the condemned lot of uncompensated, forced labor, "Nate devoted his life to getting back at the white man for the injustice of slavery . . . by inventing the Department of Motor Vehicles!"[1]

The cartoon then cuts away to a scene inside a room where a "black" Peter Griffin is seated behind a desk with a "DMV" sign prominently displayed in

176

the middle. To the left of the desk is a white male with blond hair who unsuccessfully attempts to communicate with the black civil servant, as the black government employee quickly grows obstinate and incompetent before leaving the desk abruptly. While standing in line at the Department of Motor Vehicles may be a chore to which many viewers can relate, this gag has explicit racial connotations specific to a critique of the black experience. Adding to the satirical, comical, dreadful, and exasperating nature of a typically time-consuming DMV scenario is the fact that the government employee depicted in the fantasy sequence is black.

The over-the-top belligerence and incompetence of the black government employee toward the unsuspecting and inconvenienced white patron is thus comically framed as revenge for the historically documented, perhaps equally "inconvenient" racial injustice of enslavement. In targeting a majority white viewing audience with this gag, the fact that a black government employee became the depicted "face" of public sector incompetence and insolence speaks volumes. The unspoken, but understood punch line of this gag has two parts: (1) "everyone knows" that black public sector workers are prone to inappropriate and incompetent service, and (2) such boorish conduct is so bad that it can only be contextualized and explained by reminding viewers that black civil servants behave uncivilly as a perverse way to balance the scales from over two and a half centuries of sustained systematic subjugation and enslavement.

While offered under the auspices of comedy, perhaps this depiction touches (if not tangentially) on some undergirding historical truths. Made well into the postwar era, this "joke" is indicative of how blacks are understood to have become "the face" of government employment in the modern era. Time is at a premium within mainstream network television; thus, the conscious symbology of the black government worker conveys a great deal about the joke without the producers having to burn additional screen time to explain the history behind the frustrating dynamic for the white, blond cartoon male character from whose perspective the gag originates. While not as brief, tidy, and humorous as a half-hour sitcom, this historical study explained in more detail this association of blacks with public sector work both during and after the Second World War.

While the *Family Guy*'s gross generalization associating general administrative incompetence with black presence may have been meant to be funny, what is truly ironic is that blacks—if anyone—seriously thought and believed that federal work was an honorable path to social and economic success. A "good government job" was an indispensable tool used to craft and carve out an otherwise unknown black middle class and was once regarded with hope and promise, dignity and prestige, honor and reward. Now black government

FIGURE 21. Thanks to DC's 1910 Height of Buildings Act, many can enjoy different vantage points of the U.S. Capitol building from great distances; while the neoclassical dome is easily recognizable, the top is harder to see—the face of the Statue of Freedom. Library of Congress.

employees are often seen as a joke—even possibly by the average American family guy for whom the black federal worker silently labors.

Therefore, much like the Statute of Liberty symbolized hope for incoming immigrants after the turn of the twentieth century, in the eyes of incoming black migrants, perhaps the Statue of Freedom atop the United States Capitol building in Washington, DC, symbolized the promise of both political security and economic growth in America. Especially for black Americans, this pilgrimage northward to the nation's capital was a hopeful return to original precepts of freedom initially articulated but inconsistently applied to black Americans—especially those from the South. In the private sector generally, the help that whites received from their social ties included access to prestigious jobs, gaining higher salaries, and having greater responsibility and authority in the workplace than blacks. Yet, in the public sector, a constitutional responsibility toward transparency and fairness sought to level the playing field for potential candidates so that the theoretically best candidate could be employed rather than the best-connected candidate. One looking up at the Capitol building might reflect that if there was one place in the country where fairness might get a just showing, it could very well be in Washington, DC, the home of the federal government. While the federal government's orientation toward transparency certainly challenged the traditional majority-white-power dynamic historically demonstrated within the prosperous American economy, this dynamic was ultimately difficult to change.

REAGAN'S PRESIDENTIAL RACE

On January 20, 1981, Ronald Reagan addressed an excited but cold crowd assembled in front of this very same Capitol building that possibly symbolized the promise of both political stability and economic growth in America. Not only was this Inauguration Day, but the day was also significant in that the election of President Ronald Reagan signaled the return of Republicans and conservatism to the White House after the unceremonious and ignominious exit of Richard Nixon in the early 1970s and after a long string of mostly Democratic rule stretching back to Franklin Delano Roosevelt. By 1980, the New Deal and Great Society ambitions were no longer faithfully supported by Congress. Fiscal responsibility was the new mantra that defined cost-cutting measures within the federal government, which was increasingly viewed as the chief obstacle between American efficiency and global supremacy. Accordingly, during his inaugural address Reagan declared: "In this present crisis, government is not the solution to our problem; *government is the problem.*"[2] The postwar government social growth window had now unofficially closed. It was unknown whether when Reagan saw a government that needed repair, he saw *black employees* as the face of this dysfunctional institution the way the boorish white male protagonist Peter Griffin had fantasized in the cartoon television sitcom, *Family Guy*.

While it would be unfair to speculate about what Reagan thought or felt regarding black federal employees during his tenure as president, it is fair to discern his general racial politics by analyzing the larger historical record he left. What we do know is that he publicly criticized the concept of affirmative action heavily during his 1980 presidential campaign, complaining that the "noble concept" of equal opportunity should not be "distorted into federal guidelines or quotas which require race, ethnicity or sex—rather than ability and qualifications" to be used the leading factor in employment decisions.[3] In addition, similar to the impotent implementation of Title VII of the 1964 Civil Rights Act, where its groundbreaking provisions broke little ground in being applicable to only a small percentage of eligible businesses, Reagan's secretary of labor Raymond Donovan issued new guidelines in 1981 that exempted nearly three-quarters of all federal contractors from affirmative action requirements.[4]

Reagan also appointed numerous federal judges who also consistently ruled against affirmative action policies, with only an estimated 1 percent of such total appointees being black.[5] While he hired few black judges, he did fire several U.S. Commission on Civil Rights members, among them Mary Frances Berry, who was publicly critical of his perceived anti-civil rights stances. While the concept of affirmative action disturbed Reagan, thereby prompting his initially resistant position on extending the Voting Rights Act,[6] the concept of racial segregation in education perhaps was not quite so bothersome. Reagan unsuccessfully sought a tax exemption for the private, Christian, conservative Bob Jones University in South Carolina. The university unabashedly rejected enrollment for blacks officially until 1971 and was embroiled in federal litigation over its informal segregationist practices afterward.[7] Reagan's perceived anti-civil rights stance prompted the creation of an organization, Citizens' Commission on Civil Rights. In fact, Reagan began his 1980 presidential campaign near the site where three civil rights workers were murdered in Philadelphia, Mississippi—a move that could be interpreted as tone deaf at the very least.

Further, it is not speculative to state that Reagan's actions illustrated he thought very little of civil rights, insofar as toward the tail end of his second presidency Reagan said, "Some of those [black civil rights] leaders are doing very well leading organizations based on keeping alive the feeling that they're victims of prejudice."[8] Reagan also privately questioned whether public sentiment for Dr. Martin Luther King Jr. and the push favoring a federal holiday in King's honor was "based on an image, not reality," and publicly hinted that King was a Communist dissident—comments for which he would later apologize via telephone to King's widow, Coretta Scott King.[9] He also defended notorious "Dixiecrat" senator Jesse Helms after Helms also questioned King's nationalistic loyalty.

Most famously, Reagan campaigned for his presidency by invoking a provocative story about a "Welfare Queen" who bilked the system; the story was based on a particular black woman's exceptional life of crime, yet it became an enduring image of reference and a target of populist outrage, much the way that Nixon generalized blacks as "incompetents," and much the way that the black DMV worker was the face of incompetence in the *Family Guy* fantasy sequence.[10] To Reagan's credit, he often effectively communicated his disdain for governmental waste without explicitly invoking race. Yet, in masterfully retelling stories such as that of the Welfare Queen, it did not take much on his part to further cement the negative image of blacks already held in mind by many Americans, thus it mattered little whether the underlying story was proven as true or fake news.[11] What mattered most was that the image existed. Thus, as with the *Family Guy*'s dystopian scenario, the image of black incompatibility within public administration continues to be circulated in entertaining story form, both bemusing and bewildering its audience.

Yet, if blacks were allowed to rewrite the story, or history more accurately, the idea that "government is the problem" could be appropriately reframed as "government *that somehow benefits blacks* is the problem." The Reagan administration mirrored the Wilson administration in that both the rational progressivism of the Wilson era and the "small government" movement of the Reagan era squarely placed blame on black citizens as unjustly reaping benefits they had not earned. The alluring reasoning that federal spending on social welfare represented an unnecessary form of governmental interference undergirded the dismantling of programs that specifically assisted black trainees, such as the Comprehensive Employment and Training Act.

As a direct consequence, groups such as the Center on Budget and Policy Priorities documented that programs helping black Americans suffered greatly during Reagan's presidential tenure. Furthermore, many black federal employees began to see a marked decline in economic gains during the Reagan era, with the black-white earnings inequality ratio actually increasing during the 1980s.[12] As late as 2006, black-collar worker status persisted since more than half of all black federal employees (52.7 percent) were employed at a GS-8 level or below, having occupied mostly administrative or clerical jobs with only 9.7 percent slotted in professional positions.[13]

In concert with Reagan's rhetoric about how "government is the problem," many federal, state, and municipal agencies had experienced major cutbacks in budgets and jobs in the ensuing decades, with black public sector workers being hit the hardest due to their high representation relative to their population.[14] This unfair dynamic where Americans in general were hit hard, but African Americans were hit hardest, is reminiscent of how black federal workers were the last hired but the first fired when transitioning to civilian life after wartime, having lost a disproportionate number of federal jobs in the Second

World War downsizing effort. Hence, seventy years into the postwar era, many black federal workers still found their collective position no less tenuous.

Yet, if there was change to measure, it would be in the amount of spending allocated for both military and defense. Considering that these two branches are part of the federal government, the latter did not get smaller overall as the spending rates on military and defense were astronomical. According to the Center for Strategic and Budgetary Assessments, national defense spending peaked at $456.5 billion in 1987, having ballooned 40 percent since 1980 when Reagan first took office. In retrospect, it appears the government mostly downsized in the name of fiscal responsibility in areas that primarily affected and benefited blacks, with Reagan having publicly complained that "waste and fraud" were adding unnecessarily to the costs of social welfare programs.[15] Ironically, however, it was on Reagan's watch that "government cheese" became popular.

The concept of government cheese emerged from the 1981 farm bill signed by President Reagan three days before Christmas. This subsidy gave away 560 million pounds of cheese that had been held in storage for as long as eighteen months. As executed, his maneuver turned out to be embarrassing for an administration that originally indicated that "the people" did not need food stamp programs, as the cheese was serving people who theoretically did not require the government's help. Government cheese has since been known to represent the concept of excessive waste.[16]

Nevertheless, while the Reagan era is characterized by an increase in defense spending, a decrease in social investment, and a hard stance against unionization with the shutdown of the air traffic controllers' strike, black-collar workers received a reprieve. In 1980, the Labor Department during the Reagan era quietly introduced race-norming techniques to rank within-group score conversion to eliminate disparate effects of tests and qualify more blacks for entry-level employment. Administrative maneuvers such as these supported the idea that "even though the federal government is not free from discrimination, it discriminates relatively less."[17] However, this scoring technique was subsequently made illegal with the passage of the 1991 Civil Rights Act. The delicious irony was that an innovative, structured attack against institutional racism was eventually nullified in the name of civil rights.

FINAL ANALYSIS

I, TOO, SING AMERICA

While the federal government did not precisely deliver in practice what many hoped would be an egalitarian policy, there is indeed a positive out-

FIGURE 22. Statue of Freedom, originally erected in 1863 atop the U.S. Capitol building, was brought down in 1993 for refurbishing; yet this picture encapsulates the thrust of the text—namely that (economic) freedom, while a lofty, noble ideal on which to set one's sights, was largely grounded within a sobering reality of "insufficient funds" for black-collar workers. The Statue of Freedom can also be read in three alternate words: *American Dream Deferred*. Library of Congress.

come that deserves mention. Black-collar workers did not just work for the federal government. Their collective example shows that so many of these marginalized employees worked for everything they thought the federal government stood for. The painstaking ability of African Americans to navigate and penetrate stubbornly persistent social and political barriers is unparalleled and unprecedented. In the process, African Americans demonstrated in principle and in performance, that they embodied the essence of authentic "American spirit."

African Americans, despite negative aspersions suggesting the opposite, are in fact, the "quintessential Americans" who have demonstrated, through their patient longsuffering and dogged persistence for justice, the true contours of American liberation theory. Just as the activist intellectual Hubert Harrison declared that African Americans are the "touchstone of the modern democratic idea," the collective triumphs and tribulations of American blacks have exposed in living color the evil and cruel actions wrought on them by fellow Americans.[18] These black-collar workers always endeavored to improve the flawed system for which they labored, and did not engage sustained insurrectionist tactics to dismantle it.

In the final analysis, the account of black federal workers is sobering. If the very entity that both represents and works to reinforce equity, fairness, and access for all Americans cannot provide an equitable working environment for mostly wage-scale, limited salary, nonskilled workers, then the prospects for equitable black employment elsewhere (i.e., in the private sector) are dire indeed. It was not just black federal employees who bore the brunt of the ingrained habits of social discrimination and economic stratification within federal government machinations, often it was the general American public who suffered as well.

LIFE IS FINE

For instance, in 1999 the United States Department of Agriculture (USDA) settled a lengthy, time-consuming class action lawsuit. Nearly $1 billion was paid out for discriminatory acts toward qualifying black farmers from the years 1981 to 1996. More than double that was agreed to in the largest civil rights settlement in history ($2.3 billion), wherein the USDA admitted wrongdoing in having systematically denied timely loans and other financial assistance to desperate black farmers. However, the federal government is so large and expansive that different agencies can have competing agendas while serving the same American people, as proved by the Department of Justice, which contested many claims, dismissing black farmer cases and resulting in monetary savings to the government. The plaintiffs were black farmers who asserted that they had suffered systematic, institutionalized discrimination. What is instructive about this lawsuit is that similar to systemic flaws in the discriminatory distribution of funds for returning servicemen with the G.I. Bill as enumerated by Ira Katznelson, federally appropriated USDA funds were also not distributed equitably either regionally or locally.

Yet, *during the time period for which the black farmers sued,* the USDA did not acknowledge any individual case of racism. In other words, while President Reagan did in fact push through budget cuts that resulted in the dissolution of the USDA's Office of Civil Rights, there is scant evidence that Reagan administration officials admitted discriminatory practices or acknowledged any disparate impact suffered by black farmers. When only 209 black farmers received loans to buy land out of 16,000 farmers totaling $1.3 billion during the period 1984–85, every reason except racism was provided for the steady stream of rejections for black applicants. Only in retrospect and in the contentious, litigious space of a court proceeding where financial penalties were on the line, did USDA officials admit that they "threw discrimination complaints in the trash without ever responding to or investigating them."[19] It begs the question of what black-collar workers were to believe. Faced with USDA officials who were not forthcoming, it would have been foolish for the workers to have confidence that federal officials would uphold their constitutional responsibility and remain transparent and true to the process of being fair and equitable.

The USDA's acknowledgment of racial discrimination in hindsight was similar to the 1947 release of the commissioned report, *To Secure These Rights,* which affirmed the collective discriminatory experiences of black federal workers in retrospect although so many grievances were casually dismissed by agency heads who did not see any problems at the time of reporting.[20] Only until there was an accumulation of data over a significant period of time was there "sufficient" cause to leverage a federal agency into publicly admitting fault. This dynamic cannot be underscored enough. While the black farmers were told in hindsight that they had experienced discrimination, it was not acknowledged that they were experiencing discrimination in the actual moment. Only after the fact when the period of discrimination stopped (with the threat or fulfillment of punitive legal action) did the black farmers receive confirmation that they had indeed suffered discrimination. While the black farmers were not formal black federal employees, they did consistently seek the civil services of an official federal agency. The plight of black farmers is thus instructive regarding the "cat-and-mouse games" that black-collar workers endured at the hands of official federal agencies when expressing their grievances and seeking resolution.

Many of the black farmers suffered from both opportunity costs and op-portunities lost since they did not receive in a timely manner USDA loans for which they qualified. Receiving a compensatory check several years after the fact for a fraction of the amount was insufficient to make the black farmer whole to enable the reacquisition of lands or farming equipment lost forever. As it was, black farmers represented only 2 percent of all American farmers at the time of their lawsuit, with that number in steady decline. While not dis-positive, this incident certainly might be indicative of the similar treatment experienced by black-collar workers at the hands of the federal government.

THE WEARY BLUES

In evaluating key components of other antidiscrimination policies fostered by the federal government, the truth is that Title VII of the 1964 Civil Rights Act (CRA) was not nearly as effective as advertised. Not only did it fail to convince the overwhelming majority of American companies and businesses that the new employment discrimination polices had to be applied, but it also failed to serve the target population that was the impetus for the law's creation. Studies suggest that white women have disproportionately benefited from Title VII protections since its creation.[21] The irony is that black-collar workers were not able to systematically exploit any advantage from a law originally designed for their benefit.

Although the noted historian John Hope Franklin contended in his foun-dational text *From Slavery to Freedom* that the CRA of 1964 was "the most far-reaching and comprehensive law in support of racial equality ever en-acted by Congress," it more accurately reflected only the illusion of inclu-sion.[22] After all, it is vital to point out that the strongest, most financially repercussive and punitive federal antidiscrimination measure in the post-war era comes by way of the Equal Employment Opportunity Commission (EEOC), which was created by specific mandate under Title VII of the CRA as an enforcement mechanism. Yet this commission has consistently battled moribundity and has largely been hindered by a seemingly insurmountable backlog. In outlining its history on its own website, the EEOC references it-self as a "toothless tiger."[23] A mere decade after its inception, the unresolved backlog reached as high as one hundred thousand cases. Half a century after its groundbreaking genesis, the EEOC reported that it was still experiencing a backlog in excess of seventy thousand unresolved cases in 2014.[24] Similar to the Fair Employment Practice Committee of 1941, the EEOC still lacks the independent ability to truly hold all businesses accountable for their actions—if such actions are even documented, reported, and persuasively proved in the first place.

FIGURE 23. Barack H. Obama as the forty-fourth president of the United States has one of the world's most famous faces; it is also the face of a black federal worker. Official White House photo by Pete Souza. Library of Congress.

HISTORY REPEATS ITSELF

Hence, the past plight of black federal workers specifically provides insight into the harrowing economic prospects presently facing black Americans generally. Certainly, numerous African Americans have enjoyed socially, politically, and economically rewarding careers. The unprecedented 2008 election of Barack H. Obama was further proof that America had developed into a postracial society.[25] Obama's corresponding rise in mainstream popularity as a global icon of hope, promise, and progress is significant: one of the most famous faces of American and global history is now that of a black federal employee.

Obama's exceptional success aside, the daily life of the average black American is still too often fraught with financial difficulty. America has been quite explicit about its role in promoting a capitalistic economy in the name of global supremacy. In other words, "Cash rules everything around me."[26] Thus, if American society is premised and purposed on the generation, acquisition, and accumulation of capital, then the inability to do so will significantly affect the quality and value of one's citizenship. From the beginning of the African American experience, the amicable success of this socioeconomic relationship was in doubt. In fact, blacks were objectified, seen and widely used as instruments of collective capital accumulation, not as individual recipients; their value was perverted to the point where they were traded as commodities and became capital themselves. This initial impression has certainly changed in form, but has remained consistent in substance over the years.

For instance, the entrée of blacks into the federal government was mostly due to the objectification of blacks as replacement parts to keep the war machine in operation. Once the war was over, so was the need for blacks. While many temporary black workers were made permanent ex-employees, numerous black workers did manage to stay on. But their value in the workplace has been diminished by their intractable black-collar status. Over time, even with the increased antidiscrimination policies and education and experience levels, blacks have always lagged behind white workers in lower wages and slower raises. If this disparate treatment remained consistent and unchanging even in the face of an equitable system premised on transparency in the public sector, then it raises the question: What is the true value of economic prospects that black Americans actually enjoy in general, and most especially in the more remunerative private sector?

In the modern era, it is true that more blacks are generating more income than at any other point in time. Yet romantic racialist notions that well-known blacks in sports and entertainment circles are emblematic of success or collective black success are equally foolhardy and problematic.[27] For "everyday blacks," the federal government was and is a viable career path that presumably provides a middle-class lifestyle. But the idea that their salaries as General Schedule employees will forever be capped at less than that of the chief executive officer is humbling if not damning in many respects, considering that the allure of the private sector is actually the prospect of open-ended capital accumulation. Not only are federal careers technically stunted economically, but they are further truncated by inadequate policies that provide more dignity to the process than the actual proceedings.

In other words, there is an unspoken "cost" to taking a job in the public sector. While many government employees typically enjoy more economic security than private sector firms, which can terminate employees "at will," they must now acknowledge that as black-collar workers, they will be forever financially limited in their economic prospects and lifetime earning capacity in contrast to the private sector, even if promoted to the highest levels. Black workers will never bridge the numerous and numbing socioeconomic gaps that stubbornly persist in America; working directly for the federal government will not change the overall trajectory of a historically depressed black economy.

With respect to change over time, if anything, this book highlights the ever-evolving nature of racial discrimination. Ever since the reports of the Presidential Committee and the National Committee of 1947, which initially documented discrimination by federal agencies against black employees, the methodology of racism has changed, but its effect has remained constant and consistent. After all, while the government might be commended for commissioning substantive reports, the only virtual change over time has been the alteration of names and dates, with each report essentially restating the same fundamental principles and concepts as the earlier report:

1947, *To Secure These Rights:* "In the federal government . . . the chief danger at present looms in the form of discriminatory cut-backs of Negro personnel who were hired very largely by wartime agencies, and in the refusal by other agencies in the government to hire these 'displaced employees.'"[28]

1961, *U.S. Commission on Civil Rights Report:* "Of Negro [federal] employees in Classification Act positions, 85.4 percent were in grades 1 through 4; 14.3 percent in grades 5 through 11; and 0.3 percent in grades 12 through 15 . . . 5.2 percent of the total Negro [federal] employees were in supervisory positions."[29]

1973, *The Federal Civil Rights Enforcement Effort: A Reassessment:* "Today we are releasing a third follow-up report . . . our basic conclusion is that the federal effort is highly inadequate; that it has not improved as much as we would have expected since our last report in November 1971."[30]

1996, *Fair & Equitable Treatment: A Progress Report on Minority Employment in the Federal Government:* "Minorities [who are employed by the federal government] tend to be concentrated in lower paying occupations or in the lower grades of higher paying occupations."[31]

2010, "EEOC African American Workgroup Report": "Unconscious biases and perceptions about African Americans still play a significant role in employment decisions in the federal sector."[32]

The same essential message of marginalization remained consistent over the years: black-collar workers were constantly entrenched in battles for dignity and respect in the federal workplace. What makes this consistency as amazing as it is alarming is that each of the five aforementioned reports are cross sections of different agencies comprising different individuals at different points in time essentially arriving at similar conclusions. Thus, if we look at history through the eyes of black-collar workers, perhaps we could see that their perspective of the American Dream would be that of a dream forever deferred, with virtually no option for ever being made a reality. Overt tactics of discrimination, once openly accepted, have since given way to more subtle methods of marginalization. As updated and revised agency protocols forbade blatant mistreatment, more whites grew increasingly nuanced in making discriminatory decisions that yielded similarly discriminatory results.[33] Over time, it was not just a matter of finding evidence of discrimination—for many federal actors were well aware of this gap between theory and practice for blacks both as workers and as citizens—but what became more and more difficult was to find *blatant, incontrovertible evidence* of discrimination. Racism in the federal workplace simply became less obvious, not necessarily less present, and no less pernicious.

PHOTO FINISH

In conclusion, it is appropriate to reflect once again on Langston Hughes's brief yet brave poem "Harlem (Dream Deferred)":

> What happens to a dream deferred?
> Does it dry up
> like a raisin in the sun?
> Or fester like a sore—
> And then run?
> Does it stink like rotten meat?
> Or crust and sugar over—
> like a syrupy sweet?
> Maybe it just sags
> like a heavy load.
> *Or does it explode?*

A cursory analysis allows us to see that the poem not only begins with a premise posed within a question but also concludes with another question, which ultimately suggests that there is no definitive answer to the first query. Beginning the poem with a question removes readers from a passive position and actively engages them in a dialogue. More specifically, readers are immediately repositioned as participants and asked to wrestle with the implicit question in the opening line, "What happens to a dream deferred?" The very question assumes that a dream has indeed been deferred. The "dream" referenced hearkens not to a temporal, somnambulistic state, but rather to a concrete goal, a definitive concept packaged, wrapped, and sold to all Americans, including African Americans.

Similarly, this research enterprise began with a question: No matter how hard black federal workers worked in Washington, would their collective American Dream have to defer to that of their employer? The historical evidence suggests that African Americans have experienced few fundamental, systemic changes with respect to their collective economic status relative to whites in this country. To focus exclusively on what has changed over time is to run the risk of overemphasizing minor and modest modifications to a narrative that has remained largely consistent and intractable.

For example, a shade less than two hundred years after Edward Savage memorialized the first president of the United States of America, another stately picture surfaced featuring the fortieth US president. The introductory chapter described *The Washington Family* portrait by Savage, which featured George Washington depicted in grand manner, seated in front of his plantation gardens at a table surrounded by key personal figures (introduction, fig. 1). On November 2, 1983, President Ronald Reagan is depicted seated in the Rose Garden of the White House at a table surrounded by key political figures (fig. 24). Reagan is signing in grand manner legislation to create a federal holiday in honor of the late civil rights advocate, Dr. Martin Luther King Jr.

In evaluating what is consistent versus what has changed over time in comparing the two pictures, some immediate differences jump to mind. For starters, pictures of the two US presidents invoke different images of political philosophies. George Washington espoused a philosophy of honor for public service, once stating that "every post is honorable in which a man can serve his country."[34] Conversely, Reagan believed that "government is the problem." In addition, the 1983 picture consists of Reagan photographed while engaged in a public, official action whereas the 1796 picture is an oil painting depicting Washington in private repose. Moreover, multiple individuals are depicted in Reagan's photograph but only he is in a seated position; in the Washington painting, he and Martha are depicted as sitting with only three others standing. While black people are depicted in both pictures, Savage's portrait features an unidentified male slave on the periphery, standing away from Washington while the more recent Reagan photo shows a known black female standing directly adjacent to President Reagan. That black female is Coretta Scott King, who was present at Reagan's signing of a bill that named her late husband, Dr. Martin Luther King Jr. as only the third individual to have a US federal holiday established in his name just two decades after imparting his renowned "I Have a Dream" speech.

FIGURE 24. Coretta Scott stands by in observance of the bill signing that created a federal holiday in honor of her late husband, Dr. Martin Luther King Jr. Library of Congress.

With respect to similarities, both pictures are in color and feature a US president as the central figure and object of the picture's focus. Also, both pictures demonstrate the continued presence of African Americans in American life. While a black male barely appears visible and is nearly camouflaged by the orange curtains in the Washington painting, Coretta Scott King's presence as a black female is unmistakable in the Reagan photograph. But the pictures share one striking similarity in appearance. Just as the black male slave is painted with a blank face, Coretta also appears to have a "blank face" while standing next to Reagan. Her face is nearly expressionless, and it is difficult to discern the specific emotions she harbored in that moment.

In juxtaposing these two presidential portraits, we must ask what the blank black faces, separated by nearly two hundred years, tell us about the socioeconomic ability of blacks to partake in the American Dream. One thing for certain is that Coretta Scott King's husband did not feel that the federal government had provided a "blank check" or carte blanche when it came to delivering what it promised. More succinctly, Dr. King invoked a pointed economic analysis when he famously analogized America's constitutional responsibility to that of a defaulted promissory note. King warned, "In a sense, we have come to our nation's capital to cash a check. . . . It is obvious today that America has defaulted on this promissory note insofar as her citizens of color are concerned. Instead of honoring this sacred obligation, America has given the Negro people a bad check, a check which has come back marked 'insufficient funds.'"[35]

Hence, it is no coincidence that Coretta's husband, during his shining moment in one of the most famous public speeches in human history, instinctively invoked recognition of America's constitutional responsibility to treat all citizens equitably as originally envisioned: "I have a dream that one day this nation will rise up and live out the true meaning of its creed: 'We hold these truths to be self-evident: that all men are created equal.'" More to the point, in the line immediately preceding King's allusion to federal constitutional responsibility, he stated that "even though we face the difficulties of today and tomorrow, I still have a dream. It is a dream deeply rooted in the *American dream*."[36]

Dr. Martin Luther King Jr. himself therefore publicly asserted that he ultimately answered to the same American Dream that Langston Hughes initially questioned (i.e., "What happens to a dream deferred?"). What remained unquestioned, however, was that no matter how hard black federal workers worked in Washington, their collective American Dream would have to defer to that of their employer. Accordingly, many blacks in the postwar era found a new ally in their pursuit of the American Dream: Uncle Sam. Particularly in the Washington, DC, area, as the federal government grew, so did the number of blacks employed. The federal government in time was both perceived and proven to be a more conducive environment for black workers as merit testing and established pay schedules protected many black workers from the more discriminatory tactics frequently seen in the private sector. The federal public sector thus soon became home to the majority of working black white-collar professionals in the 1940s, an absolutely amazing statistic, considering the theoretically infinite number of jobs available for blacks in the private sector. Yet the irony was that many blacks, after having migrated to the nation's capital to escape abject poverty, constant social slights, and fear of instability, found themselves in curiously similar employment positions they would have occupied had they stayed in the South (e.g., janitorial service, lawn maintenance)—*even though they had federal jobs.*

Regardless of the encouraging glimpses of access and opportunity that federal employment has provided, black-collar workers have nonetheless faced constant and consistent discrimination over the years in securing well-paying jobs and moving up the ranks. It may be telling that despite dispensing her consistent advice (i.e., "Go on and get yourself a good government job!") in support of black federal employment to those who would listen, longtime federal employee Gladys Derricotte nonetheless was able to recall the racial discrimination she herself encountered during her long public sector career. In early 1980, she joined a successful class-action lawsuit alleging that African Americans faced discrimination when it came to promotions; she retired in 1982.[37]

In other words, even after acquiring a comfortable middle-class salary, even after purchasing a home, even after having her daughters and granddaughter following in her footsteps as federal civil servants, even after three and a half decades of unfailing service to the federal government, and even after a long-standing marriage to another faithful black government employee for more than three decades, the great matriarch Mrs. Derricotte thought to conclusively prove in a court of law that she, too, was a black-collar worker. She, too, thought the federal government should honor its constitutional responsibility. She, too, had to make the best of a working relationship she likely had not preferred—*American Dream Deferred*.

NOTES

INTRODUCTION: PAINTING THE PICTURE
OF BLACK FEDERAL WORKERS

1. Martha Washington along with her two grandchildren (Eleanor Parke Custis and George Washington Parke Custis) are seen around the table. Although widely believed to be William (Billy) Lee, other evidence suggests the black male could be Christopher Sheels. See generally, Joseph Manca, "A Theology of Architecture: Edward Savage's Portrait of George Washington and His Family," *Notes in the History of Art* 31, no. 1 (Fall 2011), 29–36.

2. The "American Dream" concept of potential financial success to be enjoyed by all who pursue it and labor diligently for it was likely always present since the country's inception, but it was particularly popularized and originally coined by James Truslow Adams in his book *Epic of America* (Boston: Little, Brown, 1931), ironically, during the Depression era when belief in financial success was bleak. Lawrence R. Samuel, *The American Dream: A Cultural History* (Syracuse, NY: Syracuse University Press, 2012), 13.

3. "Racism, or the distribution of resources according to a hierarchy of race, was unfortunately woven into the fabric of American society from its inception, at least in relation to African Americans." Frederick W. Gooding Jr., *Introduction to African American Studies: A Critical Reader* (Dubuque, IA: Kendall Hunt, 2016), viii.

4. Emily Wax-Thibodeaux, "Hispanics Following African Americans' Example in Finding Government Jobs," *Washington Post*, December 3, 2013.

5. "But servile employment remained the norm, especially for the 70 percent of black women who worked in the service sector in 1940." Thomas Sugrue, *Sweet Land of Liberty: The Forgotten Struggle for Civil Rights in the North* (New York: Random House, 2008), 45.

6. Black workers were excluded from higher-paying, professional jobs even when they had an education; college educated Pullman porters are an example. "A union official informed social scientists St. Clair Drake and Horace Cayton in the early 1940s that seventy-two of the ninety black red caps in his Chicago station were college graduates." Eric Arnesen, *Brotherhoods of Color: Black Railroad Workers and the Struggle for Equality* (Cambridge, MA: Harvard University Press, 2002), 155.

7. Sugrue, *Sweet Land of Liberty*, 398.

8. E. Franklin Frazier, *Black Bourgeoisie* (Glencoe, IL: Free Press, 1957), 197–98.

9. Burleson requested the separation in the interest of efficiency since white postal railway workers complained about or refused to work in close quarters with their black coworkers, thereby threatening to disrupt mail service. Burleson was particularly bothered that white and black workers shared towels, drinking glasses, and bathrooms while working within the tight, enclosed spaces of railway cars. See Kathleen Long Wolgemuth, "Woodrow Wilson and Federal Segregation," *Journal of Negro History* 44, no. 2 (April 1959), 161–63.

10. Not until 1933 did the Twentieth Amendment to the U.S. Constitution change the Inauguration Day calendar date from March 4 to January 21.

11. Eric S. Yellin, *Racism in the Nation's Service: Government Workers and the Color Line in Woodrow Wilson's America* (Chapel Hill: University of North Carolina Press, 2013), 8.

12. Margaret C. Rung, *Servants of the State: Managing Diversity and Democracy in the Federal Workforce, 1933–1953* (Athens: University of Georgia Press, 2002), 2.

13. Andrew Kersten, "African Americans and World War II," *OAH Magazine of History* 16, no. 3 (Spring 2002), 13.

14. Rung, *Servants of the State*, 14.

15. Norma M. Riccucci and Katherine C. Naff, *Personnel Management in Government: Politics and Process* (Boca Raton, FL: CRC Press, 2017), 376.

16. MPR [Minnesota Public Radio] News, "King's 'Promissory Note' Remains in Default," August 28, 2013, accessed December 29, 2017, https://www.mprnews.org/story/2013/08/28/daily-circuit-march-on-washington.

17. Letitia Woods Brown, *Free Negroes in the District of Columbia, 1790–1846* (New York: Oxford University Press, 1972), 7.

18. Raymond H. Geselbracht, ed., *Truman, Desegregation of the Armed Forces and a Kid from the Bronx in The Civil Rights Legacy of Harry S. Truman* (Kirksville, MO: Truman State University Press, 2007), 118–19.

19. "Because the government was a national employer . . . its policies lent symbolic legitimation to racism and sexism." Rung, *Servants of the State*, 2.

20. See generally, Harvard Sitkoff, *A New Deal for Blacks: The Emergence of Civil Rights as a National Issue: The Depression Decade* (Oxford: Oxford University Press, 2008).

21. Sugrue, *Sweet Land of Liberty*, 540.

22. United States Senate, "Antidiscrimination in Employment: Hearings Before the Subcommittee on Civil Rights of the Committee on Labor and Public Welfare, United States Senate, Eighty-third Congress, Second Session, on S. 692, a Bill to Prohibit Discrimination in Employment Because of Race, Color, Religion, National Origin, Or Ancestry" (Washington, DC: Government Printing Office, 1954), 362.

23. Samuel Krislov, *The Negro in Federal Employment: The Quest for Equal Opportunity* (St. Paul: University of Minnesota Press, 1967), 5.

24. Jeffrey B. Perry, ed., *A Hubert Harrison Reader* (Middletown, CT: Wesleyan University Press, 2001), 282.

25. Sugrue, *Sweet Land of Liberty*, 13.

26. Charles S. Aiken, "A New Type of Black Ghetto in the Plantation South," *Annals of the Association of American Geographers* 80, no. 2 (June 1990), 225.

27. Joseph Slater, *Public Workers: Government Employee Unions, the Law, and the State, 1900–1962* (Ithaca, NY: Cornell University Press, 2004), 206.

28. Francine Curro Cary, ed., *Washington Odyssey: A Multicultural History of the Nation's Capital* (Washington, DC: Smithsonian Books, 1996), 216.

29. Cary, *Washington Odyssey*, 216.

30. John Hope II and Edward E. Shelton, "The Negro in the Federal Government," *Journal of Negro Education* 32, no. 4 (Autumn 1963), 372.

31. In 1946, California's population was 9,559,000 while the District of Columbia's population in 1950 was 802,178. U.S. Bureau of the Census, District of Columbia—Race and Hispanic Origin: 1800–1990, accessed May 31, 2013, http://www.census.gov/population/www/documentation/twps0056/tab23.pdf; California Department of Finance, 2008 California Statistical Abstract: Table B-1, Population of California and the United States 1940 to 2007, accessed May 31, 2013, http://www.dof.ca.gov/HTML/FS_DATA/STAT-ABS/documents/CaliforniaStatisticalAbstract2008.pdf.

32. "National Urban League Staff Report on Racial Relations," circa 1946, Part I: N30, RNUL.

33. President's Committee on Civil Rights, *To Secure These Rights* (Washington, DC: Government Printing Office, 1947), 89.

34. For additional commentary on how military and government service raised expectations of more rights and privileges for blacks, see John Modell, Marc Goulden, and Sigurour Magnusson, "World War II in the Lives of Black Americans: Some Findings and an Interpretation," *Journal of American History* 76, no. 3 (December 1989), 845; Allan M. Winkler, *Home Front U.S.A.: America During World War II*, 2nd ed. (Wheeling, IL: Harlan Davidson, 2000), 67; Mary Dudziak, *Cold War Civil Rights: Race and the Image of American Democracy*, 2nd ed. (Princeton, NJ: Princeton University Press, 2011), 243.

35. Nancy MacLean, *Freedom Is Not Enough: The Opening of the American Workplace* (Cambridge, MA: Harvard University Press, 2006), 36.

36. Philip A. Klinker and Rogers M. Smith, *The Unsteady March: The Rise and Decline of Racial Equality in America* (Chicago: University of Chicago Press, 2002).

37. Joseph McCartin, *Collision Course: Ronald Reagan, the Air Traffic Controllers, and the Strike that Changed America* (New York: Oxford University Press, 2011).

38. No base salary ever or currently listed on the official federal General Schedule Classification pay scale has eclipsed $1,000,000. U.S. Office of Personnel Management, "Pay & Leave: Salaries & Wages," January 2018, accessed January 2, 2018, https://www .opm.gov/policy-data-oversight/pay-leave/salaries-wages/salary-tables/18Tables/ html/GS.aspx.

39. Sugrue, *Sweet Land of Liberty*, 505.

CHAPTER 1: "BOY! LOOK AT ALL THESE GOVERNMENT GIRLS!"

1. Less than 1 percent of female stenographers, typists, or secretaries commanded $1,000 or more during the same period both throughout the state of Georgia and within the city of Atlanta. See U.S. Bureau of the Census, 1940 National Census, "Table 16, Wage or Salary Income Received in 1939 by all Experienced Persons in the Labor Force" (Washington, DC: Government Printing Office, 1940), 754.

2. Megan Rosenfeld, "'Government Girls': World War II's Army of the Potomac," *Washington Post*, May 10, 1999. See also Scott Hart, *Washington at War, 1941–1945* (Upper Saddle River, NJ: Prentice Hall, 1970), 35; Sara A. Evans, *Born for Liberty: A History of Women in America* (New York: Free Press, 1989), 22.

3. Rosenfeld, "Government Girls."

4. Bert Kemmerer, "15,000 Help Send Two War Planes on Way to the Fighting Fronts," *Washington Post*, May 10, 1943. The movie *Government Girl* is a 1943 comedy about a secretary who finds life (and love) made complicated when a new boss arrives; directed by Dudley Nichols starring Olivia de Havilland, Sonny Tufts, Agnes Moorehead, and Anne Shirley.

5. *Washington Times-Herald*, Jane's Journal, October 19, 1942. The series started on September 14, 1942, and ran until at least December 31, 1942. The journal was "told to" Sylvia Altman. While earlier entries were more detailed about the travails of stabilizing and securing her survival (e.g., income, shelter, food, clothing, etc.), later entries centered around Jane's frustrating attempts to find a stable and secure love life. It is unclear how much the Jane's journal entries were contrived, prompted, or suggested by the editorial staff to maximize interest and sales. Nonetheless, weekly installments of Jane's diary encouraged readers to follow along.

6. See generally, Constance McLaughlin Green, *Washington: A History of the Nation's Capital, 1800–1950* (Princeton, NJ: Princeton University Press, 1962).

7. In only one instance was race directly acknowledged in Jane's Journal, and this was when Jane reflected on an exhibition at a War Fair "showing too, that on our side everybody sticks together. The troubles of one are the troubles of all—whether it's a child orphaned by bombs in far away China or a Negro family hungry and sick in some slum here in Washington." *Washington Times-Herald*, Jane's Journal, October 28, 1942. Further, the January 1942 issue of *Good Housekeeping* magazine featured several white G-girls in a fashion spread. Not only were black women visually absent from the

entire photo shoot, but the general description of the featured workers also presumed black exclusion given the heavy use of the distinguishing adjective "Negro" during the Jim Crow era (i.e., "Negro government girl"). Rosenfeld, "Government Girls."

8. Regan E. Thornton, "Veteran with 102 Years of African-American History," U.S. Department of Veterans Affairs, February 17, 2014, accessed December 12, 2015, http://www.va.gov/health/NewsFeatures/2014/February/Veteran-with-102-Years-of-African-American-History.asp#sthash.Ybjpu1Bg.dpuf.

9. At that time, the overwhelming majority of blacks worked in service or agricultural industries; sharecropping was quite common from the end of the Civil War until the Second World War. See, Mary C. King, "Occupational Segregation by Race and Sex, 1940–88," *Monthly Labor Review* 115, no. 4 (April 1992), 30–36; see also William J. Collins, "African-American Economic Mobility in the 1940s: A Portrait from the Palmer Survey," *Journal of Economic History* 60, no. 3 (September 2000), 756–81.

10. "More often, black female domestic workers were exposed to the risk of being raped by employers." Shirley A. Hill, *Black Intimacies: A Gender Perspective on Families and Relationships* (Walnut Creek, CA: AltaMira Press, 2005), 62.

11. Karen Tucker Anderson, "Last Hired, First Fired: Black Women Workers during World War II," *Journal of American History* 69, no. 1 (June 1982), 84.

12. Barbara Franco, "The Challenge of a City Museum for Washington, DC," *Washington History* 15, no. 1 (Spring/Summer 2003), 6; see also "National Urban League Staff Report on Racial Relations," circa 1946, Part I: N30, RNUL. The Urban League also observed the continued practice of racial segregation when it noted, "Primarily, however, whites and Negroes in the District work separately, attend separate schools and other institutions, and are ignorant of each other."

13. Lucia M. Pitts, "The Federal Diary," *Washington Post*, July 25, 1942.

14. Timothy C. Dowling, *Personal Perspectives: World War II* (Santa Barbara, CA: ABC-CLIO, 2005), 200.

15. Pitts, "Federal Diary."

16. James T. Sparrow, "Freedom to Want: The Federal Government and Politicized Consumption in World War II," in *Fog of War: The Second World War and the Civil Rights Movement*, ed. Kevin M. Kruse and Stephen Tuck (New York: Oxford University Press, 2012), 19.

17. National Urban League Staff Report on Racial Relations, RNUL. According to the census, 9,382 black government workers were employed in Washington, DC, in 1940. U.S. Bureau of the Census, District of Columbia, 1940, "Table 18, Race of Employed Persons (Except on Public Emergency Work), and of Experienced Workers Seeking Work, by Industry and Sex, for the District of Columbia" (Washington, DC: Government Printing Office, 1940), 600.

18. William E. Peake, "Capital Becomes Nation's No. 1 Boom Town; 7,000 New Dwelling Units Built in Year," *Washington Times-Herald*, April 10, 1941.

19. What helped catapult the United States into the leading position as a military superpower was its extraordinary production schedule. Richard Overy documents that the United States produced over 86,000 tanks, 193,000 artillery pieces, nearly 300,000 aircraft, and 2 million army trucks. This high level of production was not possible without the added contributions of new labor force members, namely women and blacks. Richard Overy, *Why the Allies Won* (New York: Norton, 1995), 227.

20. Mark David Van Ellis, *To Only Hear Thunder Again: America's World War II Veterans Come Home* (Lanham, MD: Lexington Books, 2001), 179.

21. Bruce Nelson, "Organized Labor and the Struggle for Black Equality in Mobile during WWII," *Journal of American History* 80, no. 3 (December 1993), 952–88.

22. Section 1 of Public Law 426–62, signed into law on March 4, 1913, created the Department of Labor. Section 1 states in part: "The purpose of the Department of Labor shall be to foster, promote, and develop the welfare of the wage earners of the United States, to improve their working conditions, and to advance their opportunities for profitable employment." United States Department of Labor, The Organic Act of the Department of Labor," accessed November 19, 2012, www.dol.gov/oasam/programs/history/organact.htm#.UKptwxB5mSM.

23. Lester B. Granger, "Barriers to Negro War Employment," *Annals of the American Academy of Political and Social Science* 223, no. 1 (September 1942), 77.

24. See Joseph Young, "U.S. Pay Increases since '41 Nearly Equal Living Cost Rise," *Washington Star*, May 21, 1946.

25. "Washington Urban League First Annual Report, 1939–1940, Race Relations in the Nation's Capital. 1940," Part I: N30, RNUL. See *Washington Urban League Newsletter* 1, no. 1 (March–April 1956), 1.

26. National Urban League Staff Report on Racial Relations, RNUL.

27. "Memo from Fair Employment Practice Committee to Heads of Governmental Departments and Independent Establishments," August 10, 1942; Part 20, Papers of Philleo Nash; Folder Official Documents; Harry S. Truman Library, Independence, MO.

28. Green, *Washington*, 109.

29. "Ban on Discrimination," *Washington Tribune*, November 16, 1940.

30. Of nonwhite individuals, not in families, 89.4 percent earned $2,499 or less with 55.7 percent earning $1,499 or less. U.S. Department of Commerce, Current Population Reports, "Percent Distribution of Families and Individuals by Total Money Income Level, by Color of Head, for the Washington (D.C.) Metropolitan District: 1947," Series P-60, no. 4 (Washington, DC: Government Printing Office, 1948), 14.

31. Gordon Parks, *Voices in the Mirror: An Autobiography* (New York: Doubleday, 1990), 84.

32. Editors of TIME, *TIME 100 Photographs: The Most Influential Images of All Time* (New York: Time Inc. Books, 2015), 36.

33. Gordon Parks, *A Choice of Weapons* (New York: Harper and Row, 1966), 230–31.

34. Carl Fleishhauer and Beverly W. Brannan, eds., *Documenting America, 1935–1943* (Berkeley: University of California Press, 1988), 226–29.

35. Editors of TIME, *TIME 100 Photographs*, 36.

36. "Letters," *Washington Post*, February 18, 1997.

37. U.S. Bureau of the Census, "Changing Characteristics of the Negro Population" (Washington, DC: Government Printing Office, 1969), 116.

38. "Letter from Washington," *Washington Post*, June 11, 1944; Joseph A. Fox, "City Has Acute Problem Caring for Government Girls Arriving 100 a Day," *Washington Post*, February 8, 1942.

39. Eleanor Early, "Smart Girls Here Get Dates, Career, Culture or Husband," *Washington Times-Herald*, April 1, 1942.

40. "Senator Theodore Bilbo bragged to his Alabamian constituents that segregation in the nation's capital was the rule." Jonathon Scott Holloway, *Confronting the Veil: Abram Harris, Jr., E. Franklin Frazier and Ralph Bunche* (Chapel Hill: University of North Carolina Press, 2002), 50.

41. Dennis B. Fradin and Judith Bloom, *Fight On! Mary Church Terrell's Battle for Integration* (New York: Clarion Books: 2003), 122.

42. Cary, *Washington Odyssey*, 208.

43. Elizabeth Clark-Lewis, *Living In, Living Out: African American Domestics and the Great Migration* (New York: Kodansha America, 1996), 126.

44. Isabel Wilkerson, *The Warmth of Other Suns: The Epic Story of America's Great Migration* (New York: Vintage, 2011), 200.

45. "Midway Hall, First Negro Government Dormitory, Opens," *Washington Post*, May 2, 1943.

46. See Chalmers M. Roberts, "Peace at Last! Cheers Erupt in Washington," *Washington Post*, July 26, 1995.

47. See Carla Hall, "Remembering the Wartime Call of the Capital: At Howard, the 'Government Girls' Reunion," *Washington Post*, October 24, 1988. See also Federal Security Agency, "Washington, D.C. Eleanor Roosevelt Visiting Lucy D. Slowe Hall, Women's Dormitory for Negro War Workers," FSA-OWI Collection [LC-USW3-028297-C], Prints & Photographs Division, Library of Congress.

48. Hall, "Remembering the Wartime Call." See also Paul K. Williams, *Washington, D.C.: The World War II Years* (Charleston, SC: Arcadia, 2004), 105–6.

49. See J. Freedom du Lac, "Guidebook that Held Blacks' Hands during Segregation Reveals a Deeply Altered D.C. and Inspires a Play," *Washington Post*, September 12, 2010.

50. Green is speaking of his courtship with his eventual wife, Evelyn Coleman Green, who was living in Slowe Hall, working as a Department of Agriculture secretary at the time. See Hall, "Remembering the Wartime Call."

51. Account of Director of Personnel, Everett W. Reimer, Office of Price Administration, May 27, 1947, Part 7, Record Group (RG) 220, RPCCR.

52. The OPA employed 758 black employees during the Second World War. While this number represented only 2 percent of all OPA employees, the total number was nonetheless far and above that of many other federal agencies, whether they held a higher proportional percentage of black employees at the time or not (see chapter 2, table 2.1).

53. Account of Director of Personnel, Everett W. Reimer, Office of Price Administration, May 27, 1947, Part 7, Record Group (RG) 220, RPCCR.

54. See, Anderson, "Last Hired, First Fired."

55. "The differentiating [restroom] signs were never painted on the doors." Constance McLaughlin Green, *The Secret City: A History of Race Relations in the Nation's Capital* (Princeton, NJ: Princeton University Press, 1967), 257.

56. National Committee against Segregation in the Nation's Capital, June 23, 1947, Internal Memorandum, Correspondence with Institutions, Organizations, etc., Part 12, RG 220, RPCCR.

57. Office of Price Administration (OPA), "Internal Memorandum," May 27, 1947, General Correspondence with Government Departments and Agencies, Part 7, RG 220, RPCCR.

58. OPA, "Internal Memorandum," May 27, 1947.

59. *Historical Statistics of Black America: Volume 1* (Farmington Hills, MI: Gale Group, 1994), 1105. The UFWA affiliated with the Congress of Industrial Organizations (CIO).

60. See "Memorandum from Fact-finding Committee Appointed to Investigate Charges of Mal-administration and Racial Discrimination in the Printing and Distribution Branch to Edward N. Way, Deputy Administrator, Final Report of Committee," May 3, 1943, Record Group 188, Office of Price Administration, General Records, NARA.

61. "Memorandum from Fact-finding Committee," May 3, 1943, NARA.

62. OPA, "Internal Memorandum," May 27, 1947, General Correspondence with Government Departments and Agencies, Part 7, RG 220, RPCCR.

63. OPA, "Internal Memorandum," May 27, 1947, RPCCR.

64. OPA, "Internal Memorandum," May 27, 1947, RPCCR.

65. Clarence M. Mitchell, Jr., NAACP Lobbyist to James M. Mead, U.S. Senator, New York, November 20, 1940, Part II: A194, RNAACP.

66. OPA, "For Immediate Release," September 15, 1944, General Correspondence with Government Departments and Agencies, Part 7, RG 220, RPCCR.

67. See "May 13, 1945, Memorandum, Robert R. R. Brooks to Consumer Advisory Committee," Record Group 188, Office of the Price Administration, General Records, NARA.

68. See U.S. Bureau of the Census, "Table 4, Percent of the Population 25 Years and Over with a Bachelor's Degree or Higher by Sex, Race, and Hispanic Origin, for the United States: 1940 to 2000," accessed May 10, 2013, http://www.census.gov/hhes/soc demo/education/data/census/half-century/tables.html.

69. See "Memorandum from Fact-Finding Committee," May 3, 1943, NARA.

70. CAF stands for Clerical, Administrative, and Fiscal Service; see Young, "U.S. Pay Increases since '41."

71. See "February 15, 1943, Testimony before the Fact-finding Committee of OPA," Office of Price Administration, General Records, Record Group 188, NARA.

72. National Committee against Segregation in the Nation's Capital, June 23, 1947, Internal Memorandum, Correspondence with Institutions, Organizations, etc., Part 12, RG 220, RPCCR.

73. See "Memorandum from Fact-Finding Committee," May 3, 1943, NARA.

74. Charles D. Chamberlin, *Victory at Home: Manpower and Race in the American South during World War II* (Athens: University of Georgia Press, 2003), 134.

75. Chamberlin, *Victory at Home*, 113.

76. Ann Short Chirhart, *Torches of Light: Georgia Teachers and the Coming of the Modern South* (Athens: University of Georgia Press, 2005), 180.

77. Christopher E. Linsin, "Something More Than a Creed: Mary McLeod Bethune's Aim of Integrated Autonomy as Director of Negro Affairs," *Florida Historical Quarterly* 76, no. 1 (Summer 1997), 28.

78. See "Analysis of Reports on Negro Employment in All Field Offices as of November 30, 1945," Record Group 188, Office of the Price Administration, General Records, NARA.

79. "Letter from Chester Bowles to Commissioner Arthur S. Flemming," December 3, 1945, Record Group 188, Office of the Price Administration, General Records, NARA.

80. "Letter from Frieda Sucher to Chester Bowles," January 5, 1946, Record Group 188, Office of the Price Administration, General Records, NARA. See also "Memorandum from Frances Williams RE: Reactions to Publications of Your Letters to Flemming and Niles Regarding Discrimination Against Employment of Negroes by Federal Agencies," January 5, 1946, Record Group 188, Office of the Price Administration, General Records, NARA.

81. "Letter from T. P. Wright to Chester Bowles," December 29, 1945, Record Group 188, Office of the Price Administration, General Records, NARA.

82. Jessica Valentine letter to NAACP Legal Branch, May 9, 1945, RNAACP.

83. Neil A. Wynn, *The African American Experience during World War II* (Lanham, MD: Rowman and Littlefield, 2011), xi–xii.

84. Walter White, "The Negro Demands the Right to be Allowed to Fight for It," *Saturday Evening Post* 213, no. 24 (December 14, 1940), 27.

85. Paul Burstein, *Discrimination, Jobs and Politics: The Struggle for Equal Employment Opportunity in the United States since the New Deal* (Chicago: University of Chicago Press, 1985), 8.

86. "During the first year [FEPC] hearings involving forty-nine industries, unions, and defense training programs were conducted in Los Angeles, Washington, Chicago, New York, and Birmingham" and "served to confirm the allegation that discrimination was rampant in war industry. Seventy-five per cent of these early cases involved Negroes." Louis Coleridge Kesselman, *The Social Politics of FEPC: A Study in Reform Pressure Movements* (Chapel Hill: University of North Carolina Press, 1948), 16.

87. Herbert Hill, Testimony Before the Ad Hoc Committee Hearings on Federal Contract Compliance, House of Representatives, Washington, DC, December 5, 1968.

88. Letter from Office of Price Administration Director of Personnel, Everett W. Reimer to Robert K. Carr, Executive Secretary of PCCR, May 27, 1947, Part 7, RG 220, RPCCR.

89. Mary A. Norton, "The Federal Government and Negro Morale," *Journal of Education* 12, no. 3 (Summer 1943), 463.

90. Gunnar Myrdal, *An American Dilemma: The Negro Problem in Modern Democracy* (New York: Harper and Row, 1944), 139.

91. Perry, *Hubert Harrison Reader*, 282.

92. James E. Chinn, "Postwar D.C. Exodus of Negro Forecast in Housing Warning," *Washington Post*, April 5, 1944.

CHAPTER 2: "STUDY LONG, STUDY WRONG"

1. *Pittsburgh Courier*, "They Read about It in Paris," August 25, 1945, 9.

2. National Diet Library, Text of the Constitution and Other Important Documents: "Potsdam Declaration," accessed July 11, 2017, http://www.ndl.go.jp/constitution/e/etc/c06.html.

3. John Fousek, *To Lead the Free World: American Nationalism and the Cultural Roots of the Cold War* (Chapel Hill: University of North Carolina Press, 2000), 34.

4. Toki Schalk, "Prayers of the Righteous," *Pittsburgh Courier*, August 25, 1945, 10.

5. James T. Patterson, *Grand Expectations: The United States, 1945–1974* (Oxford: Oxford University Press, 1996), 77.

6. Philip Foner, *Organized Labor and the Black Worker: 1619–1973* (New York: International, 1976), 270.

7. "War Workers' Mass Migration Called Greatest U.S. Challenge," *Washington Post*, September 27, 1945.

8. Charles S. Johnson and Preston Valien, "The Status of Negro Labor," in *Labor in Postwar America*, ed. Colston Warne (Brooklyn, NY: Remsen Press, 1949), 568.

9. Victor Perlo, "Trends in the Economic Status of the Negro People," *Science and Society* 16, no. 2 (Spring 1950), 132.

10. "Civil Liberties Implications of the Employment, Housing, and Social Adjustment Problems of Minorities: Statement to the President's Committee on Civil Liberties," April 1, 1947, President's Committee on Civil Rights, General Correspondence with Government Departments and Agencies, Part 7, RG 220, RPCCR.

11. Rung, *Servants of the State*, 180.

12. Jerry Kluttz. "Negroes Holding 19.2% of U.S. Jobs in Capital," *Washington Post*, February 21, 1945. See also, U.S. Bureau of the Census, District of Columbia—Race and Hispanic Origin: 1800–1990.

13. "Typical Comments on Servant Problem: Some Expect Domestics' Return Since War Work Is Over; Wages Seen as Big Factor," *Washington Post*, December 3, 1945.

14. Janet M. Hooks, "Women's Occupations through Seven Decades," *Women's Bureau Bulletin*, no. 218 (Washington, DC: Government Printing Office, 1947), 35.

15. Harold H. Kassarjian, "The Negro and American Advertising, 1946–1965," *Journal of Marketing Research* 6, no. 1 (February 1969), 29–39.

16. Jonathan Birnbaum and Clarence Taylor, eds., *Civil Rights since 1787: A Reader on the Black Struggle* (New York: New York University Press, 2000), 372.

17. Laretta Henderson, *Ebony Jr! The Rise, Fall, and Return of a Black Children's Magazine* (Lanham, MD: Scarecrow Press, 2008), 49 (emphasis added).

18. General Correspondence with Government Departments and Agencies, Memorandum from Neil Dalton, Deputy Expediter (Field Operations) of FHA to All Regional Expediters on September 5, 1946, Part 7, RG 220, RPCCR.

19. Jesse Thomas Moore Jr., *A Search for Equality: The National Urban League, 1910–1961* (University Park: Pennsylvania State University Press, 1981), 133.

20. "Open Memorandum from Oliver C. Short, Director of Personnel Department of Commerce, to Heads of Bureaus and Offices," November 9, 1945, Part 12, RG 220, RPCCR.

21. See Rung, *Servants of the State*, 168; Krislov, *Negro in Federal Employment*, 34.

22. The first African American chairman of the Joint Chiefs of Staff in the United States Army, General Colin Powell, was asked by reporters if he ever envisioned such a result despite his humble origins in the impoverished South Bronx. Powell responded no "because such a dream would have been impossible for that eleven-year-old kid. But that kid didn't know that President Truman had just signed an executive order that would permit such a dream to come true. And the dream did come true, not just because President Truman signed an executive order, but also because after he signed the order, he went about the task of knocking the ears off the Pentagon to make it happen." Colin Powell, "Truman, Desegregation of the Armed Forces and a Kid from the Bronx," in *The Civil Rights Legacy of Harry S. Truman*, ed. Raymond H. Geselbracht (Kirksville, MO: Truman State University Press, 2007), 121.

23. Harvard Sitkoff, "Harry Truman and the Election of 1948: The Coming of Age

of Civil Rights in American Politics," *Journal of Southern History* 37, no. 4 (November 1971), 613.

24. Letter from Truman to Heads of All Government Departments, Agencies and Independent Establishments, December 18, 1945, Part 12, RG 220, RPCCR. "Sift Bias in Hiring, Truman Tells FEPC," *Washington Post*, December 18, 1945.

25. Letter from Truman to Heads of All Government Departments, Agencies and Independent Establishments, December 18, 1945, Part 12, RG 220, RPCCR.

26. The rejection note was dated January 27, 1946. "Testimony on Racial Discrimination in Government Agencies Before Subcommittee of President's Committee on Civil Rights by Thomas Richardson, International Vice-President, United Public Workers, CIO," April 2, 1947, Part 7, RG 220, RPCCR.

27. Myrdal, *American Dilemma*, 22.

28. PCCR Committee Members: Charles E. Wilson, chairman (president, General Electric); John S. Dickey, vice chairman (president, Dartmouth College); Franklin D. Roosevelt Jr., vice chairman (lawyer); Mrs. Sadie T. Alexander (lawyer); James B. Carey (secretary-treasurer CIO); Morris L. Ernst (lawyer); Roland B. Gittelsohn (rabbi); Dr. Frank P. Graham (president, University of North Carolina); Most Rev. Francis J. Haas (bishop); Charles Luckman (president, Lever Brothers Company); Francis P. Matthews (lawyer); Rt. Rev. Henry Knox Sherrill (bishop); Boris Shishkin (economist, AFL); Mrs. M. E. Tilly (field secretary, Southern Regional Council); Channing H. Tobias (director, Phelps-Stokes Fund).

29. Letter, John S. Dickey to Robert K. Carr, May 12, 1947, Part 7, RG 220, RPCCR; Letter from Boris Shishkin to Robert K. Carr, May 29, 1947, Part 7, RG 220, RPCCR.

30. "Memorandum, to the President's Committee from Robert K. Carr RE: Background Statement of Civil Rights in the District of Columbia, prepared by Milton Stewart and Rachel Sady," April 24, 1947, Part 7, RG 220, RPCCR.

31. Wendell E. Pritchett, "A National Issue: Segregation in the District of Columbia and the Civil Rights Movement at Mid-Century," *Georgetown Law Journal* 93, no. 4 (April 2005), 1326.

32. National Urban League Staff Report on Racial Relations, RNUL.

33. National Urban League Staff Report on Racial Relations, RNUL.

34. PCCR, *To Secure These Rights*, 58.

35. Murrey Marder, "D.C. Business Accused of Maintaining Negro Ghetto," *Washington Post*, December 11, 1948.

36. For a thorough treatment of how a federal ideal was manipulated on local levels, see Ira Kaztnelson's discussion of the G.I. Bill in *When Affirmative Action Was White* (New York: Norton, 2005).

37. "Civil Liberties Implications of the Employment, Housing, and Social Adjustment Problems of Minorities: Statement to the President's Committee on Civil Lib-

erties," April 1, 1947, General Correspondence with Government Departments and Agencies, Part 7, RG 220, RPCCR.

38. Memorandum from Mr. Stewart to Mr. Murtha, "Veterans' Administration Report," April 23, 1947, Part 7, RG 220, RPCCR.

39. "End of Racial Segregation at Airport Is Sought by U.S.," *Washington Post*, November 18, 1947.

40. Michael Gardner, *Harry Truman and Civil Rights: Moral Courage and Political Risks* (Carbondale: Southern Illinois University Press, 2003), 154; see also "Truman Held Champion of Civil Rights," *Washington Post*, June 24, 1948.

41. Anke Ortlepp, *Jim Crow Terminals: The Desegregation of American Airports* (Athens: University of Georgia Press, 2017), 16.

42. See Richard L. Lyons, "Segregation Ended at Airport," *Washington Post*, January 5, 1949.

43. Kenesaw M. Landis, *Segregation in Washington: A Report of the National Committee on Segregation in the Nation's Capital* (Chicago: NCSNC, 1948). The author, Kenesaw M. Landis II is the nephew of Kenesaw Mountain Landis, the infamous commissioner of Major League Baseball who thwarted numerous attempts to racially integrate the game. Jackie Robinson entered the league in 1947 six months after the senior Landis's death.

44. Press Release, "NAACP Scores Federal Employment Practices," November 21, 1947, Part II: B88, RNAACP.

45. Marder, "D.C. Business Accused of Maintaining Negro Ghetto."

46. Joseph Young, "U.S. Pay Increases Since '41 Nearly Equal Living Cost Rise," *Washington Star*, May 21, 1946. N.b., "employe" is an alternate spelling of "employee."

47. Memorandum from Clarence Mitchell to Walter White, RE: "Proposed Agency against Discrimination in Federal Employment," April 9, 1947, Part II: B88, RNAACP.

48. "NAACP Scores Federal Employment Practices," Press Release, RNAACP.

49. "NAACP Scores Federal Employment Practices," Press Release, RNAACP.

50. Ira Katznelson thoroughly outlines how black veterans were systematically denied benefits at a local level even though funds were federally distributed to assist all veterans with education, housing, and medical benefits. See, in general, Katznelson, *When Affirmative Action Was White*.

51. Letter from F. J. Lawton, Director, Bureau of the Budget, to Robert Carr, May 29, 1947, Part 7, RG 220, RPCCR.

52. Letter from Walter K. Scott, Director, Office of Departmental Administration, Department of State to Robert K. Carr, May 20, 1947, Part 7, RG 220, RPCCR.

53. Memorandum from Veterans Administration, August 18, 1947, Part 7, RG 220, RPCCR.

54. Letter from Keith Himebaugh, Director of Information, USDA to Robert Carr, May 21, 1947, Part 7, RG 220, RPCCR.

55. "Letter January 21, 1947 from Clarence Mitchell, NAACP Labor Secretary to Arthur S. Flemming, Civil Service Commissioner," Labor: Government Agencies, General, 1941–47, Part II: B88, RNAACP.

56. Letter from Office of Price Administration Director of Personnel, Everett W. Reimer to Robert K. Carr, Executive Secretary of PCCR, May 27, 1947, Part 7, RG 220, RPCCR.

57. Joseph D. Lohman and Edwin Embree, "The Nation's Capital," *Survey Graphic* 36, no. 1 (January 1947), 32–33.

58. Memorandum to Robert Carr, U.S. Atomic Energy Commission, August 22, 1947, Part 7, RG 220, RPCCR.

59. U.S. Department of Labor, "Negro Women and Their Jobs," *Women's Bureau Leaflet*, no. 19, January 1954 (Washington, DC: Government Printing Office, 1954), 3.

60. Transcripts April 2, 1947, Proceedings of the PCCR Committee, Statement of Thomas Richardson, Part 7, RG 220, RPCCR.

61. "Discrimination in Government Employment," Memorandum from staff of NCSNC to Members of the President's Committee on Civil Rights, June 23, 1947, 7–8, General Correspondence with Government Departments and Agencies, Part 7, RG 220, RPCCR.

62. Charles Van Devander, "What's Happening to the Negroes Who Get Jobs in Washington?" *Washington Memo*, November 17, 1947, Part II: B88, RNAACP.

63. Van Devander, "What's Happening?"

64. Van Devander, "What's Happening?"

65. Letter of Edward A. Macy, Director of Personnel to Lewis E. Williams, Director of Administrative Operations Branch, September 18, 1946, 2, Part 12, RG 220, RPCCR.

66. National Urban League Staff Report on Racial Relations, RNUL.

67. "News Reporter Finds Number of Negroes in Important Positions," *Washington Pittsburgh Courier*, August 10, 1946.

68. E. B. Henderson, "Letter to the Editor," *Washington Post*, January 1, 1946.

69. Another study by the Civil Service Commission showed that it took blacks on average seven times as long as whites to gain a promotion. Jerry Kluttz, "The Federal Diary," *Washington Post*, October 30, 1947.

70. Lula M. Fields, "Letter to the Editor," *Washington Post*, August 24, 1948.

71. Committee on Employment Discrimination, *FEPC Reference Manual* (New York: National Community Relations Council, 1948), 6–10.

72. "Civil Rights Report," *Washington Post*, October 30, 1947.

73. Memorandum from Clarence Mitchell to George Weaver, February 3, 1947, "Discrimination in Private and Federal Employment," Part II: B88, RNAACP.

74. Memorandum from Mitchell to Weaver, February 3, 1947.

75. "News Reporter Finds Number of Negroes in Important Positions," *Washington Pittsburgh Courier*, August 10, 1946.

76. Letter from Office of Price Administration Director of Personnel, Everett W. Reimer to Robert K. Carr, Executive Secretary of PCCR, May 27, 1947, Part 12, RG 220, RPCCR.

77. Memo to Thurgood Marshall from Jesse O. Dedmon, NAACP Secretary of Veterans' Affairs, RE: "Request for Legal Action in Behalf of Mr. Herman J.D. Carter," Labor: Government Agencies, General, 1941–47, July 14, 1947, Part II: B88, RNAACP.

78. NCSNC memo to PCCR, June 23, 1947, Part 7, RG 220, RPCCR.

79. NCSNC memo to PCCR, June 23, 1947.

80. Jackie Robinson broke the color line with the Brooklyn Dodgers on April 15, 1947.

81. PCCR, *To Secure These Rights*, 58.

82. PCCR, *To Secure These Rights*, 58.

83. Letter to NAACP Assistant Special Counsel Marian Wynn Perry from Phyllis Zeughauser, February 10, 1948, Part II: B88, RNAACP.

84. Harry S. Truman in letter to PCCR accepting resignation of its members, June 28, 1946, Part 7, RG 220, RPCCR.

CHAPTER 3: "THIS IS NOT WORKING"

1. "Ewing is Accused on U.S. Cook Use," *Washington Post*, August 6, 1948.

2. Associated Press, "Ewing Told to Stop Using Federal Chef," *Washington Post*, October 20, 1948.

3. "Senate Group Charges F.S.A. Head Had Hospital Cook Get His Meals," *Courier-Journal*, August 6, 1948, 15.

4. "Ewing Plans to Continue Use of Cook," *Washington Post*, August 7, 1948.

5. Social Security Administration, "Social Security History: Organizational History," n.d., accessed July 11, 2013, http://www.ssa.gov/history/orghist.html.

6. "Ewing Is Accused on U.S. Cook Use."

7. United Press International, "Bridges Kindles Legal Fire under Ewing's Borrowed Cook," *Washington Post*, August 11, 1948.

8. "Senate Group Charges F.S.A. Head Had Hospital Cook Get His Meals," *Courier-Journal*, August 6, 1948, 15.

9. U.S. Bureau of the Census, 1940 National Census, "Table 16," 594.

10. Letter to Oscar R. Ewing, Administrator, Federal Security from NAACP Labor Secretary Clarence Mitchell, February 17, 1949, Labor: Government Agencies General 1949–51, Part II: B88, RNAACP.

11. "Ewing Plans to Continue Use of Cook."

12. Social Security Administration, "Social Security History: Oscar R. Ewing," n.d., accessed December 12, 2012, http://www.ssa.gov/history/ewing.html.

13. Jess Gilbert, *Planning Democracy: Agrarian Intellectuals and the Intended New Deal* (New Haven, CT: Yale University Press, 2015), 92.

14. "Jobs Open for Negroes, Official Says," *Washington Post*, March 14, 1950. See also Susan Ware, ed., *Notable American Women: A Biographical Dictionary Completing the Twentieth Century* (Cambridge, MA: Belknap Press of Harvard University Press, 2005), 285–86.

15. Joan Cook, "Anna Hedgeman Is Dead at 90; Aide to Mayor Wagner in 1950's," *New York Times*, January 26, 1990.

16. "Jobs Open for Negroes, Official Says," *Washington Post*, March 14, 1950.

17. "Use of Army Skills Urged," *Baltimore Sun*, March 18, 1946.

18. MacLean, *Freedom Is Not Enough*, 183.

19. General Services Administration, "Special Message to the Congress on Civil Rights," *Public Papers of the Presidents: Harry S. Truman*, February 2, 1948 (Washington, DC: Government Printing Office, 1964), 124.

20. President's Committee on Civil Rights, *To Secure These Rights*, 133.

21. President's Committee on Civil Rights, *To Secure These Rights*, 133.

22. See in general, Dudziak, *Cold War Civil Rights*, 243.

23. "Same Old Slums," *Washington Post*, April 21, 1949.

24. National Council for a Permanent FEPC, News Press Release March 28–29, 1947, Part 7, RG 220, RPCCR.

25. "Capital Termed Graphic Example of Non-Democracy; Segregation Hit," *Washington Post*, October 30, 1947.

26. Executive Order 9980, Harry S. Truman Library and Museum, Executive Orders, Harry S. Truman 1945–1953, accessed October 21, 2012, http://trumanlibrary .org/executiveorders/index.php?pid=29.

27. Letter to Heads of Executive Departments and Independent Establishments from Executive Secretary L. C. Lawhorn, March 8, 1949, Part 7, RG 220, RPCCR.

28. Alvin A. Webb, "Federal Discrimination," *Washington Post*, August 30, 1948.

29. Letter to Heads of Executive Departments, March 8, 1949, RPCCR.

30. Vincent J. Browne, "Racial Desegregation in the Public Service, with Particular Reference to the U.S. Government," *Journal of Negro Education* 23, no. 3 (Summer 1954), 244.

31. Michael R. Belknap, *Employment of Blacks by the Federal Government* (New York: Routledge, 1991), 80.

32. Press Release, September 30, 1949, Job Recommendations, Part II: A326, RNAACP.

33. While the event was advertised for all government employees, no specific agency was cited as the primary sponsor. Jerry Kluttz, "The Federal Diary," *Washington Post,* July 2, 1951.

34. Violette K. Taylor, "Post Office Cafeterias," *Washington Post,* February 28, 1952.

35. "Segregated Farewell," *Washington Post*, December 26, 1950.

36. Donald Dewey, "Negro Employment in Southern Industry," *Journal of Political Economy* 60, no. 4 (1952), 283.

37. Press release, "Promote Only on Basis of Merit [Board Orders Norfolk Navy Yard]," Labor: Naval Yard and Bases, August 13, 1953, Part II: A326, RNAACP.

38. "Promote Only on Basis of Merit," RNAACP.

39. "Digest of Press Clippings in the Civil Rights Field, Memo from Robert Carr to Members of the PCCR," April 16, 1947, Part 7, RG 220, RPCCR.

40. U.S. Civil Service Commission, Fair Employment Board, Washington, D.C., August 10, 1953—Decision by Fred C. Croxton, Acting Chairman, Fair Employment Board RE: appellant Elmer Harris, August 10, 1953, Labor: Naval Yard and Bases, Part II: A326, RNAACP.

41. Decision by Fred C. Croxton, RNAACP.

42. See William A. Sundstrom, "The Color Line: Racial Norms and Discrimination in Urban Labor Markets, 1910–1950," *Journal of Economic History* 54, no. 2 (1994), 382–96.

43. The four service categories were Clerical, Administrative, Fiscal Service (CAF); Custodial (which included all mechanical positions, CU); Professional/Scientific (P); and Sub-Professional/Sub-Scientific (SP).

44. Grades GS 16–18 were eventually replaced by the Senior Executive Service (SES) level due to the Civil Service Reform Act of 1978.

45. Public Administration Review, "Federal Position Classification and Pay Legislation," *Public Administration Review* 9, no. 4 (Autumn 1949), 298–99.

46. Public Administration Review, "Federal Position Classification and Pay Legislation," 298–99.

47. Committee on Employment Discrimination, *Fair Employment Practices Commission Reference Manual* (New York: National Community relations Council, 1948), 6–10, Phileo Nash Files, Part 26, RPCCR.

48. William Edward Burghardt DuBois, *Souls of Black Folk: Essays and Sketches* (Cambridge, MA: A.C. McClurg, 1903), 204.

49. Jessica Valentine letter to NAACP Legal Branch, May 9, 1945, RNAACP.

50. Foner, *Organized Labor*, 536. See also Belknap, *Employment of Blacks*, 27.

51. Green, *Washington*, 329.

52. "Monthly Report of Labor Secretary," September 3, 1947, "NAACP Labor Department, Monthly Reports, 1945–49," Part II: A341, Part 7, RG 220, RPCCR.

53. Branch Rickey, general manager of the Brooklyn Dodgers, who broke the color barrier in Major League Baseball by hiring Jackie Robinson in 1947. Harold W. Pfautz, "The New 'New Negro': Emerging American," *Phylon* 24, no. 4 (1963), 360–68.

54. "Meeting Community Needs," NUL Annual Report for 1953, RNUL.

55. National Urban League, "Jottings," November 1954, 5, RNUL.

56. National Urban League, "Jottings," November 1954, 5, RNUL.

57. Robert C. Weaver was the first black American to hold an official cabinet position from 1966 to 1968 with the Department of Housing and Urban Development.

58. S. L. Fishbein, "Race Issues Cleared Up Here, Wilkins Says," *Washington Post,* April 13, 1955.

59. Simeon Booker, "The Last Days of J. Ernest Wilkins: A Victim of Political Bickering, Unbending Fighter Dies a Lonely Man," *Ebony* 15, no. 5 (March 1960), 143.

60. Simeon Booker, "Washington Notebook," *Ebony* 36, no. 1 (November 1980), 27.

61. Booker, "Washington Notebook," 27.

62. See "Ike Denies Asking J. Ernest Wilkins To Quit," *Chicago Defender,* August 30, 1958.

63. Fishbein, "Race Issues Cleared Up Here."

64. Drew Pearson, "Wilkins' Ouster Raises Problem," *Washington Post,* August 15, 1958. See also, Booker, "Washington Notebook."

65. Sugrue, *Sweet Land of Liberty,* 267.

66. Letter from Dwight D. Eisenhower read into record by Vice-President at the first meeting of the Presidential Committee on Government Contracts, September 14, 1953, Part 7, RG 220, RPCCR.

67. See "Bias Banned in U.S. Hiring," *Washington Post,* November 14, 1953; see also Wolgemuth, "Woodrow Wilson." At a presidential cabinet meeting on April 11, 1913, Burleson expressed intolerable conditions in Railway Mail Service (i.e., same drinking glasses, towels, and washrooms) and announced gradual implementation of racial segregation.

68. Kluttz, "Federal Diary."

CHAPTER 4: "RATS! DISCRIMINATED AGAIN"

1. "Hobson Specialty: Successful Hoaxes," *Washington Post,* July 4, 1972.

2. Helen Thompson, "In the 1960s, One Man Took Washington, D.C.'s Rat Problem into His Own Hands, Literally," Smithsonian.com, July 21, 2015, accessed July 11, 2017. http://www.smithsonianmag.com/smart-news/1960s-julius-hobson-took-dcs-rat-problem-his-own-hands-180955961/ (emphasis added).

3. "Hobson Specialty."

4. Burt Solomon, *The Washington Century: Three Families and the Shaping of the Nation's Capital* (New York: HarperCollins, 2004), 154–55.

5. "Hobson Specialty."

6. The photograph requirement for the "Rule of Three" was abolished in 1941 with the aid of the NAACP, which made the persuasive case that black workers who were selected among the three finalists were disproportionately affected on account of the photographs included with their applications that verified that they were not white.

The rule of three was in existence until 2010 when it was abandoned for a more stream-lined "category rating." Joe Davidson, "President Obama's Hiring Reforms Draw Applause at Personnel Agency," *Washington Post*, May 12, 2010.

7. Robert H. Zieger, *For Jobs and Freedom: Race and Labor in America since 1865* (Lexington: University Press of Kentucky, 2007), 191.

8. In 1964 *Business Week* magazine declared, "The basic cause of negro poverty is discrimination." Nicholas Lemann, *The Promised Land: The Great Black Migration and How It Changed America* (New York: Vintage Books, 1992), 112.

9. Carol Honsa, "Negro GSA Workers Charge Administration with Discrimination," *Washington Post*, June 22, 1969.

10. August C. Bolino, *Manpower and the City* (Cambridge, MA: Schenkman, 1969), 33.

11. Robert E. Baker, "Job Picture Still Far from Rosy to Negroes Here," *Washington Post*, August 13, 1963.

12. Derived from a table attached to letter to Roy Wilkins NAACP from Lee White, Special Counsel to the President, November 13, 1965, Part III: A144, Folder Government, National Civil Service 1958–65, RNAACP.

13. Letter to Robert E. McLaughlin, President, Board of Commissioners, District of Columbia from Sterling Tucker, Executive Director, August 8, 1960, Part III: A144, RNAACP.

14. U.S. Bureau of the Census, 1940 National Census (Washington, DC: Government Printing Office, 1940), 609–12.

15. Jerry Kluttz, "Policy on Jobs Stirs Hill Clash," *Washington Post*, October 4, 1966.

16. Solomon, *Washington Century*, 154.

17. *Hobson v. Hansen*, 269 F. Supp., 401 (D.D.C. 1967).

18. Robert E. Baker, "Fragmented Leadership Frustrates Achievement of D.C. Negroes' Goals," *Washington Post*, August 16, 1963.

19. Solomon, *Washington Century*, 135, 155. See "SNCC, Dick Gregory Snub White," *Jet Magazine* 30, no. 9 (June 9, 1966), 8.

20. Cynthia Gorney, "Julius Hobson Sr. Dies: Activist Stirred Up City for 25 Years," *Washington Post*, March 24, 1977.

21. Gorney, "Julius Hobson Sr. Dies."

22. Solomon, *Washington Century*, 151.

23. "D.C. Core Unit Gets New Look," *Washington Post*, December 10, 1964.

24. "Authorization Form," n.d., Papers of Julius Hobson.

25. Martin Weil, "Government Discriminates in Hiring, D.C. Negroes Say," *Washington Post*, December 4, 1968.

26. Daniel Stevens, "Public Opinion and Public Policy: The Case of Kennedy and Civil Rights," *Presidential Studies Quarterly* 32, no. 1 (March 2002), 113.

27. David Stebenne, *Arthur J. Goldberg: New Deal Liberal* (New York: Oxford University Press, 1996), 246.

28. Stebenne, *Arthur J. Goldberg*, 246.

29. "Text of President's Civil Rights Message," *Washington Post*, March 1, 1963.

30. See Table 1: Union Membership as a Percent of U.S. Labor Force: Private and Public Sectors; Selected Years, 1900–1984, in Melvin W. Reder, "The Rise and Fall of Unions: The Public Sector and the Private," *Journal of Economic Perspectives* 2, no. 2 (Spring 1988), 106.

31. "Text of President Kennedy's Speech to Mayors," *Washington Post*, June 10, 1963.

32. "Text of President Kennedy's Speech to Mayors."

33. "Landmark Legislation: The Civil Rights Act of 1964," United States Senate, n.d., accessed April 20, 2018, https://www.senate.gov/artandhistory/history/common/generic/CivilRightsAct1964.htm.

34. Kenneth Y. Chay, "The Impact of Federal Civil Rights Policy on Black Economic Progress: Evidence from the Equal Employment Opportunity Act of 1972," *Industrial and Labor Relations Review* 51, no. 4 (July 1998), 609–10.

35. Chay, "Impact of Federal Civil Rights Policy," 610.

36. Andy Kiersz, "The Impact of Small Business on the US Economy in 2 Extreme Charts," *Business Insider*, June 16, 2015, accessed July 11, 2017, http://www.businessinsider.com/us-employment-by-firm-size-has-a-fat-tailed-distribution-2015–6.

37. Seven years later, available data from 1979 provides an idea of just how many employees were exempt from Title VII's 1964 provisions. Excluding government employees, railroad employees, self-employed people, 86 percent of total employees nationwide worked at enterprises or businesses containing twenty or fewer employees, whereas only 1.4 percent had one hundred or more employees. U.S. Department of Commerce Bureau of the Census, "No. 901 Establishments, Employees and Payroll by Industry and Employment-Size, Class: 1979," in *Statistical Abstract of the United States, 1981* (Washington, DC: Government Printing Office, 1981), 536.

38. Andrea H. Beller, "The Economics of Enforcement of an Antidiscrimination Law: Title VII of the Civil Rights Act of 1964," *Journal of Law and Economics* 21, no. 2 (October 1978), 361.

39. See Donald J. McCrone and Richard J. Hardy, "Civil Rights Policies and the Achievement of Racial Economic Equality, 1948–1975," *American Journal of Political Science* 22, no. 1 (February 1978), 1–17 (some impact observed, but the effects of closing the black-white income gap were largely limited to the South); Larry Isaac and Lars Christiansen, "How the Civil Rights Movement Revitalized Labor Militancy," *American Sociological Review* 67, no. 5 (October 2002), 722–46 (the civil rights movement, but not the Civil Rights Act is credited with causing economic change); Charles Brown, "Black-White Earnings Ratios since the Civil Rights Act of 1964: The Impor-

tance of Labor Market Dropouts," *Quarterly Journal of Economics* 99, no. 1 (February 1984), 31–44 (legislation may have improved blacks' economic condition, but scant evidence demonstrates a direct policy impact); John J. Donohue III and James Heckman, "Continuous Versus Episodic Change: The Impact of Civil Rights Policy on the Economic Status of Blacks," *Journal of Economic Literature* 29, no. 4 (December 1991), 1603–43 (no major economic impact observed as blacks collectively benefit from marginal changes in relative income).

40. John David Skrentny, "Pragmatism, Institutionalism, and the Construction of Employment Discrimination," *Sociological Forum* 9, no. 3 (September 1994), 354–55.

41. Harvard Law Review Association, "Developments in the Law: Employment Discrimination and Title VII of the Civil Rights Act of 1964," *Harvard Law Review* 84, no. 5 (March 1971), 1202.

42. "Developments in the Law," 1207.

43. Dave Zirin, *What's My Name, Fool? Sports and Resistance in the United States* (Chicago: Haymarket Books, 2005), 157.

44. Baker, "Job Picture Still Far from Rosy."

45. Skrentny, "Pragmatism," 353–54.

46. Solomon, *Washington Century*, 62.

47. Memo: RE: 1966 Employee Attitude and Opinion Survey, June 14, 1966, AFGE Lodge 1092, PJH.

48. U.S. Civil Service Commission on Civil Rights, *To Know or Not to Know: Collection and Use of Racial and Ethnic Data in Federal Assistance Programs* (Washington, DC: Government Printing Office, 1973), 7.

49. Letter to Hobson from John W. Macy, Jr., Chairman, US Civil Service Commission, April 13, 1966, PJH.

50. Philip Shandler, "Hobson to Seek US Job Quotas," *Evening Star*, September 1, 1969.

51. U.S. Civil Service Commission, *Challenge and Change: Annual Report, 1968* (Washington, DC: Government Printing Office, 1968), 17.

52. Tristram Coffin, "USDA Story Untold," *Washington Examiner*, June 8, 1968.

53. Kluttz, "Policy on Jobs Stirs Hill Clash."

54. Letter to the Honorable Joseph S. Clark, Jr., Chairman of the Subcommittee on Employment and Manpower, June 17, 1968, signed by Wm. F. Ryan, Charles C. Diggs, Edward R. Rogbal, Phillip Burton, John Conyers, Jr., PJH.

55. "Developments in the Law," 1202.

56. Weil, "Government Discriminates in Hiring."

57. Weil, "Government Discriminates in Hiring."

58. Underwater acoustics was an emerging field in the late 1960s; scientists in the medical field used the techniques to conduct auditory experiments or gauge medical ultrasound efficacy. Letter to Rep. Wm. F. Ryan from John Macy, September 30, 1968, PJH.

59. Julius Hobson, *Education Reporter*, March 1968, PJH

60. Ben W. Gilbert, *Ten Blocks from the White House: Anatomy of the Washington Riots of 1968* (New York: Praeger, 1968), 152.

61. Dr. Martin Luther King Jr. was assassinated April 4, 1968. Columnist William Raspberry reported in late June: "For several weeks, Hobson has been circulating petitions among Federal employees across the country in support of his contention. He says that he has received more than 3000 letters from aggrieved civil servants." William Raspberry, "Hobson Tilts with Uncle Sam," *Washington Post*, June 26, 1968.

62. King Petition, Circa 1968, PJH.

63. Julius Hobson, "Uncle Sam Is a Bigot," *Saturday Evening Post* 241, no. 8 (April 20, 1968), 16.

64. Letter from Brad Johnson of Detroit to Julius Hobson, June 10, 1968, PJH.

65. Johnson to Hobson, June 10, 1968, PJH.

66. Letter to Julius Hobson from Malissa J. Bozman, August 25, 1969, PJH.

67. On S23453, August 11–12, 1969, Washington, DC: Government Printing Office, 1969, testimony of J. Hobson is on 178–92, PJH.

68. "Minority Perspectives on Bureaucracy" *Bureaucrat* 2, no. 2 (Summer 1973), 139.

69. Letter to Julius Hobson from Berl I. Bernhard, staff director, U.S. Commission on Civil Rights, April 15, 1963, PJH.

70. Outside the federal government, blacks could obtain only laborer or service-type jobs in a crowded metropolitan area like the District of Columbia. For example, the city's Work Training Opportunity Center reported in 1968 that 98.4 percent of all applicants seeking training for new jobs were "Negro." While the city's black population was still growing in the postwar era, this 98.4 percent suggests overrepresentation among the disenfranchised and continued stagnation of black capitalistic development without federal protection. Department of Public Welfare, "Work Training Opportunity Center" 3, no. 5 (May 1968), 3, PJH.

71. Letter to Hobson from Kent Corey, Director of Manpower & Training, Commission on Economic Opportunities, June 8, 1968, PJH.

72. Ken W. Clawson and Robert C. Maynard, "U.S. Tried to Delay Bias Blast: U.S. Tried to Delay Rights Report," *Washington Post*, October 13, 1970.

73. Mike Causey, "New Code Readied in Race Data: The Federal Diary," *Washington Post*, October 11, 1969. This guessing procedure was later dropped in favor of voluntary disclosure during the hiring process. See Causey, "U.S. Again to Ask Sex and Race Data: Held Aid to Recruiting Women, Minorities U.S. Will Require Sex, Race, Ethnic Data for Jobs," *Washington Post*, December 7, 1977.

74. Joseph Young, The Federal Spotlight," *Sunday Star*, July 6, 1969.

75. Letter to Julius Hobson from John Craven, April 26, 1968, PJH.

76. Hobson to Craven, April 26, 1968, PJH.

77. Gorney, "Julius Hobson Sr. Dies."

CHAPTER 5: "I WAS HURTING"

1. *National Alliance* 19, no. 4 (April 1970), 4; see also *National Alliance* 19, no. 5 (May 1970), 5.

2. Government Research Corporation, "Dinner Date on Labor Day," *National Journal* 3, no. 38 (January 30, 1971), 239.

3. "Nixon Snubs White; Black Labor Leader," *Daily Defender*, September 1, 1970.

4. "A New Design for the Postal Service: A Private Corporation," speech delivered before the Magazine Publishers Association and the American Society of Magazine Editors, Shoreham Hotel, Washington, DC, April 3, 1967. See Lawrence O'Brien, "A New Design for the Postal Service," *Vital Speeches of the Day* 33, no. 14 (May 1, 1967), 418–21.

5. Philip F. Rubio, *There's Always Work at the Post Office: African American Postal Workers and the Fight for Jobs, Justice and Equality* (Chapel Hill: University of North Carolina Press, 2010), 274 (emphasis added).

6. "The NIH Task Force against Racism and Discrimination," *A.C.E. Newsletter* (All Concerned Employees) 1, no. 1, July 12, 1971.

7. George Lardner Jr., "On Tapes, Nixon Sounds Off on Women, Blacks, Cabinet," *Washington Post*, December 27, 1998.

8. Alf J. Mapp Jr., *Thomas Jefferson: Passionate Pilgrim* (Lanham, MD: Rowman and Littlefield, 1991), 12.

9. "Chocolate City" is the name of a song from a similarly titled album of George Clinton and his funk band Parliament in 1975. See also Kenneth Carroll, "As Chocolate City Gathered Confidence after the Success of the Civil Rights Movement, D.C.'s Varied Black Communities Found a Common Anthem," *Washington Post*, February 1, 1998.

10. By 1980, the black proportion decreased slightly to 70.3 percent (448,906). Campbell Gibson and Kay Jung, "Table 23, District of Columbia—Race and Hispanic Origin: 1800 to 1990," *Historical Census Statistics on Population Totals by Race, 1790 to 1990, and by Hispanic Origin, 1970 to 1990, for the United States, Regions, Divisions, and States*, U.S. Bureau of the Census, Working Paper Series no. 56, September 2002, accessed November 30, 2012, www.census.gov/population/wwwdocumentation/twps0056/twps0056.htm.

11. "7 Unions Are Accused of Working against Black Postal Employes," *New York Times*, August 11, 1971.

12. "Hardships Plague Federal Employees," *Afro American*, May 19, 1970.

13. "Hardships Plague Federal Employees."

14. U.S. Commission on Civil Rights, *Equal Opportunity in Suburbia: A Report of the United States Commission on Civil Rights* (Washington, DC: Government Printing Office, 1974), 12.

15. U.S. Commission on Civil Rights, *The Movement of Federal Facilities to the Suburbs* (Washington, DC: Government Printing Office, 1971), vi.

16. DC's black population peaked at 71.5 percent in 1970. See U.S. Bureau of the Census, *District of Columbia—Race and Hispanic Origin: 1800—1990.*

17. Internal memorandum from Executive Assistant to the Postmaster General circa July 2, 1971, RG 28, NARA.

18. A postal service spokesman said, "Admittedly, the move to the suburbs works hardship on some employees, white and black. But we have tried to soften the impact when it does occur." Bart Barnes, "Blacks Said Losing Jobs in Post Office," *Washington Post*, August 3, 1971.

19. U.S. Bureau of the Census, Maryland: Population of Counties by Decennial Census, 1900–1990, accessed June 23, 2013, http://www.census.gov/population/cen counts/md190090.txt.

20. U.S. Commission on Civil Rights, *Equal Opportunity in Suburbia* (Washington, DC: Government Printing Office, 1974), 7.

21. U.S. Commission on Civil Rights, *Federal Installations and Equal Housing Opportunity* (Washington, DC: Government Printing Office, 1970), 21.

22. U.S. Commission on Civil Rights, *Federal Installations*, 21.

23. E.O. 11512 was revoked with issuance of EO 12072 on August 16, 1978, which requires all federal agencies to first consider central business areas without any consideration of housing, parking, or adequate access to the central business area, in contrast to E.O. 11512.

24. Executive Order 11512 signed on February 27, 1970 by President Richard M. Nixon. American Presidency Project, "Executive Order 11512—Planning, Acquisition, and Management of Federal Space," accessed November 25, 2012, http://www .presidency.ucsb.edu/ws/index.php?pid=60482.

25. U.S. Commission on Civil Rights, *Equal Opportunity in Suburbia*, 48.

26. U.S. Commission on Civil Rights, *Equal Opportunity in Suburbia*, 48.

27. Based on consistent patterns of disparate treatment for black-collar workers, the presumption of nonracist intentions must be questioned and the uglier alternative seriously considered.

28. William Raspberry, "'White Noose' Grips Suburban Housing," *Washington Post*, March 24, 1967.

29. "The positive impact of race on probability of employment, together with the low Black/White earnings ratio, suggests that discrimination against black males occurs mainly in upgrading or in hiring to fill relatively well-paying positions." James E. Long, "Employment Discrimination in the Federal Sector," *Journal of Human Resources* 11, no. 1 (Winter 1976), 96.

30. U.S. Department of Commerce, Bureau of the Census, "Current Population Reports, Series P-60, Money Income of Families and Persons in the United States" (Washington, DC: Government Printing Office, 1970), nos. 105 and 157.

31. Only 16,318 or 11.8 percent of black federal employees were slotted in grades GS 9–11 ($9,320–$14,599) while 6,511 or 4.7 percent were found in grades GS 12–18 ($13,389–$33,495). U.S. Civil Service Commission, "Study of Minority Group Employment in the Federal Government," November 30, 1969 (Washington, DC: Government Printing Office, 1969), 30.

32. By 1980, the black proportion decreased slightly to 70.3 percent (448,906). Gibson and Jung, "Table 23, District of Columbia."

33. U.S. Bureau of the Census, Characteristics of the Population, part 10 District of Columbia, "Table 92, Employment Characteristics of the Negro Population for Areas and Places, 1970" (Washington, DC: Government Printing Office, 1973).

34. That is, 3,063 out of 118,856 males. Data are unavailable for black federal worker salaries working in the nation's capital during this same period. U.S. Bureau of the Census, Government Workers. "Census of Population: 1970, Subject Reports, Final Report PC(2)-7D." (Washington, DC: Government Printing Office, 1970), 315.

35. Robert Sadacca, *The Validity and Discriminatory Impact of the Federal Service Entrance Examination* (Washington, DC: Urban Institute, 1971), 22.

36. *Douglas v. Hampton*, 512 F.2d 976 (D.C. Cir. 1975), 982.

37. Timothy S. Robinson, "Police, Job Tests Adjudged Biased," *Washington Post*, February 28, 1975.

38. Claudia Levy, "Job Bias by U.S. Is Talks Topic," *Washington Post*, September 20, 1972.

39. U.S. Department of Commerce Bureau of the Census, "No. 477, Minority Group Full-Time Employment in the Federal Government, All Agencies, by Pay System: 1972 and 1978." *Statistical Abstract of the United States, 1980* (Washington, DC: Government Printing Office, 1980), 284.

40. "Whites are much less likely to support concrete implementation of principles than principles themselves . . . the principles have some force but often lose out when they conflict with other principles (such as 'individualism'), with personal goals or with personal preferences." See Howard Schuman et al., *Racial Attitudes in America: Trends and Interpretations* (Cambridge, MA: Harvard University Press, 1985), 205.

41. U.S. Commission on Civil Rights, *The Federal Civil Rights Enforcement Effort: A Reassessment* (Washington, DC: Government Printing Office, 1973), 42–43.

42. Paul Delaney, "Top Black Woman Is Ousted by NASA," *New York Times*, October 28, 1973.

43. Ruth Bates Harris, *Harlem Princess: The Story of Harry Delaney's Daughter* (New York: Vantage Press, 1999), 4; Kim McQuaid, "'Racism, Sexism, and Space Ventures': Civil Rights at NASA in the Nixon Era and Beyond," in *Societal Impact of Space-flight*, ed. Steven J. Dick and Roger D. Launius (Washington, DC: NASA Office of External Relations, History Division, 2007), 427.

44. Sociologist Robert Hauser finds that "the college entry chances of white men declined in the last half of the 1970s and then rose by 1988 to a peak above that of the

1970s. In the mid-1970s, about 53 percent of white men entered college; the college entry rate dropped to 50 percent by 1980 but increased to 60 percent in 1988. The series shows growth in black college entry chances relative to those of whites during the 1970s, with a peak late in the decade. At the peak, the college-going chances of blacks were almost equal to those of whites." Robert M. Hauser, "Trends in College Entry among Whites, Blacks and Hispanics," in *Studies of Supply and Demand in Higher Education*, ed. Charles T. Clotfelter and Michael Rothschild (Chicago: University of Chicago Press, 1993), 70. See also Steve Curwood, "Harmful Effects Feared as Enrollments Drop," *Boston Globe*, May 20, 1986.

45. Alex Poinsett, "Annual Progress Report, 1973: Year of Watergate," *Ebony Magazine* 30, no. 3 (January 1974), 33.

46. Mark Lawrence, "At GPO, 15-Year Job Bias Fight Ends; $2.4 Million Settlement Reached in Black Workers' Suit," *Washington Post*, August 12, 1987.

47. Tim O'Brien, "NASA Official Fights Ouster," *Washington Post*, October 29, 1973.

48. McQuaid, "'Racism, Sexism, and Space Ventures,'" 423.

49. *Minority Employees at NASA (MEAN) v. James M. Beggs*, 723 F.2d 958 (D.C. Cir. 1983).

50. Kim McQuaid, "Race, Gender, and Space Exploration: A Chapter in the Social History of the Space Age," *Journal of American Studies* 41, no. 2 (July 2007), 405.

51. McQuaid, "Race, Gender, and Space Exploration," 434.

52. "Ruth Bates Harris Assumes New Post at NASA," *Astrogram* 16, no. 25 (September 12, 1974), 1.

53. Miles Waggoner, "Remarks of Ruth Bates Harris at Summer Institute Closing Activity," *NASA News*, Release no. 75–239, September 15, 1975.

54. McQuaid, "'Racism, Sexism, and Space Ventures,'" 442. Harris's son died of what was later diagnosed as AIDS. See also *New York Times Book Review* 98 (August 1, 1993), 14.

55. *Womack v. Lynn*, 504 F.2d 267 (D.C. Cir. 1974).

56. "Samuel Simmons Appointed President of Black Aged," *Jet Magazine* 62, no. 5 (April 12, 1982), 6.

57. Simeon Booker, "Ticker Tape U.S.A.," *Jet Magazine* 54, no. 24 (August 31, 1978), 11.

58. Gail Fineberg, "Court Clears Way for Cook Case Payout," Library of Congress, November 18, 1996, accessed July 11, 2017, http://www.loc.gov/loc/lcib/9620/cook.html.

59. R. C. Newell, "Rap GPO Job Bias," *Afro American*, November 15, 1975.

60. *McKenzie v. McCormick*, 425 F.Supp. 137 (D.D.C.1977); see also "Judge finds GPO Bosses Guilty of Racism in Promotion Evaluations," *Washington Star*, January 26, 1977.

61. *McKenzie v. McCormick*, p. 139.

62. Todd Richissin, "Alfred McKenzie, 80, Airman Who Fought for Civil Rights," *Baltimore Sun*, April 6, 1998.

63. "Racism Found Lingering in Printing Office Unit," *Washington Post*, January 13, 1977.

64. Mark Lawrence, "At GPO, 15-Year Job Bias Fight Ends," *Washington Post*, August 12, 1987.

65. Richard Goldstein, "Alfred McKenzie, Who Fought for Rights, Dies at 80," *New York Times*, April 11, 1998.

66. Booker, "Ticker Tape U.S.A.," 10.

67. "ACLU Cites Gardener," *Afro American*, December 9, 1978.

68. Nancy Ferris, "A Long Discrimination Fight Finally," *Washington Star*, November 20, 1977.

69. William Raspberry, "Can't Make Reparations, NIH Claims," *Washington Post*, October 13, 1969.

70. U.S. Congress House Committee on Education, Discrimination in Employment (Oversight), "Testimony of Hoover Rowel," Ninety-Second Congress, Second Session, October 20, 1972 (Washington, DC: Government Printing Office, 1972), 273.

71. Raspberry, "Lawyer Says NIH Words, Deeds Don't Jibe."

72. William Raspberry, "Lawyer Says NIH Words, Deeds Don't Jibe on Job Equality," *Washington Post*, October 12, 1969.

73. Raspberry, "Lawyer Says NIH Words, Deeds Don't Jibe."

74. William Raspberry, "Discrimination at NIH: Winning and Waiting," *Washington Post*, October 24, 1975.

75. Ferris, "Long Discrimination Fight Finally."

76. U.S. Commission on Civil Rights, *The Federal Civil Rights Enforcement Effort*, 42–43.

77. Perlo, "Trends in the Economic Status of the Negro People," 234.

78. Clarence Hunter, "New Group Seeks Place in Sun with Black Federal Workers," *Baltimore Afro-American*, September 11, 1982, 14.

79. Johnny Scott's Answers to Interview Questions about BIG National Training Conference, August 2010, RBIG.

80. Black WWII soldiers of the 92nd Infantry reclaimed the moniker "Buffalo Soldiers," as it also refers to the nickname given to black soldiers by Native Americans after the Civil War in the late nineteenth century. Abby Callard, "Memoirs of a World War II Buffalo Soldier," *Smithsonian.com*, November 6, 2009, accessed September 16, 2012, http://www.smithsonianmag.com/history-archaeology/Memoirs-of-a-World-War-II-Buffalo-Soldier-.html.

81. Jason Tomassini, "Buffalo Soldier Chronicles his Battles in Europe and at Home," *Montgomery Gazette*, July 8, 2009.

82. 156 Cong. Rec. E439, "Honoring James Harden 'Pat' Daugherty and the Buffalo Soldiers," *Congressional Record* 155, no. 182, (Washington, DC: Government Printing Office, 2010).

83. Pritchett, "National Issue," 1325.

84. Papers of Blacks in Government, Memorandum, "The History of the Formation of Blacks in Government (BIG) (Parklawn Chapter, December 1975 and the National Organization, January 1977), James Daugherty, n.d., RBIG.

85. U.S. Commission on Civil Rights, *To Eliminate Employment Discrimination: The Federal Civil Rights Enforcement Effort–1974* (Washington, DC: Government Printing Office 1975), 5.

86. Karlyn Barker, "Blacks Allegedly Pressured to Quit U.S. Jobs," *Washington Post*, September 3, 1982.

87. "NAACP, UL, Labor Groups Go after Black Voters," *Jet Magazine*, 51, no. 1 (September 23, 1976), 21.

88. Letter from BIG Chairman Pat Daugherty to Thomas McFee, Acting Assistant Secretary for Administration and Management, DHEW, March 16, 1977, RBIG.

89. Daugherty to McFee, March 16, 1977, RBIG.

90. Letter from Thomas McFee, Acting Assistant Secretary for Administration and Management, DHEW to BIG Chairman Pat Daughtery, March 30, 1977, RBIG.

91. "Documenting Your EEO Complaint," n.d., RBIG.

92. Patricia A. Taylor, "Income Inequality in the Federal Civilian Government," *American Sociological Review* 44, no. 3 (June 1979), 469.

93. Internal National Memorandum from BIG President Rubye Fields, "A Message from BIG," *Blacks in Government Winning Ways*, ca. 1979, RBIG.

94. "Our Town," *Washington Post*, October 18, 1979.

95. "First National Conference Attracts over 2,200," *BIG News* 1, no. 1 (December 1980), 1. Also underscoring the sensitivity around attendance, BIG national historian Jacqueline Beatty relays the following anecdote: BIG published two separate conference programs: one listing the daily workshops and another listing the social activities. Conference organizers feared that any mention of social activities would diminish the legitimacy of the conference in the eyes of white supervisors responsible for approving and authorizing official travel on the job. BIG National Historian, C. Jacqueline Beatty's Answers to Interview Questions about BIG National Training Conference, August 2011, RBIG.

96. The second annual conference, also held in Washington, DC, in September 1980, attracted more than 4,200 participants. "First National Conference Attracts over 2,200."

97. Dan Elasky, "Civil Rights During the Carter Administration, 1977–1981: Part 1: Papers of the Special Assistant for Black Affairs, Section A," 17, accessed May 17, 2012 http://cisupa.proquest.com/ksc_assets/catalog/102657.pdf.

98. "Next National Conference!" *BIG News* 1, no. 1 (March 1980), 2.

99. Mark W. Huddleston and William W. Boye, *The Higher Civil Service in the United States: Quest for Reform* (Pittsburgh: University of Pittsburgh Press, 1996), 109.

100. Peter K. Eisinger, *Black Employment in City Government, 1973–1980* (Washington, DC: Joint Center for Political Studies, 1983), 1.

101. Congressional Budget Office, "Educational Attainment of Salaried Full-Time Permanent Federal Civilian Employees, by Occupational Category, 1975 to 2005." *Characteristics and Pay of Federal Civilian Employees,* (Washington, DC: Government Printing Office, 2007), 18.

102. U.S. Bureau of the Census, *Statistical Abstract of the United States, 1970* (Washington, DC: Government Printing Office, 1970), 397. The value of $8,000 to $12,000 in 1975 roughly equates to $34,000 to $51,000 in 2012. Office of Price Administration, Rates of Pay Under the General Schedule, Effective the First Pay Period Beginning on or after October 1, 1975, accessed November 20, 2012, www.opm.gov/oca/pre1994/1975_GS.pdf.

103. U.S. Department of Commerce Bureau of the Census, "No. 477 Minority Group Full-Time Employment in the Federal Government, All Agencies, by Pay System: 1972 and 1978" (Washington, DC: Government Printing Office, 1980), 284.

104. Businesses with fewer than 250 workers or with a federal contract less than $1 million in value would be exempt from generating written summaries of their affirmative action programs. This plan was eventually abandoned two years later thanks in part to pressure from Congress and the EEOC. Frank Dobbin, *Inventing Equal Opportunity* (Princeton, NJ: Princeton University Press, 2009), 136.

105. Kathy Sawyer, "Proposal to Ease Job Bias Rules Draws Criticism from Both Sides," *Washington Post*, August 26, 1981. Also note that the affirmative action reduction proposal came only three weeks after President Ronald Reagan's administration communicated its hard-line stance against federal workplace improvements when he fired over 11,000 striking air traffic controllers. See also, McCartin, *Collision Course.*

106. Quote from U.S. Chamber of Commerce attorney John B. Brandenburg. Sawyer, "Proposal to Ease Job Bias Rules."

107. Nancy M. Modesitt, "Reinventing the EEOC," *SMU Law Review* 63 (2010), 1241.

EPILOGUE: A MOVING PICTURE OF BLACK WORKERS, 1980–1981

1. "Family Guy DMV," YouTube video, 0:33, posted by "aleguzmanb," October 2, 2009, https://www.youtube.com/watch?v=CS4DnwrXThU. This episode first aired May 14, 2006.

2. American Presidency Project, "Ronald Reagan Inaugural Address: January 20, 1981," accessed June 23, 2017, http://www.presidency.ucsb.edu/ws/?pid=43130 (emphasis added).

3. Kevin L. Lyles, *The Gatekeepers: Federal District Courts in the Political Process* (Westport, CT: Praeger, 1997), 133.

4. Lyles, *Gatekeepers*, 133. The Office of Federal Contract Compliance voluntarily limited its jurisdiction to "government contractors with 250 or more employees and a federal contract of one million dollars or more."

5. CNN Politics data indicate that only 7 of a total of 353 federal judiciary appointees during Reagan's tenure were black, with less than 7 percent total being nonwhite. Joan Biskupic, Aaron Kessler and Ryan Struyk, "Trump Judicial Picks Lack Decades-Long Diversity Drive," *CNN Politics*, November 30, 2017, accessed December 12, 2017, http://www.cnn.com/2017/11/30/politics/trump-judges-courts-race/index .html.

6. With the signing of the twenty-five-year extension, the "grass-roots lobbying and legislative campaign had forced Mr. Reagan and Attorney General William French Smith to abandon their plan to ease the restrictions in the landmark civil rights legislation." Howell Raines, "Voting Rights Act Signed by Reagan," *New York Times*, June 30, 1982.

7. Reagan only reversed his stance after public opposition as part of a "salvage operation" to repair his image as nonracist. Steven R. Weisman, "Reagan Acts to Bar Tax Break to Schools in Racial Bias Cases," *New York Times*, January 19, 1982.

8. Andrew Rosenthal, "Reagan Hints Civil Rights Leaders Exaggerate Racism to Preserve Cause," *New York Times*, January 14, 1989.

9. Francis X. Clines, "Reagan's Doubts on Dr. King Disclosed," *New York Times*, October 22, 1983.

10. The *Chicago Tribune* actually first invoked the term "welfare queen" when covering the true story of career con artist Linda Taylor. Josh Levin, "The Real Story of Linda Taylor, America's Original Welfare Queen," *Chicago Tribune*, December 19, 2013.

11. "'The Welfare Queen driving a pink Cadillac to cash her welfare checks at the liquor store fits a narrative that many white, working-class Americans had about inner-city blacks,' [history professor John] Hinshaw says. 'It doesn't matter if the story was fabricated, it fit the narrative, and so it felt true, and it didn't need to be verified.'" This disparaging imaging helped to stereotype welfare during the Reagan era along racial lines, and was increasingly seen as a burdensome waste, although welfare was not seen as causing poverty during the Depression era when the federal government made strategic investments to help mostly white citizens. John Blake, "Return of the 'Welfare Queen,'" *CNN*, January 23, 2012, accessed September 14, 2017, http://www .cnn.com/2012/01/23/politics/weflare-queen/index.html.

12. John F. Zipp, "Government Employment and Black-White Earnings Inequality, 1980–1990," *Social Problems* 41, no. 3 (August 1994), 378.

13. U.S. Office of Personnel Management, "Annual Report to Congress: Federal Equal Opportunity and Recruitment Program," January 2007, accessed July 11, 2017,

https://www.opm.gov/policy-data-oversight/diversity-and-inclusion/reports/feorp 2006.pdf.

14. Patricia Cohen, "Public-Sector Jobs Vanish, Hitting Blacks Hard," *New York Times*, May 24, 2015.

15. Greg Schneider and Renae Merle, "Reagan's Defense Buildup Bridged Military Eras," *Washington Post*, June 9, 2004; Robert Pear, "Reagan's Social Impact," *New York Times*, August 25, 1982.

16. Associated Press, "Government Cheese Goes to Poor as President Signs Farm Bill," *New York Times*, December 23, 1981.

17. Zipp, "Government Employment," 380.

18. Jeffrey B. Perry, ed., *A Hubert Harrison Reader* (Middletown, CT: Wesleyan University Press, 2001) 282.

19. *Congressional Record Online*, "Pigford Settlement," *Congressional Record* 156, no. 118 (Thursday, August 5, 2010), accessed September 14, 2017, https://www.gpo.gov/fdsys/pkg/CREC-2010-08-05/html/CREC-2010-08-05-pt1-PgS6836.htm, S6836-S6837.

20. President's Committee on Civil Rights (PCCR), *To Secure These Rights* (Washington, DC: Government Printing Office, 1947).

21. Sally Kohn, "Affirmative Action Has Helped White Women More Than Anyone," *TIME*, June 17, 2013.

22. Horace Huntley and David Montgomery, eds., *Black Workers' Struggle for Equality in Birmingham* (Champaign: University of Illinois Press, 2007), 228.

23. *EEOC History: 35th Anniversary: 1965–2000*, "1965–1971: A 'Toothless Tiger' Helps Shape the Law and Educate the Public," circa 2000, accessed December 28, 2017, https://www.eeoc.gov/eeoc/history/35th/1965-71/index.html.

24. A "house subcommittee held hearings on the commission having run up a backlog of nearly 100,000 cases last September (1973)," a mere decade after the EEOC's inception. Marilyn Bender, "Job Discrimination, 10 Years Later," *New York Times*, November 10, 1974. "The [Health, Education, Labor and Pensions] HELP minority report points out that the EEOC has a pending inventory of 70,781 complaints of discrimination as of March 2014," U.S. Equal Employment Opportunity Commission, "EEOC Response to Senate HELP Minority Staff Report," November 28, 2014, accessed October 25, 2017, https://www.eeoc.gov/eeoc/legislative/report_response_final.cfm.

25. John McWhorter, "Racism in America Is Over," *Forbes*, December 30, 2008.

26. "Wu-Tang Clan—C.R.E.A.M.," YouTube video, 4:51, posted by "WuTangClan-VEVO," January 21, 2014, https://www.youtube.com/watch?v=PBwAxmrE194.

27. See generally, George M. Fredrickson, *Black Image in the White Mind: The Debate on Afro-American Character and Destiny, 1817–1914* (New York: Harper and Row, 1971).

28. PCCR, *To Secure These Rights*, 59.

29. U.S. Commission on Civil Rights, *Employment: 1961 United States Commission on Civil Rights Report, Book. 3* (Washington, DC: Government Printing Office, 1961), 27.

30. U.S. Commission on Civil Rights, *The Federal Civil Rights Enforcement Effort: A Reassessment* (Washington, DC: Government Printing Office, 1973), 42–43.

31. U.S. Merit Systems Protection Board, "Fair & Equitable Treatment: A Progress Report on Minority Employment in the Federal Government" (Washington, DC: Office of Policy and Evaluation, 1996), viii, accessed June 23, 2017, https://www.mspb.gov/MSPBSEARCH/viewdocs.aspx?docnumber=253658&version=253945&application=ACROBAT.

32. U.S. Equal Employment Opportunity Commission, "EEOC African American Workgroup Report," January, 2010, accessed October 21, 2017, https://www.eeoc.gov/federal/reports/aawg.cfm.

33. "In many instances, although the committee or the agencies felt that the evidence did not support a finding of discrimination, investigation disclosed discriminatory practices which needed correction." U.S. Commission on Civil Rights, *Employment*, 23.

34. General George Washington inscribed the phrase in a letter to Colonel Benedict Arnold dated September 14, 1775. Edwin Anderson Alderman, Joel Chandler Harris and Charles William Kent, *Library of Southern Literature: Biography* (Atlanta, GA: Martin and Hoyt, 1907), 5647.

35. MPR News, "King's 'Promissory Note' Remains in Default," August 28, 2013.

36. Gary Younge, *The Speech: The Story behind Dr. Martin Luther King Jr.'s Dream* (Chicago: Haymarket Books, 2013), xv (emphasis added).

37. Emily Wax-Thibodeaux, "Hispanics Following African Americans' Example in Finding Government Jobs," *Washington Post*, December 3, 2013.

BIBLIOGRAPHY

ARCHIVAL AND MANUSCRIPT COLLECTIONS

Harry S. Truman Presidential Library, Independence, MO

  Records of the President's Committee on Civil Rights (RPCCR)

Library of Congress, Washington, DC

  Manuscript Division

Records of the National Association for the Advancement of Colored People (RNAACP)

Records of the National Urban League (RNUL)

National Archives and Records Administration, College Park, College Park, MD (NARA)

Papers of Julius Hobson, Washingtoniana Division. Martin Luther King Jr. Memorial Library, Washington, DC (PJH)

Records of Blacks in Government, BIG National Headquarters, Washington, DC (RBIG)

Records of the National Alliance for Postal and Federal Employees, NAPFE National Headquarters, Washington, DC (RNAPFE)

GOVERNMENT DOCUMENTS

California Department of Finance. 2008 California Statistical Abstract: Table B-1, Population of California and the United States 1940 to 2007. Accessed May 31, 2013. http://www.dof .ca.gov/HTML/FS_DATA/STAT-ABS/documents/CaliforniaStatisticalAbstract2008.pdf.

Committee on Employment Discrimination. *Fair Employment Practices Commission Reference Manual.* New York: National Community Relations Council, 1948.

Congressional Budget Office. "Educational Attainment of Salaried Full-Time Permanent Federal Civilian Employees, by Occupational Category, 1975 to 2005." *Characteristics and Pay of Federal Civilian Employees.* Washington, DC: Government Printing Office, 2007.

Congressional Record Online. "Pigford Settlement." *Congressional Record* 156, no. 118 (Thursday, August 5, 2010). Accessed September 14, 2017. https://www.gpo.gov/fdsys/pkg/CREC -2010-08-05/html/CREC-2010-08-05-pt1-PgS6836.htm.

Douglas v. Hampton, 512 F.2d 976 (D.C. Cir. 1975).

Equal Employment Opportunity Commission (EEOC) EEOC History: 35th Anniversary: 1965–2000, "1965–1971: A 'Toothless Tiger' Helps Shape the Law and Educate the Public," ca. 2000. Accessed April 20, 2018. https://www.eeoc.gov/eeoc/history/35th/1965-71/index .html.

Executive Order 9980. Harry S. Truman Library and Museum, Executive Orders, Harry S. Tru-
    man 1945–1953. Accessed October 21, 2012. http://trumanlibrary.org/executiveorders/in
    dex.php?pid=29.

Executive Order 11512. February 27, 1970. "American Presidency Project." Accessed November
    25, 2012. http://www.presidency.ucsb.edu/ws/index.php?pid=60482.

Federal Security Agency. "Washington, D.C. Eleanor Roosevelt Visiting Lucy D. Slowe
    Hall, Women's Dormitory for Negro War Workers." FSA-OWI Collection [LC-USW3–
    028297-C], May 1943. Prints & Photographs Division, Library of Congress.

General Services Administration. "Special Message to the Congress on Civil Rights." February
    2, 1948. *Public Papers of the Presidents: Harry S. Truman*. Washington, DC: Government
    Printing Office, 1964.

Hobson v. Hansen, 269 F. Supp. 401 (D.D.C. 1967).

McKenzie v. McCormick, 425 F.Supp. 137 (D.D.C. 1977).

Minority Employees at NASA v. James M. Beggs, 723 F.2d 958 (D.C. Cir. 1983).

National Diet Library (Japan). Text of the Constitution and Other Important Documents. "Pots-
    dam Declaration." Accessed July 11, 2017. http://www.ndl.go.jp/constitution/e/etc/c06.html.

Office of Price Administration (OPA). "Rates of Pay Under the General Schedule, Effective the
    First Pay Period Beginning on or after October 1, 1975." Accessed November 20, 2012. www
    .opm.gov/oca/pre1994/1975_GS.pdf.

President's Committee on Civil Rights (PCCR). *To Secure These Rights*. Washington, DC: Gov-
    ernment Printing Office, 1947.

Public Administration Review. "Federal Position Classification and Pay Legislation." *Public Ad-
    ministration Review* 9, no. 4 (Autumn 1949), 298–99.

Social Security Administration. "Social Security History: Organizational History." N.d. Ac-
    cessed July 11, 2013. http://www.ssa.gov/history/orghist.html.

Social Security Administration. "Social Security History: Oscar R. Ewing." N.d. Accessed De-
    cember 12, 2012. http://www.ssa.gov/history/ewing.html.U.S. Bureau of the Census. *Chang-
    ing Characteristics of the Negro Population*. Washington, DC: Government Printing Office,
    1969.

U.S. Bureau of the Census. Characteristics of the Population, part 10 District of Columbia. "Ta-
    ble 92, Employment Characteristics of the Negro Population for Areas and Places, 1970."
    Washington, DC: Government Printing Office, 1973.

U.S. Bureau of the Census. District of Columbia, 1940. "Table 18, Race of Employed Persons (Ex-
    cept on Public Emergency Work), and of Experienced Workers Seeking Work, by Industry
    and Sex, for the District of Columbia." Washington, DC: Government Printing Office, 1940.

U.S. Bureau of the Census. "District of Columbia—Race and Hispanic Origin: 1800–1990." Ac-
    cessed May 31, 2013. http://www.census.gov/population/www/documentation/twps0056/
    tab23.pdf.

U.S. Bureau of the Census. "Education & Social Stratification Branch Percent of People 25 Years
    and Over Who Have Completed High School or College, by Race, Hispanic Origin and
    Sex: Selected Years 1940 to 2008." Washington, DC: U.S. Government Printing Office, 2008.

U.S. Bureau of the Census. Government Workers. "Census of Population: 1970, Subject Reports, Final Report PC(2)-7D." Washington, DC: Government Printing Office, 1970.

U.S. Bureau of the Census. "Maryland: Population of Counties by Decennial Census, 1900— 1990." Accessed May 12, 2013. http://www.census.gov/population/cencounts/md190090. txt.

U.S. Bureau of the Census. 1940 National Census. "Table 16, Wage or Salary Income Received in 1939 by all Experienced Persons in the Labor Force." Washington, DC: Government Printing Office, 1940.

U.S. Bureau of the Census. *Statistical Abstract of the United States, 1970.* Washington, DC: Government Printing Office, 1970.

U.S. Bureau of the Census. "Table 4, Percent of the Population 25 Years and Over with a Bachelor's Degree or Higher by Sex, Race, and Hispanic Origin, for the United States: 1940 to 2000." Accessed May 10, 2013. http://www.census.gov/hhes/socdemo/education/data/census/half-century/tables.html.

U.S. Bureau of the Census. "Table 23, District of Columbia—Race and Hispanic Origin: 1800 to 1990." Historical Census Statistics on Population Totals by Race, 1790 to 1990, and by Hispanic Origin, 1970 to 1990, for the United States, Regions, Divisions, and States. September 2002. Accessed November 30, 2012. www.census.gov/population/wwwdocumentation/twps0056/twps0056.htm.

U.S. Civil Service Commission. *Challenge and Change: Annual Report, 1968.* Washington, DC: Government Printing Office, 1968.

U.S. Civil Service Commission. "Study of Minority Group Employment in the Federal Government." Washington, DC: Government Printing Office, 1969.

U.S. Civil Service Commission. *To Know or Not to Know: Collection and Use of Racial and Ethnic Data in Federal Assistance Programs.* Washington, DC: Government Printing Office, 1973.

U.S. Commission on Civil Rights. *Employment: 1961 United States Commission on Civil Rights Report, Book 3.* Washington, DC: Government Printing Office, 1961.

U.S. Commission on Civil Rights. *Equal Opportunity in Suburbia: A Report of the United States Commission on Civil Rights.* Washington, DC: Government Printing Office, 1974.

U.S. Commission on Civil Rights. *Federal Installations and Equal Housing Opportunity.* Washington, DC: Government Printing Office, 1970.

U.S. Commission on Civil Rights. *The Federal Civil Rights Enforcement Effort: A Reassessment.* Washington, DC: Government Printing Office, 1973.

U.S. Commission on Civil Rights. *The Movement of Federal Facilities to the Suburbs.* District of Columbia Advisory Committee. Washington, DC: Government Printing Office, 1971.

U.S. Commission on Civil Rights. *To Eliminate Employment Discrimination: The Federal Civil Rights Enforcement Effort–1974.* Washington, DC: Government Printing Office 1975.

U.S. Congress House Committee on Education, Discrimination in Employment (Oversight). "Testimony of Hoover Rowel." Ninety-Second Congress, Second Session, October 20, 1972. Washington, DC: Government Printing Office, 1972.

U.S. Department of Commerce. Bureau of the Census. "Current Population Reports, 1970." Series P-60, Money Income of Families and Persons in the United States. Washington, DC: Government Printing Office, 1970, nos. 105 and 157.

U.S. Department of Commerce. Bureau of the Census. "No. 477, Minority Group Full-Time Employment in the Federal Government, All Agencies, by Pay System: 1972 and 1978." *Statistical Abstract of the United States, 1980*. Washington, DC: Government Printing Office, 1980.

U.S. Department of Commerce. Bureau of the Census. "No. 901 Establishments, Employees and Payroll by Industry and Employment-Size, Class: 1979." *Statistical Abstract of the United States, 1981*. Washington, DC: Government Printing Office, 1981.

U.S. Department of Commerce. Current Population Reports. "Percent Distribution of Families and Individuals by Total Money Income Level, by Color of Head, for the Washington (DC) Metropolitan District: 1947." Series P-60, no. 4. Washington, DC: Government Printing Office, 1948.

U.S. Department of Labor. "The African American Labor Force in the Recovery." February 19, 2012. Accessed May 14, 2013. http://www.dol.gov/_sec/media/reports/blacklaborforce/.

U.S. Department of Labor. "Negro Women and Their Jobs." *Women's Bureau Leaflet*, no. 19, January 1954. Washington, DC: Government Printing Office, 1954.

U.S. Department of Labor. The Organic Act of the Department of Labor. Accessed November 19, 2012. www.dol.gov/oasam/programs/history/organact.htm#.UKptwxB5mSM.

U.S. Equal Employment Opportunity Commission (EEOC). "EEOC African American Workgroup Report." January, 2010. Accessed October 21, 2017. https://www.eeoc.gov/federal/reports/aawg.cfm.

U.S. Equal Employment Opportunity Commission (EEOC). "EEOC Response to Senate HELP Minority Staff Report." November 28, 2014. Accessed October 25, 2017. https://www.eeoc.gov/eeoc/legislative/report_response_final.cfm.

U.S. Equal Employment Opportunity Commission (EEOC). Section A. "Equal Opportunity in the Federal Work Force, as part of the Equal Employment Opportunity Commission's Annual Report on the Federal Work Force, Fiscal Year 2004." N.d. Accessed February 21 2013. http://www.eeoc.gov/federal/reports/fsp2004/section1a.html.

U.S. Merit Systems Protection Board. "Fair & Equitable Treatment: A Progress Report on Minority Employment in the Federal Government." Washington, DC: Office of Policy and Evaluation, 1996. Accessed June 13, 2017. https://www.mspb.gov/MSPBSEARCH/viewdocs.aspx?docnumber=253658&version=253945&application=ACROBAT.

U.S. Office of Personnel Management (OPA). "Pay & Leave: Salaries & Wages." January 2018. Accessed January 2, 2018. https://www.opm.gov/policy-data-oversight/pay-leave/salaries-wages/salary-tables/18Tables/html/GS.aspx.

U.S. Office of Personnel Management (OPA). "Annual Report to Congress: Federal Equal Opportunity and Recruitment Program," January 2007. Accessed July 11, 2017. https://www.opm.gov/policy-data-oversight/diversity-and-inclusion/reports/feorp2006.pdf.

U.S. Postal Service, "History of the U.S. Postal Service." N.d. Accessed April 3, 2012. http://www.usps.com/history/history/his3.htm#REORG.

United States Senate. "Antidiscrimination in Employment: Hearings Before the Subcommit-
    tee on Civil Rights of the Committee on Labor and Public Welfare, United States Senate,
    Eighty-third Congress, Second Session, on S. 692, a Bill to Prohibit Discrimination in Em-
    ployment Because of Race, Color, Religion, National Origin, Or Ancestry." Washington,
    DC: Government Printing Office, 1954.
United States Senate. "Landmark Legislation: The Civil Rights Act of 1964." N.d. Accessed April
    20, 2018. https://www.senate.gov/artandhistory/history/common/generic/CivilRightsAct
    1964.htm.
Womack v. Lynn, 504 F.2d 267, 8 FEP Cases 841 (D.C. Cir. 1974).

NEWSPAPERS AND PERIODICALS

Afro American

Astrogram

Baltimore Afro-American

Baltimore Sun

BIG News

Black Enterprise

Boston Globe

Bureaucrat

Chicago Defender

Congressional Record

Daily Defender

Ebony Magazine

Education Reporter

Evening Star

Federal Register

Forbes

Jet Magazine

Montgomery Gazette

National Alliance

New York Times

New York Times Book Review

Pittsburgh Courier

Pittsburgh Post-Gazette

Postal Alliance

Springfield Star

Sunday Star

TIME

Vital Speeches of the Day

Washington Examiner

Washington Pittsburgh Courier

Washington Post

Washington Star

Washington Times-Herald

Washington Tribune

PUBLICATIONS, BOOKS, AND ARTICLES

A.C.E. Newsletter (All Concerned Employees). "The NIH Task Force against Racism and Discrimination" 1, no. 1, July 12, 1971.

Adams, James Truslow. *Epic of America*. Boston: Little, Brown, 1931.

Aiken, Charles S. "A New Type of Black Ghetto in the Plantation South." Annals of the Association of American Geographers 80, no. 2 (Jun., 1990): 223–246.

Alderman, Edwin Anderson, Joel Chandler Harris, and Charles William Kent. *Library of Southern Literature: Biography*. Atlanta, GA: Martin and Hoyt, 2015.

American Postal Workers Union. "APWU History." Accessed May 2, 2013. http://www.apwu.org/apwu-history.

American Presidency Project. "Executive Order 11512: Planning, Acquisition, and Management of Federal Space." Accessed November 25, 2012. http://www.presidency.ucsb.edu/ws/index.php?pid=60482.

American Presidency Project. "Ronald Reagan Inaugural Address: January 20, 1981." Accessed June 23, 2017. http://www.presidency.ucsb.edu/ws/?pid=43130.

Anderson, Karen Tucker. "Last Hired, First Fired: Black Women Workers during World War II." *Journal of American History* 69, no. 1 (June 1982), 82–97.

Arnesen, Eric. *Brotherhoods of Color: Black Railroad Workers and the Struggle for Equality*. Cambridge, MA: Harvard University Press, 2002.

Arnesen, Eric. "The Evolution of the World's Largest Postal Union." Accessed May 2, 2013. http://www.apwu.org/labor-history-articles/evolution-world's-largest-postal-union.

Baldwin, James. *Nobody Knows My Name*. New York: Penguin Books, 1954.

Belknap, Michael R. *Employment of Blacks by the Federal Government*. New York: Routledge, 1991.

Beller, Andrea H. "The Economics of Enforcement of an Antidiscrimination Law: Title VII of the Civil Rights Act of 1964." *Journal of Law and Economics* 21, no. 2 (October 1978), 359–80.

Biondi, Martha. *To Stand and Fight: The Struggle for Civil Rights in Postwar New York City*. Cambridge, MA: Harvard University Press, 2003.

Birnbaum, Jonathan, and Clarence Taylor, eds. *Civil Rights since 1787: A Reader on the Black Struggle*. New York: New York University Press, 2000.

Bolino, August C. *Manpower and the City*. Cambridge, MA: Schenkman, 1969.

Brown, Charles. "Black-White Earnings Ratios since the Civil Rights Act of 1964: The Importance of Labor Market Dropouts." *Quarterly Journal of Economics* 99, no. 1 (February 1984), 31–44.

Brown, Letitia Woods. *Free Negroes in the District of Columbia, 1790–1846.* New York: Oxford University Press, 1972.

Browne, Vincent J. "Racial Desegregation in the Public Service, with Particular Reference to the U.S. Government." *Journal of Negro Education* 23, no. 3 (Summer 1954), 242–48.

Bureaucrat. "Minority Perspectives on Bureaucracy." *Bureaucrat* 2, no. 2 (Summer 1973), 127–91.

Burstein, Paul. *Discrimination, Jobs and Politics: The Struggle for Equal Employment Opportunity in the United States since the New Deal.* Chicago: University of Chicago Press, 1985.

Callard, Abby. "Memoirs of a World War II Buffalo Soldier." Smithsonian.com, November 6, 2009. Accessed September 16, 2012. http://www.smithsonianmag.com/history-archaeology/Memoirs-of-a-World-War-II-Buffalo-Soldier-.html.

Cary, Francine Curro, ed. *Washington Odyssey: A Multicultural History of the Nation's Capital.* Washington, DC: Smithsonian Books, 1996.

Chamberlin, Charles D. *Victory at Home: Manpower and Race in the American South during World War II.* Athens: University of Georgia Press, 2003.

Chay, Kenneth Y. "The Impact of Federal Civil Rights Policy on Black Economic Progress: Evidence from the Equal Employment Opportunity Act of 1972." *Industrial and Labor Relations Review* 51, no. 4 (July 1998), 608–32.

Chirhart, Ann Short. *Torches of Light: Georgia Teachers and the Coming of the Modern South.* Athens: University of Georgia Press, 2005.

Clark-Lewis, Elizabeth. Living *In, Living Out: African American Domestics and the Great Migration.* New York: Kodansha America, 1996.

Collins, William J. "African-American Economic Mobility in the 1940s: A Portrait from the Palmer Survey." *Journal of Economic History* 60, no. 3 (September 2000), 756–81.

Cullinan, Gerald. *The United States Postal Service.* New York: Praeger, 1968.

Davis, John A. "Negro Employment in the Federal Government." *Phylon* 6, no. 4 (1945), 337–46.

Delaney, Paul. "Top Black Woman is Ousted by NASA." *New York Times*, October 28, 1973.

Dewey, Donald. "Negro Employment in Southern Industry. *Journal of Political Economy* 60, no. 4 (1952), 279–93.

Dobbin, Frank. *Inventing Equal Opportunity.* Princeton, NJ: Princeton University Press, 2009.

Doherty, Brian. "Affirmative Action: Interethnic Wars and the Absurdity of Racial Classification." October 1994. Accessed April 28, 2013. http://reason.com/archives/1994/10/01/affirmative-reaction.

Donohue, John J. III, and James Heckman. "Continuous Versus Episodic Change: The Impact of Civil Rights Policy on the Economic Status of Blacks." *Journal of Economic Literature* 29, no. 4 (December 1991), 1603–43.

Dowling, Timothy C. *Personal Perspectives: World War II.* Santa Barbara, CA: ABC-CLIO, 2005.

Du Bois, William Edward Burghardt. *Souls of Black Folk: Essays and Sketches.* Cambridge, MA: A. C. McClurg, 1903.

Dudziak, Mary. *Cold War Civil Rights: Race and the Image of American Democracy,* 2nd ed. Princeton, NJ: Princeton University Press, 2011.

Editors of TIME. *TIME 100 Photographs: The Most Influential Images of All Time*. New York: Time Inc. Books, 2015.

Eisinger, Peter K. *Black Employment in City Government, 1973–1980*. Washington, DC: Joint Center for Political Studies, 1983.

Elasky, Dan. "Civil Rights during the Carter Administration, 1977–1981: Part 1: Papers of the Special Assistant for Black Affairs, Section A." Accessed May 17, 2012. http://cisupa.proquest.com/ksc_assets/catalog/102657.pdf.

Evans, Sara A. *Born for Liberty: A History of Women in America*. New York: Free Press, 1989.

"Family Guy DMV." YouTube video, 0:33, posted by "aleguzmanb." October 2, 2009. https://www.youtube.com/watch?v=CS4DnwrXThU.

Fineberg, Gail. "Court Clears Way for Cook Case Payout." Library of Congress, November 18, 1996. Accessed July 11, 2017. http://www.loc.gov/loc/lcib/9620/cook.html.

Fleishhauer, Carl, and Beverly W. Brannan, eds. *Documenting America, 1935–1943*. Berkeley: University of California Press, 1988.

Foner, Philip S. *Organized Labor and the Black Worker: 1619–1973*. New York: International, 1976.

Fousek, John. *To Lead the Free World: American Nationalism and the Cultural Roots of the Cold War*. Chapel Hill: University of North Carolina Press, 2000.

Fradin, Dennis B., and Judith Bloom. *Fight On! Mary Church Terrell's Battle for Integration*. New York: Clarion Books, 2003.

Franco, Barbara. "The Challenge of a City Museum for Washington, DC." *Washington History* 15, no. 1 (Spring/Summer 2003), 4–25.

Frank, Sue A., and Gregory B. Lewis. "Government Employees: Working Hard or Hardly Working?" *American Review of Public Administration* 34, no. 1 (March 2004), 36–51.

Frazier, E. Franklin. *Black Bourgeoisie*. Glencoe, IL: Free Press, 1957.

Fredrickson, George M. *Black Image in the White Mind: The Debate on Afro-American Character and Destiny, 1817–1914*. New York: Harper and Row, 1971.

Gardner, Michael. *Harry Truman and Civil Rights: Moral Courage and Political Risks*. Carbondale: Southern Illinois University Press, 2003.

Gibson, Campbell, and Kay Jung. "Table 23, District of Columbia—Race and Hispanic Origin: 1800 to 1990." *Historical Census Statistics on Population Totals by Race, 1790 to 1990, and by Hispanic Origin, 1970 to 1990, for the United States, Regions, Divisions, and States*. U.S. Bureau of the Census, Working Paper Series no. 56, September 2002. Accessed November 30, 2012. www.census.gov/population/wwwdocumentation/twps0056/twps0056.htm.

Gilbert, Ben W. *Ten Blocks from the White House: Anatomy of the Washington Riots of 1968*. New York: Praeger, 1968.

Gilbert, Jess. *Planning Democracy: Agrarian Intellectuals and the Intended New Deal*. New Haven, CT: Yale University Press, 2015.

Glenn, A. L. Sr. *History of the National Alliance of Postal Employees: 1913–1955*. Washington, DC: National Alliance of Postal Employees, 1956.

Gooding, Frederick W. Jr. *Introduction to African American Studies: A Critical Reader.* Dubuque, IA: Kendall Hunt, 2016.

Gooding, Frederick W. Jr. *You Mean, There's RACE in My Movie? The Complete Guide to Understanding Race in Mainstream Hollywood*, 2d ed. Silver Spring, MD: On the Reelz Press, 2017.

Government Research Corporation. "Dinner Date on Labor Day." *National Journal* 3, no. 38 (January 30, 1971), 239.

Granger, Lester B. "Barriers to Negro War Employment." *Annals of the American Academy of Political and Social Science* 223, no.1 (September 1942), 72–80.

Green, Constance McLaughlin. *The Secret City: A History of Race Relations in the Nation's Capital.* Princeton, NJ: Princeton University Press, 1967.

Green, Constance McLaughlin. *Washington: A History of the Nation's Capital, 1800–1950.* Princeton, NJ: Princeton University Press, 1962.

Greenhouse, Steve. "Most U.S. Union Members Working for the Government, New Data Shows." *New York Times*, September 10, 2010.

Harris, Ruth Bates. *Harlem Princess: The Story of Harry Delaney's Daughter.* New York: Vantage Press, 1999.

Hart, Scott. *Washington at War, 1941–1945.* Upper Saddle River, NJ: Prentice Hall, 1970.

Harvard Law Review Association. "Developments in the Law: Employment Discrimination and Title VII of the Civil Rights Act of 1964." *Harvard Law Review* 84, no. 5 (March 1971), 1109–316.

Hauser, Robert M. "Trends in College Entry among Whites, Blacks and Hispanics." In *Studies of Supply and Demand in Higher Education*, edited by Charles T. Clotfelter and Michael Rothschild, 61–120. Chicago: University of Chicago Press, 1993.

Henderson, Laretta. *Ebony Jr! The Rise, Fall, and Return of a Black Children's Magazine.* Lanham, MD: Scarecrow Press, 2008.

Hill, Shirley A. *Black Intimacies: A Gender Perspective on Families and Relationships.* Walnut Creek, CA: AltaMira Press, 2005.

Historical Statistics of Black America. Vol. 1. Farmington Hills, MI: Gale Group, 1994.

Hobson, Julius. "Uncle Sam Is a Bigot." *Saturday Evening Post* 241, no. 8 (April 20, 1968), 16.

Holloway, Jonathan Scott. *Confronting the Veil: Abram Harris Jr., E. Franklin Frazier, and Ralph Bunche.* Chapel Hill: University of North Carolina Press, 2002.

Honey, Michael Keith. *Black Workers Remember: An Oral History of Segregation, Unionism, and the Freedom Struggle.* Berkeley: University of California Press, 1999.

Hooks, Janet M. "Women's Occupations through Seven Decades." *Women's Bureau Bulletin*, no. 218. Washington, DC: U.S. Government Printing Office, 1947.

Hope, John II, and Edward E. Shelton. "The Negro in the Federal Government." *Journal of Negro Education* 32, no. 4 (Autumn 1963), 367–74.

Huddleston, Mark W., and William W. Boye. *The Higher Civil Service in the United States: Quest for Reform.* Pittsburgh: University of Pittsburgh Press, 1996.

Huntley, Horace, and David Montgomery, eds. *Black Workers' Struggle for Equality in Birmingham*. Champaign: University of Illinois Press, 2007.

Isaac, Larry, and Lars Christiansen. "How the Civil Rights Movement Revitalized Labor Militancy." *American Sociological Review* 67, no. 5 (October 2002), 722–46.

Johnson, Charles, and Preston Valien. "The Status of Negro Labor." In *Labor in Postwar America*, edited by Colston Warne, ch. 26. Brooklyn, NY: Remsen Press, 1949.

Jones, Joyce. "Does Working for Uncle Sam Still Make Sense?" *Black Enterprise* 27, no. 7 (February 1996), 110–16.

Kassarjian, Harold H. "The Negro and American Advertising, 1946–1965." *Journal of Marketing Research* 6, no. 1 (February 1969), 29–39.

Katznelson, Ira. *When Affirmative Action Was White*. New York: Norton, 2005.

Kersten, Andrew. "African Americans and World War II." *OAH Magazine of History* 16, no. 3 (Spring 2002), 13–17.

Kesselman, Louis Coleridge. *The Social Politics of FEPC: A Study in Reform Pressure Movements*. Chapel Hill: University of North Carolina Press, 1948.

Kiersz, Andy. "The Impact of Small Business on the US Economy in 2 Extreme Charts." *Business Insider*, June 16, 2015.

King, Mary C. "Occupational Segregation by Race and Sex, 1940–88." *Monthly Labor Review* 115, no. 4 (April 1992), 30–36.

Klinker, Philip A., and Rogers M. Smith. *The Unsteady March: The Rise and Decline of Racial Equality in America*. Chicago: University of Chicago Press, 2002.

Krislov, Samuel. *The Negro in Federal Employment: The Quest for Equal Opportunity*. St. Paul: University of Minnesota Press, 1967.

Landis, Kenesaw M. *Segregation in Washington: A Report of the National Committee on Segregation in the Nation's Capital*. Chicago: NCSNC, 1948.

Lemann, Nicholas. *The Promised Land: The Great Black Migration and How It Changed America*. New York: Vintage Books, 1992.

Linsin, Christopher E. "Something More Than a Creed: Mary McLeod Bethune's Aim of Integrated Autonomy as Director of Negro Affairs." *Florida Historical Quarterly* 76, no. 1 (Summer, 1997), 20–41.

Lohman, Joseph D., and Edwin Embree. "The Nation's Capital." *Survey Graphic* 36, no. 1 (January 1947), 32–37.

Long, James E. "Employment Discrimination in the Federal Sector." *Journal of Human Resources* 11, no. 1 (Winter 1976), 86–97.

Lunardini, Christine A. "Standing Firm: William Monroe Trotter's Meetings with Woodrow Wilson, 1913–1914." *Journal of Negro History* 64, no. 3 (Summer 1979), 244–64.

Lyles, Kevin L. *The Gatekeepers: Federal District Courts in the Political Process*. Westport, CT: Praeger, 1997.

MacLean, Nancy. *Freedom Is Not Enough: The Opening of the American Workplace*. Cambridge, MA: Harvard University Press, 2006.

Manca, Joseph. "A Theology of Architecture: Edward Savage's Portrait of George Washington and His Family." *Notes in the History of Art* 31, no. 1 (Fall 2011), 29–36.

Mangum, Garth L., and John Walsh. *Union Resilience in Troubled Times: The Story of the Operating Engineers, AFL-CIO, 1960–1993.* Armonk, NY: M. E. Sharpe, 1994.

Mapp, Alf J. Jr. *Thomas Jefferson: Passionate Pilgrim.* Lanham, MD: Rowman and Littlefield, 1991.

McAllister, Bill. "Consultants to Make Postal Diversity Study." *Washington Post*, November 13, 1996.

McCartin, Joseph. *Collision Course: Ronald Reagan, the Air Traffic Controllers, and the Strike that Changed America.* New York: Oxford University Press, 2011.

McCrone, Donald J., and Richard J. Hardy. "Civil Rights Policies and the Achievement of Racial Economic Equality, 1948–1975." *American Journal of Political Science* 22, no. 1 (February 1978), 1–17.

McQuaid, Kim. "Race, Gender, and Space Exploration: A Chapter in the Social History of the Space Age." *Journal of American Studies* 41, no. 2 (July 2007), 405–34.

McQuaid, Kim. "'Racism, Sexism, and Space Ventures': Civil Rights at NASA in the Nixon Era and Beyond." In *Societal Impact of Spaceflight*, edited by Steven J. Dick and Roger D. Launius. Washington, DC: NASA Office of External Relations, History Division, 2007, 421–51.

Modell, John, Marc Goulden, and Sigurour Magnusson. "World War II in the Lives of Black Americans: Some Findings and an Interpretation." *Journal of American History* 76, no. 3 (December 1989), 838–48.

Modesitt. Nancy M. "Reinventing the EEOC." *SMU Law Review* 63 (2010), 1237–77.

Moore, Jesse Thomas Jr. *A Search for Equality: The National Urban League, 1910–1961.* University Park: Pennsylvania State University Press, 1981.

MPR [Minnesota Public Radio] News. "King's 'Promissory Note' Remains in Default." August 28, 2013. Accessed December 29, 2017. https://www.mprnews.org/story/2013/08/28 daily-circuit-march-on-washington.

Mullen, Shannon. "Race Remains Hot Topic Despite Obama Presidency." *USA Today.* October 17, 2010.

Myrdal, Gunnar. *An American Dilemma: The Negro Problem in Modern Democracy.* New York: Harper and Row, 1944.

Nelson, Bruce. "Organized Labor and the Struggle for Black Equality in Mobile during WWII." *Journal of American History* 80, no. 3 (December 1993), 952–88.

Norton, Mary A. "The Federal Government and Negro Morale." *Journal of Education* 12, no. 3 (Summer 1943), 452–63.

O'Brien, Lawrence. "A New Design for the Postal Service." *Vital Speeches of the Day* 33, no. 14 (May 1, 1967), 418–21.

Ortlepp, Anke. *Jim Crow Terminals: The Desegregation of American Airports.* Athens: University of Georgia Press, 2017.

Overy, Richard. *Why the Allies Won.* New York: Norton, 1995.

Parks, Gordon. *A Choice of Weapons.* New York: Harper and Row, 1966.

Parks, Gordon. *Voices in the Mirror: An Autobiography.* New York: Doubleday, 1990.

Patterson, James T. *Grand Expectations: The United States, 1945–1974.* Oxford: Oxford University Press, 1996.

Perlo, Victor. "Trends in the Economic Status of the Negro People." *Science and Society* 16, no. 2 (Spring 1950), 115–60.

Perry, Jeffrey B., ed. *A Hubert Harrison Reader.* Middletown, CT: Wesleyan University Press, 2001.

Persky, Anna Stolley. "State of the Union: The Role of Labor in America's Future." *Washington Lawyer* (July/August 2011). Accessed April 20, 2018. https://www.dc bar.org/bar-resources/publications/washington-lawyer/articles/july-august-2011-labor -union.cfm.

Pfautz, Harold W. "The New 'New Negro': Emerging American." *Phylon* 24, no. 4 (1963), 360–68.

Pitts, Steven. "Research Brief: Black Workers and the Public Sector." Berkeley Center for Labor Research and Education, 2011.

Powell, Colin. "Truman, Desegregation of the Armed Forces and a Kid from the Bronx." In *The Civil Rights Legacy of Harry S. Truman*, edited by Raymond H. Geselbracht, 117–25. Kirksville, MO: Truman State University Press, 2007.

Pritchett, Wendell E. "A National Issue: Segregation in the District of Columbia and the Civil Rights Movement at Mid-Century." *Georgetown Law Journal* 93, no. 4 (April 2005), 1321–33.

Reder, Melvin W. "The Rise and Fall of Unions: The Public Sector and the Private." *Journal of Economic Perspectives* 2, no. 2 (Spring 1988), 89–110.

Reid, Ira De A. "Special Problems of Negro Migration during the War." *Milbank Memorial Fund Quarterly* 25, no. 3 (July 1947), 284–92.

Riccucci, Norma M., and Katherine C. Naff, *Personnel Management in Government: Politics and Process.* Boca Raton, FL: CRC Press, 2017.

Royster, Deirdre A. "Race, Ethnicity and Inequality in the US Labor Market: Critical Issues in the New Millennium: What Happens to Potential Discouraged? Masculinity Norms and the Contrasting Institutional and Labor Market Experiences of Less Affluent Black and White Men." *Annals of the American Academy of Political and Social Science* 609, no. 153 (January 2007).

Rubio, Phillip F. *There's Always Work at the Post Office: African American Postal Workers and the Fight for Jobs, Justice, and Equality.* Chapel Hill: University of North Carolina Press, 2010.

Rung, Margaret C. *Servants of the State: Managing Diversity and Democracy in the Federal Workforce, 1933–1953.* Athens: University of Georgia Press, 2002.

Sadacca, Robert. *The Validity and Discriminatory Impact of the Federal Service Entrance Examination.* Washington, DC: Urban Institute, 1971.

Samuel, Lawrence R. *The American Dream: A Cultural History.* Syracuse, NY: Syracuse University Press, 2012.

Schuman, Howard et al. *Racial Attitudes in America: Trends and Interpretations.* Cambridge, MA: Harvard University Press, 1985.

Sitkoff, Harvard. *A New Deal for Blacks: The Emergence of Civil Rights as a National Issue: The Depression Decade.* Oxford: Oxford University Press, 2008.

Sitkoff, Harvard. "Harry Truman and the Election of 1948: The Coming of Age of Civil Rights in American Politics." *Journal of Southern History* 37, no. 4 (November 1971), 597–616.

Skrentny, John David. "Pragmatism, Institutionalism, and the Construction of Employment Discrimination." *Sociological Forum* 9, no. 3 (September 1994), 343–69.

Slater, Joseph. *Public Workers: Government Employee Unions, the Law, and the State, 1900–1962.* Ithaca, NY: Cornell University Press, 2004.

Solomon, Burt. *The Washington Century: Three Families and the Shaping of the Nation's Capital.* New York: HarperCollins, 2004.

Sparrow, James T. "Freedom to Want: The Federal Government and Politicized Consumption in World War II." In *Fog of War: The Second World War and the Civil Rights Movement*, edited by Kevin M. Kruse and Stephen Tuck, 15–31. New York: Oxford University Press, 2012.

Stebenne, David. *Arthur J. Goldberg: New Deal Liberal.* New York: Oxford University Press, 1996.

Stevens, Daniel. "Public Opinion and Public Policy: The Case of Kennedy and Civil Rights." *Presidential Studies Quarterly* 32, no. 1 (March 2002), 111–36.

Sugrue, Thomas. *Sweet Land of Liberty: The Forgotten Struggle for Civil Rights in the North.* New York: Random House, 2008.

Sundstrom, William A. "The Color Line: Racial Norms and Discrimination in Urban Labor Markets, 1910–1950." *Journal of Economic History* 54, no. 2 (1994), 382–96.

Taylor, Patricia A. "Income Inequality in the Federal Civilian Government." *American Sociological Review* 44, no. 3 (June 1979), 468–79.

Thompson, Helen. "In the 1960s, One Man Took Washington, D.C.'s Rat Problem into His Own Hands, Literally." Smithsonian.com, July 21, 2015. Accessed July 11, 2017. http://www.smithsonianmag.com/smart-news/1960s-julius-hobson-took-dcs-rat-problem-his-own-hands-180955961/.

Thornton, Regan E. "Veteran with 102 Years of African-American History." U.S. Department of Veterans Affairs, February 17, 2014. Accessed December 12, 2015. http://www.va.gov/health/NewsFeatures/2014/February/Veteran-with-102-Years-of-African-American-History.asp#sthash.Ybjpu1Bg.dpuf.

Van Ellis, Mark David. *To Only Hear Thunder Again: America's World War II Veterans Come Home.* Lanham, MD: Lexington Books, 2001.

Waggoner, Miles. "Remarks of Ruth Bates Harris at Summer Institute Closing Activity." *NASA News*, Release no. 75–239, September 15, 1975.

Ware, Susan, ed. *Notable American Women: A Biographical Dictionary Completing the Twentieth Century.* Cambridge, MA: Belknap Press of Harvard University Press, 2005.

Weiss, Nancy J. "The Negro and the New Freedom: Fighting Wilsonian Segregation." *Political Science Quarterly* 84, no. 1 (March 1969), 61–79.

White, Walter. "The Negro Demands the Right to Be Allowed to Fight for It." *Saturday Evening Post* 213, no. 24 (December 14, 1940), 27.

Wilkerson, Isabel. *The Warmth of Other Suns: The Epic Story of America's Great Migration.* New York: Vintage, 2011.

Williams, Paul K. *Washington, D.C.: The World War II Years.* Charleston, S.C.: Arcadia, 2004.

Winkler, Allan M. *Home Front U.S.A.: America during World War II.* Wheeling, IL: Harlan Davidson, 2000.

Wolgemuth, Kathleen Long. "Woodrow Wilson and Federal Segregation." *Journal of Negro History* 44 (April 1959), 158–73.

"Wu-Tang Clan—C.R.E.A.M." YouTube video, 4:51, posted by "WuTangClanVEVO," January 21, 2014. https://www.youtube.com/watch?v=PBwAxmrE194.

Wynn, Neil A. *The African American Experience during World War II.* Lanham, MD: Rowman and Littlefield, 2011.

Yellin, Eric S. *Racism in the Nation's Service: Government Workers and the Color Line in Woodrow Wilson's America.* Chapel Hill: University of North Carolina Press, 2013.

Younge, Gary. *The Speech: The Story behind Dr. Martin Luther King Jr.'s Dream.* Chicago: Haymarket Books, 2013.

Zieger, Robert H. *For Jobs and Freedom: Race and Labor in America since 1865.* Lexington: University Press of Kentucky, 2007.

Zieger, Robert H., and Gilbert J. Gall. *American Workers, American Unions: The Twentieth Century.* Baltimore: Johns Hopkins University Press, 1986.

Zipp, John F. "Government Employment and Black-White Earnings Inequality, 1980–1990." *Social Problems* 14, no. 3 (August 1994), 363–82.

Zirin, Dave. *What's My Name, Fool? Sports and Resistance in the United States.* Chicago: Haymarket Books, 2005.

Zwerling, Craig, and Hilary Silver. "Race and Job Dismissals in a Federal Bureaucracy." *American Sociological Review* 57, no. 5 (October 1992), 651–60.

INDEX